Comments from readers of the previous edition of this book...

"Mike Smart's Excel books have a visible structure and flow smoothly, easily, and progressively from one topic to the next - it is unlikely that a reader (of his books) will get 'stuck' because of a missing prerequisite. It has been a blessing to have stumbled upon his books.

Mike's books are easy to read not because the subject matter is easy. They are easy because he has put in the effort to understand a student's mind and a reader's mind. They are easy because he has put in the effort to anticipate questions before they arise and delights the reader of his books with answers just as those questions begin to surface".
– *A reader from Blue Ash, OH, USA*

"This beautifully crafted book has given me enormous insight into the subtle workings of Excel. It is so well put together in eight sessions. If you are unclear on anything, you just keep going through the session until it falls into place. I had never used pivot tables or macros before and now I have the confidence to use them in my work as a financial consultant. My small business clients are mesmerized by how quickly I can analyze data exported to excel".
– *A reader from Canterbury, Kent, UK*

"This book is perfect for those who are proficient in Excel, but want to expand their skills to become more efficient and utilize Excel's advanced features. I knew there were better ways to accomplish the work I did in Excel and was frustrated by my limitations.

Completing this program has not only allowed me to do a better job in less time, but also to do things I never dreamed possible".
– *A reader from Maryville, TN, USA*

"Finally a book on Excel that cuts to the chase and teaches you the advanced skills expected of people who use this spreadsheet on a daily basis. It does an exceptional job teaching pivot tables which, incredibly, many other books on Excel leave out. I have a few books on Excel but this one is the best I have so far to get you using Excel's intermediate to advanced features right away".
– *A reader from North Bay, ON, Canada*

"If you wanted to really understand things you always pretended to, then buy this book. Easy to use and understand. Highly recommended".
– A reader from London, UK.

"Clearly it's a `technical' book, but the style is very friendly and approachable (this is not a book just for geeks). There are plenty of `ahhhhh' moments, when you discover a quick way to do something that has taken you ages to complete in the past, or suddenly have your eyes opened to something Excel is capable of that you never knew before.

Overall I think this is well worth buying if you are new to more advanced Excel functions or want a refresher. I would be very surprised if anyone works through this book and doesn't find at least one thing they can use to make them more efficient or effective in the future, that more than justifies the cost".
– A reader from Somerset UK.

"I teach Excel, and found this book very useful. The book is for those who know their way around in Excel.

It's a great book for the right audience: to the point. It's up to you and your time schedule if *you want to read the extra information*. The "extras" and in-depth are placed so you may choose to read it.

If you complete each lesson, you'll become a resource for your company!"
– A reader from Norway

Who Is This Book For?

If you can already use all of Excel's essential features but want to raise your skills to true Expert level, you've found the right book.

This book isn't for absolute beginners. If you're just starting out with Excel you should buy our *Essential Skills* book to learn all of Excel's most important features.

This book will give you advanced Excel skills that are rarely mastered by the average user. By the end of the book, you'll be a true Excel expert, able to use all of the power available from the world's most powerful business tool. Your Excel skills will be greater and broader than almost all other Excel users in the workplace.

This book is for Excel 2010 users who:

- Are already comfortable with Excel 2010's basic features (ideally by completing all of the lessons in our *Essential Skills* course).

- Want to use *all* of Excel 2010's more powerful and complex features.

Use of this book as courseware

This book is also the official courseware for The Smart Method's Excel 2010 Expert Skills course.

Smart Method courses have been taken by a varied cross-section of the world's leading companies. We've had fantastic feedback from the vast number of professionals we've empowered with advanced Excel skills.

This book is also suitable for use by other training organizations, teachers, schools and colleges to provide structured, objective-led, and highly effective classroom courses.

Learn Excel 2010 Expert Skills with The Smart Method

Mike Smart

Published by:

The Smart Method® Ltd
Burleigh Manor
Peel Road
Douglas, IOM,
Great Britain
IM1 5EP

Tel: +44 (0)845 458 3282 Fax: +44 (0)845 458 3281

E-mail: sales@LearnMicrosoftExcel.com
Web: www.LearnMicrosoftExcel.com (this book's dedicated web site)

Printed and bound in the United States of America

FIRST EDITION

International Standard Book Number (ISBN10): 0-9554599-8-2
International Standard Book Number (ISBN13): 978-0-9554599-8-6

The Smart Method® is a registered trade mark of The Smart Method Ltd.

2 4 6 8 10 9 7 5 3 1

Author's Acknowledgements

O would some Power, the gift to give us, To see ourselves as others see us!

Robert Burns, Scottish poet (1759-1796)

Many people will read this book. Some will be confronting advanced concepts, such as pivot tables and macros, for the very first time. Others will be seasoned professionals with an IT background. Readers will include students, office workers, accountants, administrators, doctors, scientists, engineers, bankers… and many other professions.

The book aims to communicate how to use Excel's advanced features in a way that is comprehensible to all.

I couldn't have written the original Excel 2007 version of this book without the help of many pairs of eyes. I have been extremely lucky to have had this help, throughout the writing process, from a wonderful group of international readers who kindly agreed to test drive the course prior to going to print.

I'm very grateful to Nate Barber (from San Antonio, Texas, USA). Nate was already a seasoned Excel power user and provided some wonderful technical insights. He also highlighted many cases where my British English didn't quite make the journey across the Atlantic. His feedback really helped me to improve the book in so many ways.

Many thanks are also due to Valérie Rousseau (from Quebec, Canada). Valérie spotted an embarrassing number of grammatical errors in my writing, and managed to discover errors that had been missed by all other reviewers.

Huge thanks also go out to Mark Casey (from London, England). Mark provided clear and concise feedback that caused me to completely re-write some of the lessons. His excellent command of the written word enabled me to eloquently re-phrase some of my more clumsy sentences.

I'd like to show great appreciation to Lorna Henderson (from Auckland, New Zealand). Lorna provided fantastically detailed feedback, resulting in hundreds of improvements to the book. There's hardly a page in the book that has not benefited from her suggestions and comments.

Many thanks also to Heidi Hembree (from Maryville, Tennessee, USA). Heidi highlighted many areas where I hadn't communicated concepts as well as I should have. Her feedback had a significant impact upon every session.

I'm also extremely grateful to Rosalind Johnson (from Pantymwyn, Wales). Rosalind's useful suggestions helped me to improve the readability of many lessons.

Thanks are also due to Jennifer Lashely (from London, England). Jennifer highlighted many potential pitfalls when working through the lessons that I was then able to eliminate from the final copy.

Special thanks are also due to Simon Smart (my son) who took time out of his own busy software development schedule to undertake a very comprehensive technical proof read.

Huge thanks also to Sue Ferrario (from Douglas, Great Britain) who tirelessly completed the final proofread of the book prior to going to print.

I'd also like to thank the many others that have helped to shape the content of this book that I have not mentioned by name. Your contributions were greatly appreciated.

Contents

Session Two: Data Integrity, Subtotals and Validations   65

Session Three: Advanced Functions   99

Session Four: Using Names and the Formula Auditing Tools   153

Session Five: Pivot Tables   191

Session Six: What If Analysis and Security   243

Appendix A: Skills Covered in the Essential Skills Course   359

Index   365

Introduction

Welcome to *Learn Excel 2010 Expert Skills With The Smart Method®*. This book has been designed to enable students to master Excel 2010 advanced skills by self-study. The book is equally useful as courseware in order to deliver classroom courses.

Smart Method® publications are continually evolving as we discover better ways of explaining or teaching the concepts presented.

Feedback

At The Smart Method we love feedback – both positive and negative. If you have any suggestions for improvements to future versions of this book, or if you find content or typographical errors, the author would always love to hear from you via e-mail to:

feedback@LearnMicrosoftExcel.com

Future editions will always incorporate your feedback so that there are never any known errors at time of publication.

If you have any difficulty understanding or completing a lesson, or if you feel that anything could have been more clearly explained, we'd also love to hear from you. We've made hundreds of detail improvements to our books based upon reader's feedback and continue to chase the impossible goal of 100% perfection!

Downloading the sample files

In order to use this book it is sometimes necessary to download sample files from the Internet. The sample files are available from:

http://www.LearnMicrosoftExcel.com

Type the above URL into your web browser and you'll see the link to the sample files at the top of the home page.

Problem resolution

If you encounter any problem downloading or using the sample files please send an e-mail to:

feedback@LearnMicrosoftExcel.com

We'll do everything possible to quickly resolve the problem.

Typographical Conventions Used In This Book

This guide consistently uses typographical conventions to differentiate parts of the text.

When you see this	Here's what it means
Click *Line Color* on the left-hand bar and then click *No line.*	Italics are used to refer to text that appears in a worksheet cell, an Excel dialog, on the Ribbon, or elsewhere within the Excel application. Italics may sometimes also be used for emphasis or distinction.
Click: Home→Font→Underline. 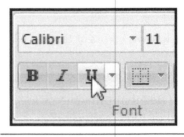	Click on the Ribbon's *Home* tab and then look for the *Font* group. Click the *Underline* button within this group (that's the left-hand side of the button, not the drop-down arrow next to it).
Click: Home→Font→ Underline Drop Down→Double Underline. 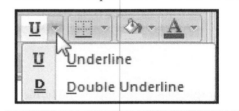	Click on the Ribbon's *Home* tab and then look for the *Font* group. Click the drop-down arrow next to the *Underline* button (that's the right-hand side of the button) within this group and then click *Double Underline* on the drop-down list.
Click: File→Options→ Advanced→General→ Edit Custom Lists→Import	This is a more involved example. 1. Click the *File* tab on the Ribbon, and then click the *Options* button towards the bottom of the left-hand pane. The *Excel Options* dialog appears. 2. Choose the *Advanced* list item in the left-hand pane and scroll down to the *General* group in the right-hand pane. 3. Click the *Edit Custom Lists...* button. Yet another new dialog pops up. Click the *Import* button.
Type **European Sales** into the cell.	Whenever you are supposed to actually type something on the keyboard it is shown in bold faced text.
Press <Ctrl> + <Z>.	You should hold down the **Ctrl** key and then press the **Z** key.

Σ AutoSum ▾

When a lesson tells you to click a button, an image of the relevant button will often be shown either in the page margin or within the text itself.

note

In Excel 2007/2010 there are a possible 16,585 columns and 1,048,476 rows. This is a great improvement on previous versions.

If you want to read through the book as quickly as possible, you don't have to read notes.

Notes usually expand a little on the information given in the lesson text.

important

Do not click the Delete button at this point as to do so would erase the entire table.

Whenever something can easily go wrong, or when the subject text is particularly important, you will see the *important* sidebar.

You should always read important sidebars.

tip

Moving between tabs using the keyboard

You can also use the <Ctrl>+<PgUp> and <Ctrl>+<PgDn> keyboard shortcuts to cycle through all of the tabs in your workbook.

Tips add to the lesson text by showing you shortcuts or time-saving techniques relevant to the lesson.

The bold text at the top of the tip box enables you to establish whether the tip is appropriate to your needs without reading all of the text.

In this example you may not be interested in keyboard shortcuts so do not need to read further.

anecdote

I ran an Excel course for a small company in London a couple of years ago...

Sometimes I add an anecdote gathered over the years from my Excel classes or from other areas of life.

If you simply want to learn Excel as quickly as possible you can ignore my anecdotes.

trivia

The feature that Excel uses to help you out with function calls first made an appearance in Visual Basic 5 back in 1996 and had the wonderful name: *IntelliSense*. The Excel...

Sometimes I indulge myself by adding a little piece of trivia in the context of the skill being taught.

Just like my anecdotes you can ignore these if you want to. They won't help you to learn Excel any better!

The World's Fastest Cars

When there is a sample file (or files) to accompany a lesson, the file name will be shown in a folder icon.

You can download the lesson or file from: *www.LearnMicrosoftExcel.com.* Detailed instructions are given in: *Lesson 1-2: Apply a simple filter to a range.*

Putting the Smart Method to Work

Excel version and service pack

This edition was written using *Microsoft Excel 2010 Service Pack 1* running under the *Windows 7 Service Pack 1* operating system. You'll discover how to confirm that your computer is running these versions in: *Lesson 1-1: Check your program and operating system version*.

If you are using an earlier or later operating system (for example Windows XP or Windows Vista) this book will be equally relevant, but you may notice small differences in the appearance of some of the screen grabs in the book. This will only occur when describing an operating system (rather than an Excel) feature.

This book is written purely for Excel 2010 and, due to huge changes in this version, will not be useful for earlier versions (97, 2000, 2002 and 2003). If you are using Excel 2007 you should either upgrade to Excel 2010 or purchase the earlier version of this book: *Learn Excel 2007 Expert Skills with The Smart Method*.

Sessions and lessons

The book is arranged into Sessions and Lessons. In a *Smart Method* course a Session would generally last for between sixty and ninety minutes. Each session would represent a continuous period of interactive instruction followed by a coffee break of ten or fifteen minutes.

When you use this book for self-instruction I'd recommend that you do the same. You'll learn better if you lock yourself away, switch off your telephone and complete the whole session without interruption. The memory process is associative, and we've ensured that each lesson within each session is very closely coupled (contextually) with the others. By learning the whole session in one sitting, you'll store all of that information in the same part of your memory and should find it easier to recall later.

The experience of being able to remember all of the words of a song as soon as somebody has got you "started" with the first line is an example of the memory's associative system of data storage.

We'd also highly recommend that you do take a break between sessions and spend it relaxing rather than catching up on your e-mails. This gives your brain a little idle time to do some data sorting and storage.

Read the book from beginning to end

Many books consist of disassociated self-contained chapters, often all written by different authors. This approach works well for pure reference books (such as encyclopedias). The problem with this approach is that there's no concept of building knowledge upon assumed prior knowledge, so the text is either confusing or unduly verbose as instructions for the same skill are repeated in many parts of the book.

This book is more effective as a learning tool because it takes a holistic approach. You will learn Excel in the same way you would be taught during one of our *Smart Method* courses.

In our classroom courses it's often the case that a delegate turns up late. One golden rule is that we can't begin until everybody is present, as each hands-on lesson builds upon skills taught in the previous lesson.

I strongly recommend that you read the book from beginning to end in the order that it is written. Because of the unique presentational style, you'll hardly waste any time reading about things that you already know and even the most advanced Excel user will find some nugget of extremely useful information in every session.

How this book avoids wasting your time

> Nobody has things just as he would like them. The thing to do is to make a success with what material I have.
>
> *Dr. Frank Crane (1861–1928), American clergyman and journalist*

The only material available to me in teaching you Excel is the written word and sample files. I'd rather have you sitting next to me in a classroom, but Frank Crane would have told me to stop complaining and use the tools I have in the most effective way.

Over the years I have read many hundreds of computer text books and most of my time was wasted. The big problem with most books is that I have to wade through thousands of words just to learn one important technique. If I don't read everything I might miss that one essential insight.

This book utilizes some of the tried and tested techniques developed after teaching vast numbers of people to learn Excel during many years of delivering *Smart Method* classroom courses.

As you'll see in this section, many presentational methods are used to help you to avoid reading about things you already know how to do, or things that are of little interest to you.

Why our classroom courses work so well

In *Smart Method* classroom courses we have a 100% success rate training delegates to *Essential Skills* level in one day (the subject matter of our *Essential Skills* book) and to *Expert* level in a further single day (the subject matter of this book).

One of the reasons we can teach so much in a single day is that we don't waste time teaching skills that the delegates already know. Class sizes are small (six maximum) and the instructor stands behind the delegates monitoring their screens. The instructor will say "Open the sample file *Sales* that you'll find in the *Samples* folder on the C drive". If everybody does this, no time is wasted explaining how. If anybody has difficulty, more information is given until all delegates demonstrate success.

Another key to learning effectively is to only teach the best way to accomplish a task. For example, you can save a workbook by clicking the *Save* button on the *Quick Access Toolbar* or you can press the **<Ctrl>+<S>** keys on the keyboard. Because clicking the *Save* button is the easiest, fastest and most intuitive method we only teach this in the classroom. In the book we do mention the alternatives, but only in a sidebar.

How this book mimics our classroom technique

Here's a lesson step:

	1	Save the workbook.
Note You can also use the **<Ctrl>+<S>** keyboard shortcut to save your work.		When you are editing a workbook the changes you make are only held in the computer's memory. If there is a power cut or your computer crashes, you will lose any work that has been done since the last save. For this reason you should get into the habit of regularly saving your work. Click the *Save button* on the *Quick Access Toolbar* at the top left of the screen.

If you already know how to save a workbook read only the line: *Save the workbook* and just do it. Don't waste your time reading anything else.

Read the smaller print only when you don't already know how to do something.

If you're in a hurry to learn only the essentials, as fast as possible, don't bother with the sidebars either unless they are labeled **important**.

Read the sidebars only when you want to know everything and have the time and interest.

Avoiding repetition

	2 Convert the table into a range. *This was covered in: Lesson 1-9: Format a table using table styles and convert a table into a range.*

A goal of this book (and our classroom courses) is not to waste your time by explaining any skill twice.

In a classroom course, a delegate will sometimes forget something that has already been covered earlier in the day. The instructor must then try to get the student to remember and drop little hints reminding them about how they completed the task earlier.

This isn't possible in a book, so I've made extensive use of cross references in the text pointing you back to the lesson in which the relevant skill was learned. The cross references also help when you use this book as a reference work but have forgotten the more basic skills needed to complete each step.

Use of American English

American English (rather than British English) spelling has been used throughout. This is because the Excel help system and screen elements all use American English spelling, making the use of British English confusing.

Examples of differences are the British English spelling: *Colour* and *Dialogue* as opposed to the American English spelling: *Color* and *Dialog*.

Because this book is used all over the world, much care has been taken to avoid any country-specific terminology. In most of the English speaking world, apart from North America, the symbol # is referred to as the **hash sign**. I use the term *hash* throughout this book.

First page of a session

1/ The first page begins with a quotation, often from an era before the age of the computer, that is particularly pertinent to the session material. As well as being fun, this helps us to remember that all of the real-world problems we solve with technology have been around for a long time.

3/ The session objectives *formally* state the precise skills that you will learn in the session.

At the end of the session you should re-visit the objectives and not progress to the next session until you can honestly agree that you have achieved them.

In a *Smart Method* course we never progress to the next session until all delegates are completely confident that they have achieved the previous session's objectives.

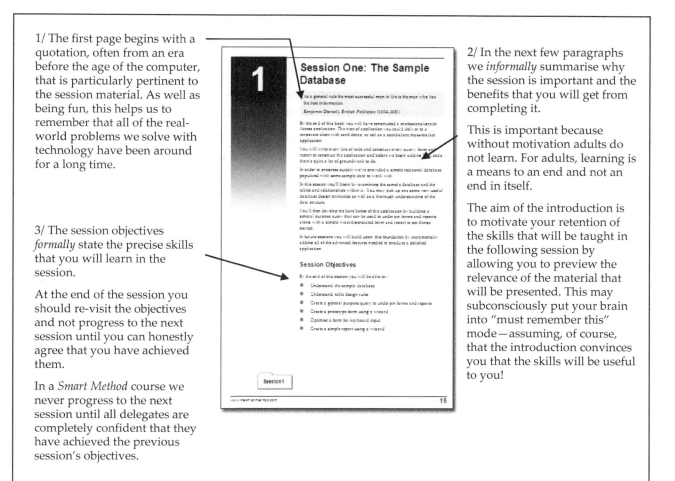

2/ In the next few paragraphs we *informally* summarise why the session is important and the benefits that you will get from completing it.

This is important because without motivation adults do not learn. For adults, learning is a means to an end and not an end in itself.

The aim of the introduction is to motivate your retention of the skills that will be taught in the following session by allowing you to preview the relevance of the material that will be presented. This may subconsciously put your brain into "must remember this" mode—assuming, of course, that the introduction convinces you that the skills will be useful to you!

Every lesson is presented on two facing pages

Pray this day, on one side of one sheet of paper, explain how the Royal Navy is prepared to meet the coming conflict.
Winston Churchill, Letter to the Admiralty, Sep 1, 1939

Winston Churchill was well aware of the power of brevity. The discipline of condensing thoughts into one side of a single sheet of A4 paper resulted in the efficient transfer of information.

A tenet of our teaching system is that every lesson is presented on *two* facing sheets of A4. We've had to double Churchill's rule as they didn't have to contend with screen grabs in 1939!

If we can't teach an essential concept in two pages of A4 we know that the subject matter needs to be broken into two smaller lessons.

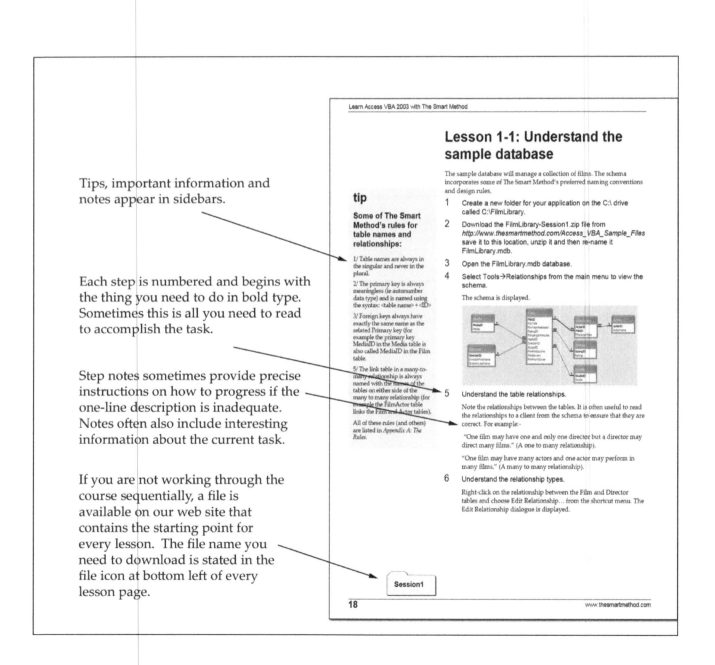

Learning by participation

Tell me, and I will forget. Show me, and I may remember. Involve me, and I will understand.

Confucius (551-479 BC)

Confucius would probably have agreed that the best way to teach IT skills is hands-on (actively) and not hands-off (passively). This is another of the principal tenets of the Smart Method® teaching system. Research has backed up the assertion that you will learn more material, learn more quickly, and understand more of what you learn, if you learn using active, rather than passive methods.

For this reason pure theory pages are kept to an absolute minimum with most theory woven into the hands-on sessions either within the text or in sidebars. This echoes the teaching method in Smart Method courses, where snippets of pertinent theory are woven into the lessons themselves so that interest and attention is maintained by hands-on involvement, but all necessary theory is still covered.

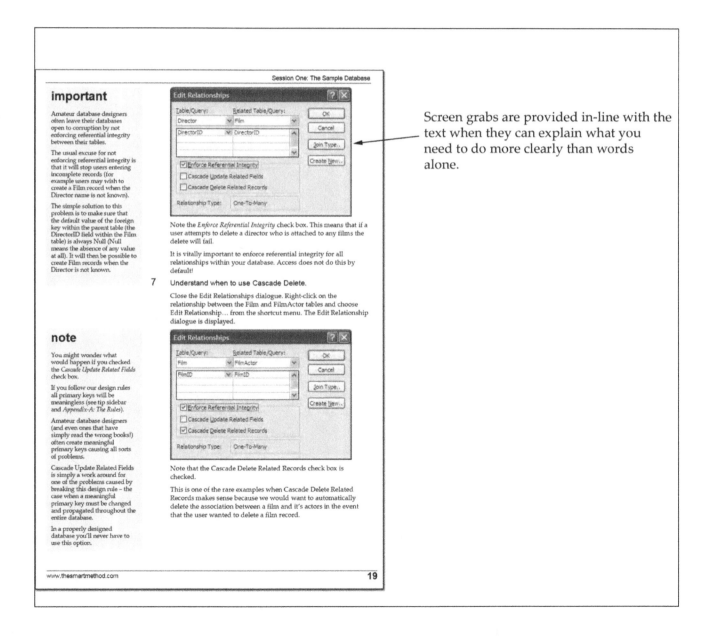

Screen grabs are provided in-line with the text when they can explain what you need to do more clearly than words alone.

Session One: Tables, Ranges and Databases

As a general rule the most successful man in life is the man who has the best information.

Benjamin Disraeli, British Politician (1804-1881)

Excel was never designed to be a relational database. Excel is a tool for analyzing data and not for data storage. This hasn't stopped corporate users all over the world from erroneously using Excel to store data in order to support their business operations.

Excel now has a fantastic new *table* feature (introduced for the first time in Excel 2007) making it possible to implement many features previously only available in true relational database products (such as Access, SQL Server and Oracle).

In this session you'll learn all about tables, how they differ from ranges, and how to use them effectively to manage data.

This lesson also introduces *structured table references* that provide a completely new way to reference dynamic table data. This has eliminated the need for the complex workarounds previously required to work with dynamic ranges.

Session Objectives

By the end of this session you will be able to:

- Check your program and operating system version
- Apply a simple filter to a range
- Apply a top 10 and custom filter to a range
- Apply an advanced filter with multiple OR criteria
- Apply an advanced filter with complex criteria
- Apply an advanced filter with function-driven criteria
- Extract unique records using an advanced filter
- Convert a range into a table and add a total row
- Format a table using table styles and convert a table into a range
- Create a custom table style
- Sort a range or table by rows
- Sort a range by columns
- Sort a range or table by custom list
- Name a table and create an automatic structured table reference
- Create a manual structured table reference
- Use special items in structured table references
- Understand unqualified structured table references

Lesson 1-1: Check your program and operating system version

If you are using Windows XP or Windows Vista, the procedure is almost the same as described here for Windows 7. You should easily be able to figure out the differences between the earlier versions and Windows 7.

1   Start Excel.

2   Check your program version.

1. Click the *File* button [File] at the top left of the screen.

   The Backstage View is displayed. Backstage View is a major new Excel 2010 feature and allows you to do a huge number of common tasks from one simple window.

2. Click the *Help* button [Help] towards the bottom-left pane of the Backstage View window.

3. Notice the *About Microsft Excel* information at the bottom right of the dialog:

   About Microsoft Excel

   Version: 14.0.6106.5005 (32-bit)
   Additional Version and Copyright Information
   Part of Microsoft Office Professional 2010

   It's almost certain that you will have the 32-bit version of Microsoft Excel installed but a very small number of users may find that they have the 64-bit version of Excel 2010 (see sidebar facing page). All of the lessons in this book should work in exactly the same way with both 32-bit and 64-bit versions.

4. Click the *Additional Version and Copyright Information* link just below the version number.

   The *About Microsoft Excel* dialog appears.

   You'll see the Excel version number at the top of the dialog. In this example the Excel version is:

   Microsoft® Excel® 2010 (14.0.6106.5005) SP1 MSO (14.0.6106.5005)

   The important part is the *SP1* denoting that you have *service pack one* installed (for more on this see sidebar). If this says SP2, SP3 or an even larger number this is also fine. It simply means that Microsoft have fixed even more bugs in their product since this book was published.

   If you do not see any reference to SPn, you have an early, un-patched version of Excel 2010 and you should update it (the update is free) via the Internet.

note

What is the 64-bit version of Excel 2010?

Until recently all computers used 32-bit microprocessors. This type of microprocessor cannot easily work with more than about 4 Gigabytes of memory.

64-bit microprocessors can typically work with around 4 Petabytes of memory. If you've never heard of a Petabyte that's because it is enormous! A Petabyte is actually a million Gigabytes. It is currently believed that this is more memory than you could ever need (but we used to say that about 4 Gigabytes too)!

While 64-bit microprocessors have been around for a long time, it was only with the release of Windows 7 (available in both 32-bit and 64-bit versions) that 64-bit operating systems became widely used.

The problem with 64-bit computers is that most of the software in the world is 32-bit. In Windows 7 64-bit edition this isn't a problem, because it can run both 32 and 64 bit software.

Office 2010 is the first Office release that is available in both a 32-bit and a 64-bit version.

For most users, (even those with 64-bit Windows 7), Microsoft still recommend the use of their 32-bit Office version because the 64-bit version may not allow some add-ins to function correctly. For this reason the 64-bit version of Excel will remain a rarity for some time.

The 64-bit version is specifically recommended for Excel expert users who need to work with Excel spread sheets that are larger than 2 Gigabytes or that have more than a million rows.

The other big advantage of the 64-bit version is that it is able to use multi-core processors to increase processing speed.

3   Check the Operating System version.

Click the *System Info…* button. The Operating System (OS) Name and Version will then be visible at the top right of the dialog:

Warning: This computer program is protected by copyright law and international treaties. Unauthorized reproduction or distribution of this program, or any portion of it, may result in severe civil and criminal penalties, and will be prosecuted to the maximum extent possible under the law.

[OK]
[System Info…]
[Tech Support…]

Windows 7

Item	Value
OS Name	Microsoft Windows 7 Professional
Version	6.1.7601 Service Pack 1 Build 7601

Windows Vista

Item	Value
OS Name	Microsoft® Windows Vista™ Ultimate
Version	6.0.6001 Service Pack 1 Build 6001

Windows XP

Item	Value
OS Name	Microsoft Windows XP Professional
Version	5.1.2600 Service Pack 2 Build 2600

It doesn't matter if you have Vista running a later service pack than SP1, Windows XP running a later service pack than SP2, or Windows 7 running a later service pack than SP1.

If you're running Windows 7, Vista or Windows XP, any edition will suffice (it doesn't have to be the Ultimate or Professional edition).

4   Close the *About Microsoft Excel* dialog.

5   Click the *Home* tab on the ribbon to return to the normal Excel screen.

<table>
<tr><td>

important

Organizing your sample files folder

When you complete a lesson involving a sample file that is changed, you will be asked to save the file with a suffix.

By the time you've completed the course you'll have sample files such as:

Sales-1
Sales-2
Sales-3 ... etc

The first file is a sample file that you downloaded, and the others (with the number suffix) are interim versions as you complete each lesson.

The sample file set includes the sample file *and all interim versions*.

The interim versions are provided for two reasons:

1. If your work-in-progress becomes unusable (for example after a system crash) you can continue without starting from the beginning again.

2. If a lesson doesn't seem to give the results described, you can open the finished example to get some clues about what has gone wrong.

It is a good idea to place the sample files in a different folder to your saved work. If you don't do this you'll be over-writing the sample interim files (such as Sales-1, Sales-2 etc) with your own finished work.

</td><td>

Lesson 1-2: Apply a simple filter to a range

1 Download the sample files (if you haven't already done so).

1. Open your web browser and type in the URL:

    www.learnmicrosoftexcel.com

2. Click the download link on the top left of the home page.

3. Download the sample files (also see sidebar: *Organizing your sample files folder*).

2 Open *Inventory-1* from your sample files folder.

Notice the yellow *Protected View* bar at the top of the screen:

> ⓘ Protected View   This file originated from an Internet location and might be unsafe. Click for more details.   [Enable Editing]

Protected view is a brand new feature for Excel 2010. Click the *Enable Editing* button to allow you to edit the workbook. See facing page sidebar for more on *Protected View*.

This workbook contains a list showing all goods in stock.

	A	B	C	D	E	F
				Unit	In	
1	Product Name	Supplier	Category	Price	Stock	Value
2	Aniseed Syrup	Exotic Liquids	Condiments	10.00	13	130.00
3	Boston Crab Meat	New England Seafood Cannery	Seafood	18.40	123	2,263.20
4	Camembert Pierrot	Gai pâturage	Dairy Products	34.00	19	646.00
5	Carnarvon Tigers	Pavlova, Ltd.	Seafood	62.50	42	2,625.00
6	Chai	Exotic Liquids	Beverages	18.00	39	702.00

3 Add a filter to the range.

1. Click anywhere inside the range.

2. Click: Data→Sort & Filter→Filter.

Notice that small drop-down arrow buttons have appeared in the range header row:

	A	B	C	D	E	F
				Unit	In	
1	Product Name ▾	Supplier ▾	Category ▾	Price ▾	Sto ▾	Value ▾
2	Aniseed Syrup	Exotic Liquids	Condiments	10.00	13	130.00
3	Boston Crab Meat	New England Seafood Cannery	Seafood	18.40	123	2,263.20

4 Use the filter to display products in the *Seafood* category.

1. Click the drop-down arrow to the right of *Category* in C1.

2. Uncheck the *(Select All)* check box.

3. Check the *Seafood* checkbox.

4. Click the OK button.

Only Seafood products are now displayed:

</td></tr>
</table>

Inventory-1

	A	B	C	D	E	F
				Unit	In	
1	Product Name ▾	Supplier ▾	Category ▾	Price ▾	Sto ▾	Value ▾
3	Boston Crab Meat	New England Seafood Cannery	Seafood	18.40	123	2,263.20
5	Carnarvon Tigers	Pavlova, Ltd.	Seafood	62.50	42	2,625.00
12	Escargots de Bourgog	Escargots Nouveaux	Seafood	13.25	62	821.50
20	Gravad lax	Svensk Sjöföda AB	Seafood	26.00	11	286.00

Notice that the filter button next to *Category* in cell C1 has changed to show that a filter condition is in effect. 🔽

Notice also that the row numbers along the left of the worksheet are now shaded blue and are no longer sequential.

5 **Add a second filter condition to show items in the *Seafood* category with an inventory value greater than 1,000.**

1. Click the drop-down arrow to the right of *Value* in cell F1.

2. Click: Number Filters→Greater Than... from the drop-down menu.

3. Type **1000** into the text box.

Custom AutoFilter

Show rows where:
Value

| is greater than | ▾ | 1000 | ▾ |

◉ And   ○ Or

| | ▾ | | ▾ |

Use ? to represent any single character
Use * to represent any series of characters

OK   Cancel

4. Click the OK button.

Only rows that are in the *Seafood* category and exceed a value of 1,000 are now shown.

	A	B	C	D	E	F
				Unit	In	
1	Product Name ▾	Supplier ▾	Category ▾	Price ▾	Sto ▾	Value ▾
3	Boston Crab Meat	New England Seafood Cannery	Seafood	18.40	123	2,263.20
5	Carnarvon Tigers	Pavlova, Ltd.	Seafood	62.50	42	2,625.00
26	Inlagd Sill	Svensk Sjöföda AB	Seafood	19.00	112	2,128.00
51	Röd Kaviar	Svensk Sjöföda AB	Seafood	15.00	101	1,515.00
59	Spegesild	Lyngbysild	Seafood	12.00	95	1,140.00

6 **Remove the filter from the range.**

1. Click anywhere inside the range.

2. Click: Data→Sort & Filter→Filter.

Notice that the small drop-down handles have disappeared from the range header row and that all rows are now displayed.

Lesson 1-3: Apply a top 10 and custom filter to a range

Filter

1 Open *Inventory-1* from your sample files folder (if it isn't already open).

2 Add a filter to the range.

Click anywhere inside the range and then click:

Data→Sort & Filter→Filter

3 Apply a top ten filter to identify the ten items that have the most expensive inventory.

   1. Click the drop-down arrow to the right of *Value* in cell F1.

   2. Click: *Number Filters.*

   3. Click: *Top 10...* on the fly-out menu.

      The *Top 10 AutoFilter* dialog is displayed:

Top 10 AutoFilter		
Show		
Top	10	Items
	OK	Cancel

      It is possible to use this dialog to filter to a number other than ten or to filter to the *Bottom* values (if you wanted to show the items with the least expensive inventory).

   4. Click OK.

      The ten items with the most expensive inventory are shown. Note that they are still sorted alphabetically, in ascending order, by *Product Name.* You'd probably want to sort the rows by value in descending order. Sorting will be covered later in: *Lesson 1-11: Sort a range or table by rows.*

4 Clear the filter condition from the Value column.

   1. Click the button to the right of *Value* in cell F1.

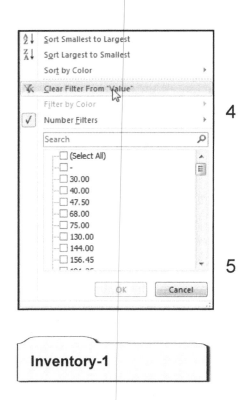

      Value

   2. Click *Clear Filter from "Value"* on the shortcut menu.

      The filter condition is removed and all items in the list are shown.

5 Use a custom filter to show items that have a value between 1,000 and 3,000.

   1. Click the drop-down arrow to the right of *Value* in cell F1.

   2. Click: Number Filters→Custom Filter on the drop-down menu.

Inventory-1

note

Filtering by color

Excel 2010 also has the ability to filter by cell color.

The *Filter by Color* option only lights up when at least one cell in the column has a background color.

You can then click the filter arrow at the top of the column and choose *Filter by Color*. This brings up a fly-out menu listing every color in the column:

Filter by Cell Color

No Fill

Filter by Font Color

Automatic

The *Custom Filter* dialog is displayed.

3. Set the filter condition: *is greater than or equal to 1000 And is less than or equal to 3000*.

4. Click the OK button.

Only products with a value between 1,000 and 3,000 are shown.

6   Remove the filter from the range.

1. Click anywhere inside the range.

2. Click: Data→Sort & Filter→Filter.

    Notice that the small drop-down arrows have disappeared from the range header row and that all rows are now displayed.

Lesson 1-4: Apply an advanced filter with multiple OR criteria

1 Open *Inventory-1* from your sample files folder (if it isn't already open).

2 Create the criteria range.

The criteria range is the area on your worksheet where you define the advanced filter criteria.

1. Insert five blank rows at the top of the worksheet.

2. Copy the range headers from row 6 to row 1.

Your worksheet should now look like this:

	A	B	C	Unit Price	In Stock	Value
1	Product Name	Supplier	Category			
2						
3						
4						
5						
6	Product Name	Supplier	Category	Unit Price	In Stock	Value
7	Aniseed Syrup	Exotic Liquids	Condiments	10.00	13	130.00

Each of the rows 2-4 can now be used to define the criteria needed for each column in the range.

3 Add filter criteria to show all products in the *Condiments*, *Seafood* and *Confections* categories.

This is an example of a filter with three OR criteria. The filter can be defined as:

Condiments OR Seafood OR Confections.

Add the three filter criteria by typing (or copy and pasting) the three category names into cells C2:C4.

	A	B	C
1	**Product Name**	**Supplier**	**Category**
2			Condiments
3			Seafood
4			Confections

4 Apply the criteria using an advanced filter.

1. Click anywhere in the range to be filtered (any cell in the range A6:F75).

2. Click: Data→Sort & Filter→Advanced.

The *Advanced Filter* dialog is displayed with the range already defined. Because you clicked within the range in step one you have saved yourself the trouble of manually selecting the range.

Inventory-1

note

Using wildcards in criteria

Sometimes you will want to filter using a subset of the letters in a text column.

In this case, you can use the wildcard characters – the asterisk (*) and the question mark (?).

It is easiest to explain how wildcards work with a few examples:

C*g   Finds **Containing**
         Finds **Citing**
         Finds **Changing**

S?d   Finds **Sid**
         Finds **Sad**
         Finds **Syd**
         Finds **Sud**

The asterisk means that any number of wildcard letters can occur between the letters.

The question mark means that only one wildcard letter can occur between the letters.

note

Text filters are inexact by default

This lesson's example works just fine but it would have worked just as well if you had entered the filter expression **Cond** instead of **Condiments**.

For the same reason, the filter expression **Dairy** would return the category **Dairy Products**.

Sometimes this isn't what you want and you need an exact match. In this case, you need to enter the filter conditions like this:

=″=Seafood″

=″=Dairy Products″

Unlike **Con**, The filter condition

=″=Con″

... doesn't return the *Condiments* category.

3. Click in the *Criteria range:* text box.

4. Select the range A1:F4 with the mouse.

The criteria range appears as: A1:F4.

5. Click the OK button.

The range is now filtered to display only *Condiments, Seafood* and *Confections*.

6	Product Name	Supplier	Category	Unit Price	In Stock	Value
7	Aniseed Syrup	Exotic Liquids	Condiments	10.00	13	130.00
8	Boston Crab Meat	New England Seafood Cannery	Seafood	18.40	123	2,263.20
10	Carnarvon Tigers	Pavlova, Ltd.	Seafood	62.50	42	2,625.00
14	Chef Anton's Cajun S	New Orleans Cajun Delights	Condiments	22.00	53	1,166.00
15	Chocolade	Zaanse Snoepfabriek	Confections	12.75	15	191.25

5   Remove the advanced filter from the range.

1. Click anywhere inside the range.

2. Click: Data→Sort & Filter→Clear.   [✄ Clear]

The advanced filter is cleared and all records are displayed.

6   Save your work as *Inventory-2*.

Lesson 1-5: Apply an advanced filter with complex criteria

1 Open *Inventory-2* from your sample files folder (if it isn't already open).

2 Create complex advanced filter criteria.

This time we are going to create a criteria with both AND and OR criteria. This is an example of a criteria that is beyond the scope of a simple filter. Here are the criteria we are going to apply:

WHERE

Category equals Condiments

OR

(Category equals Seafood AND Value is greater than 2,000)

OR

Value is greater than 3,000

This will list everything in the *Condiments* category.

It will also list products in the *Seafood* category but only if their value is greater than 2,000.

It will also list all products that have a value greater than 3,000 irrespective of what category they are in.

1. Set the criteria range as follows:

	C	D	E	F
		Unit	In	
1	Category	Price	Stock	Value
2	Condiments			
3	Seafood			>2000
4				>3000

2. Apply the advanced filter using the skills learned in: *Lesson 1-4: Apply an advanced filter with multiple OR criteria.*

3. You will see the following values in the *Advanced Filter* dialog:

List range:	$A$6:$F$75
Criteria range:	Inventory!Criteria

You may wonder why the Criteria range displays as *Inventory!Criteria* this time instead of *Inventory!$A$1:$F$4.*

The reason is that Excel has created something called a *Range Name* behind the scenes. You'll learn all about Range Names later, in: *Session Four: Using Names and the Formula Auditing Tools.*

Inventory-2

Let's now audit the results:

	A	B	C	D	E	F
6	**Product Name**	Supplier	Category	Unit Price	In Stock	Value
7	Aniseed Syrup	Exotic Liquids	Condiments	10.00	13	130.00
8	Boston Crab Meat	New England Seafood Cannery	Seafood	18.40	123	2,263.20
10	Carnarvon Tigers	Pavlova, Ltd.	Seafood	62.50	42	2,625.00
14	Chef Anton's Cajun Seasoning	New Orleans Cajun Delights	Condiments	22.00	53	1,166.00
16	Côte de Blaye	Aux joyeux ecclésiastiques	Beverages	263.50	17	4,479.50
21	Genen Shouyu	Mayumi's	Condiments	15.50	39	604.50
24	Grandma's Boysenberry Spread	Grandma Kelly's Homestead	Condiments	25.00	120	3,000.00
27	Gula Malacca	Leka Trading	Condiments	19.45	27	525.15
31	Inlagd Sill	Svensk Sjöföda AB	Seafood	19.00	112	2,128.00
38	Louisiana Fiery Hot Pepper Sauce	New Orleans Cajun Delights	Condiments	21.05	76	1,599.80
39	Louisiana Hot Spiced Okra	New Orleans Cajun Delights	Condiments	17.00	4	68.00
45	Northwoods Cranberry Sauce	Grandma Kelly's Homestead	Condiments	40.00	6	240.00
47	Original Frankfurter grüne Soße	Plutzer Lebensmittelgroßmärkte AG	Condiments	13.00	32	416.00
52	Queso Manchego La Pastora	Cooperativa de Quesos 'Las Cabras'	Dairy Products	38.00	86	3,268.00
53	Raclette Courdavault	Gai pâturage	Dairy Products	55.00	79	4,345.00
61	Sir Rodney's Marmalade	Specialty Biscuits, Ltd.	Confections	81.00	40	3,240.00
63	Sirop d'érable	Forêts d'érables	Condiments	28.50	113	3,220.50
73	Vegie-spread	Pavlova, Ltd.	Condiments	43.90	24	1,053.60

- All eleven *Condiments* products are listed irrespective of their value.

- Only three *Seafood* products are shown – only the items with a value greater than 2,000.

- Items such as *Sir Rodney's Marmalade* are listed even though they do not appear in the *Condiment* or *Seafood* categories. This is because their value is greater than 3,000.

3 Remove the advanced filter from the range.

1. Click anywhere inside the range.

2. Click: Data→Sort & Filter→Clear. [Clear]

The advanced filter is cleared and all records are displayed.

4 Save your work as *Inventory-3*.

Lesson 1-6: Apply an advanced filter with function-driven criteria

When a company conducts a physical stock check of its inventory there will always be some errors in the count. Auditors have to verify the accuracy of a stock check. To do this they extract some random samples in order to establish the likely margin of error.

In this lesson, we'll take the Inventory workbook and extract an auditing sample by using an advanced filter in conjunction with a MOD (Modulus or Remainder) function.

Excel's MOD function returns the whole number (or integer) part of a number after it has been divided by another number. It is often used in conjunction with the INT (integer) function to convert minutes into hours and minutes. For example, to convert 170 minutes into 2 hours 50 minutes you would use the functions like this:

=INT(170/60)   This returns 2, as the whole number part of 2.83 is 2.

=MOD(170,60)   This returns 50, because 60 only divides evenly into 170 twice (120) leaving 50 over.

We're going to use the MOD function in conjunction with an advanced filter to show one transaction in every five, so that we can sample one in five (20%) of the products to check during the audit.

1   Open *Inventory-3* from your sample files folder (if it isn't already open).

2   Add a column to the left of the range and fill it with incremental numbers.

	A	B	C
6	No	Product Name	Supplier
7	1	Aniseed Syrup	Exotic Liquids
8	2	Boston Crab Meat	New England Seafood Cannery
9	3	Camembert Pierrot	Gai pâturage
10	4	Carnarvon Tigers	Pavlova, Ltd.

3   Add a MOD function to cell A2 that will return True when the value in cell A7 is divisible by five.

1. Type the following function into cell A2.

	A	B
1		Product Name
2	=MOD(A7,5)=0	
3	MOD(**number**, divisor)	

2. Press the **<Enter>** key.

The cell contains the value: *False.*

note

Using a function-driven criteria to implement a case sensitive filter

Filters are case insensitive by default.

The filters:

Category=Seafood

And

Category=SEAFOOD

… will produce exactly the same result.

You can implement a case sensitive filter using the EXACT function.

The filter condition:

=EXACT(D7, "Seafood")

… would extract the *Seafood* records in this table.

The filter condition:

=EXACT(D7, "SEAFOOD")

… would not extract any records.

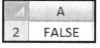

◢	A
2	FALSE

This is because the number in cell A7 (1) is not evenly divisible by five.

Here's how the MOD function works:

- The value in cell A7 is divided by five and the remainder is returned. In this case the remainder is 1 because the number 1 is not evenly divisible by 5.

- The expression 1=0 is not true so the cell displays a result of FALSE.

- If cell A7 had contained a value that is evenly divisible by 5 (such as 5 or 10) the MOD function would have returned zero (because the remainder is zero). This would result in the cell displaying a True result because the expression 0=0 is true.

4 Apply the advanced filter.

Notice that we didn't type the word **No** into cell A1. For a function driven filter you must leave the cell above the formula blank. This tells the advanced filter to work directly upon the result of the function.

1. Apply an advanced filter in the same way you did in: *Lesson 1-4: Apply an advanced filter with multiple OR criteria,* using A1:A2 as the *Criteria range.* The *Advanced Filter* dialog should look like this:

> **Advanced Filter**
>
> Action
> ◉ Filter the list, in-place
> ○ Copy to another location
>
> List range: `$A$6:$G$75`
> Criteria range: `$A$1:$A$2`
> Copy to:
>
> ☐ Unique records only
>
> OK   Cancel

2. Click the OK button.

6	No	Product Name	Supplier
11	5	Chai	Exotic Liquids
16	10	Côte de Blaye	Aux joyeux ecclésiastiques
21	15	Genen Shouyu	Mayumi's
26	20	Gudbrandsdalsost	Norske Meierier
31	25	Inlagd Sill	Svensk Sjöföda AB

Note that the numbers in column A now read 5,10,15,20...

The list now contains the 20% sample needed for the audit.

5 Save your work as *Inventory-4*.

Lesson 1-7: Extract unique records using an advanced filter

1   Open *Inventory-4* from your sample files folder (if it isn't already open).

2   Click: Data→Sort & Filter→Clear to show all items in the range.

In the Inventory workbook you will notice that one supplier often provides multiple products. For example *Speciality Biscuits, Ltd.* supplies more than one product:

	A	B	C
6	No	Product Name	Supplier
60	54	Scottish Longbreads	Specialty Biscuits, Ltd.
61	55	Sir Rodney's Marmalade	Specialty Biscuits, Ltd.
62	56	Sir Rodney's Scones	Specialty Biscuits, Ltd.

In this lesson we'll extract a list of suppliers from the workbook using an advanced filter. The advanced filter's *Unique records only* feature will be used to ensure that each supplier is only listed once.

You will be amazed at how often you'll find this feature useful in your day-to-day business use of Excel.

3   Delete rows 1-5 (the cells that were previously used to define the advanced filter criteria condition).

After deleting these rows your worksheet should look like this:

	A	B	C
1	No	Product Name	Supplier
2	1	Aniseed Syrup	Exotic Liquids
3	2	Boston Crab Meat	New England Seafood Cannery
4	3	Camembert Pierrot	Gai pâturage
5	4	Carnarvon Tigers	Pavlova, Ltd.

4   Bring up the *Advanced Filter* dialog.

Click: Data→Sort & Filter→Advanced.

5   Set the *List range* to all cells in column C within the range.

   1.   Click in the *List range* text box.

   2.   Click into cell C1.

   3.   Press: **<Ctrl>+<Shift>+<DownArrow>**

      The range C1:C70 appears in the *List Range* text box.

List range:	$C$1:$C$70	

Inventory-4

6   Leave the *Criteria Range* box blank and check the *Unique records only* check box.

> ☑ Unique records only

7   Click the *Copy to another location* option button.

8   Click in the *Copy to:* box and then click once in cell I1.

The dialog should now look like this:

9   Click the OK button.

A list of suppliers appears in column I:

	F	G	H	I	J	K
1	In Stock	Value		Supplier		
2	13	130.00		Exotic Liquids		
3	123	2,263.20		New England Seafood Cannery		
4	19	646.00		Gai pâturage		
5	42	2,625.00		Pavlova, Ltd.		
6	39	702.00		Aux joyeux ecclésiastiques		
7	17	323.00		New Orleans Cajun Delights		

Notice that there are no duplicate entries in the list. *The Unique records only* feature has ensured that each supplier is only listed once.

10   Delete column I.

11   Save your work as *Inventory-5*.

Lesson 1-8: Convert a range into a table and add a total row

This lesson introduces tables (originally introduced in Excel 2007). Tables provide a completely new way to work with tabular data and are particularly powerful when dealing with dynamic data. A table is very similar to a range but incorporates several very useful extra features.

You can freely convert a table to a range, or a range to a table. The key difference between ranges and tables is that table references shrink and grow dynamically.

For example, if you create a chart from a table and then add more rows to the table, the source data will automatically adjust to include the new rows. This doesn't happen with a range.

1 Open *Inventory-5* from your sample files folder (if it isn't already open).

2 Convert the range into a table.

note

You can also convert a range into a table using the keyboard shortcut:

<Ctrl>+<T>

1. Click anywhere inside the range

2. Click: Insert→Tables→Table.

The *Create Table* dialog is displayed:

Create Table	
Where is the data for your table?	
=$A$1:$G$70	
☑ My table has headers	
OK	Cancel

3. Click the OK button.

The range has now been converted to a table. The appearance of the range has changed and filter arrows have appeared in the header row.

	A	B	C
1	No ▾	Product Name ▾	Supplier ▾
2	1	Aniseed Syrup	Exotic Liquids
3	2	Boston Crab Meat	New England Seafood Cannery
4	3	Camembert Pierrot	Gai pâturage
5	4	Carnarvon Tigers	Pavlova, Ltd.

3 Scroll down the table and note the "sticky" column headers.

1. Click inside the table

2. Scroll down the table until the headers disappear from the top row.

In a range you would have to freeze panes in order to continue to view the range headers (freeze panes was covered in the Essential Skills book in this series). Tables are much easier to work with. The table headers and filter buttons are always visible as they replace the column letters when scrolled off the screen:

Inventory-5

No		Product Name	Supplier	Category
14	13	Fløtemysost	Norske Meierier	Dairy Products
15	14	Geitost	Norske Meierier	Dairy Products
16	15	Genen Shouyu	Mayumi's	Condiments
17	16	Gnocchi di nonna Alice	Pasta Buttini s.r.l.	Grains/Cereals
18	17	Gorgonzola Telino	Formaggi Fortini s.r.l.	Dairy Products

note

Excel's use of the quirky SUBTOTAL function

When Excel adds a total row it uses the quirky SUBTOTAL function by default.

The SUBTOTAL function has a very odd syntax. It is:

SUBTOTAL(function_num, ref1, [ref2], ...)

The *function_num* argument causes massive confusion as it has been implemented in a very quirky way!

The *function_num* can be a value of 1 to 11, each corresponding to a different function. For example function_num *9* is the SUM function.

The *function_num* can also be the same numbers with 100 added to them (ie 101-111) and these correspond to the same functions. For example function_num 9 is the SUM function and so is function_num 109.

So why do we have 109 and 9 both meaning the SUM function?

The reason is that a 109 SUM function ignores any rows that are hidden, while a 9 SUM function will include any hidden rows. (You'll learn about hidden rows in: *Lesson 6-7: Hide and unhide worksheets, columns and rows*).

You need to know this because the total row ignores any rows hidden by default meaning that (in this lesson's example) the function used to total (or sum) the column is:

=SUBTOTAL(109,[Value])

This will ignore all hidden rows and, most of the time that is what you want.

If you wanted to include any hidden rows in the total you would have to change the formula to:

=SUBTOTAL(9,[Value])

4 Add a total row.

Tables have a built-in ability to add total rows.

1. Click anywhere inside the table.

   The *Table Tools* tab appears on the ribbon.

2. Click: Table Tools→Design→Table Style Options→Total Row.

   A total row appears at the bottom of the table.

	Category	Unit Price	In Stock	Value
69	Grains/Cereals	33.25	22	731.50
70	Confections	9.50	36	342.00
71				69,598.25

3. Re-size the *Value* column if needed to view the total.

By default the total row contains the SUM of all values in the right-most column. Excel uses the SUM function indirectly via the SUBTOTAL function (see sidebar).

5 Change the total from SUM to AVERAGE and add a total for the *In Stock* column.

1. Click cell G71 (the cell containing the total).

   A drop-down arrow appears next to the total.

2. Click the drop-down arrow and choose *Average* from the function list.

3. Click on cell F71 at the bottom of the *In Stock* column (the cell in the dark blue total row).

   A drop-down arrow appears next to the empty cell.

4. Click the drop-down arrow and then click *Sum* from the function list.

   The sum of units in stock is now also displayed.

6 Change the AVERAGE in cell G71 back to a SUM.

33.25	22	731.50
9.50	36	342.00
	3018	69,598.25

7 Save your work as *Inventory-6*.

Lesson 1-9: Format a table using table styles and convert a table into a range

When you have formatted your data as a table, you can customize the appearance of the table using Excel's powerful *table styles* feature.

You can either apply a table style from the *table styles gallery* or you can create your own custom table styles.

All of the pre-defined styles in the *table styles gallery* follow best practice by restricting color choice to theme colors. Themes are covered in great depth in the *Essential Skills* book in this series.

In this lesson we'll explore the simpler of the two options by applying some of the standard pre-defined table styles. Later (in *Lesson 1-10: Create a custom table style),* we'll create a hand-designed table style.

1 Open *Inventory-6* from your sample files folder (if it isn't already open).

2 Apply the *module* theme to the workbook.

Click: Page Layout→Themes→Themes→Module.

The module theme is applied and the colors used in the table change.

The reason they change is that Microsoft used best practice when creating the built-in table styles and restricted their color choices to theme colors.

3 Change the theme back to the default *Office* theme.

4 Choose a new table style from the *Table Styles Gallery*.

1. Click anywhere inside the table.

2. Click: Table Tools→Design→Table Styles→More.

The *More* button is located on the bottom right hand corner of the Table Styles group:

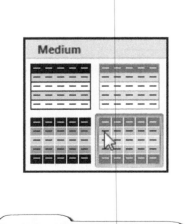

The table styles gallery is displayed.

3. Click any of the table styles that you find attractive.

The chosen table style is applied.

4. Restore the table style to the default *Table Style Medium 9.*

5 Change the table's appearance using *Table Style Options*.

1. Click inside the table.

2. Click the Table Tools→Design tab and focus upon the *Table Style Options* group.

Inventory-6

note

Formatting mayhem when converting tables to ranges and back

When you convert a table to a range, all of the formatting applied to the table remains.

Removing this formatting after conversion can be problematic.

The biggest problem occurs if you need to convert the range back into a table again.

Because each cell contains formatting information, Excel politely refuses to change any of the colors. This makes it impossible to change the table style using the table style gallery.

The table appearance then becomes very strange when you add rows to the table. The added rows will use the table style while the rows imported from the range will keep their old formatting (because Excel thinks that the formatting has been manually applied).

The simple solution is to always obey the important rule:

Apply the None style before converting a table to a range, except when you are sure that you will never want to convert the range back to a table again.

tip

How to quickly identify tables and ranges

A quick way to tell tables from ranges is to click inside the table/range.

If you see the Table Tools tab on the Ribbon you will immediately know that you are looking at a table.

The easiest way to understand the options is to experiment by switching each option on and off. The function of each option will then be obvious.

6   Apply the *None* quick table style to remove all table style formatting.

The *None* style is extremely useful.

In a moment we're going to convert the table back into a range. You'll nearly always want to remove table style formatting prior to conversion (see sidebar for more on this).

1.   Click anywhere inside the table.

2.   Click: Table Tools→Design→Table Styles→ More→None.

The *None* style is the one in the top left corner of the gallery.

The table now looks more like a range but it is still a table and still provides all table features.

7   Set the *None* style as the default.

I always like to work with the *None* style as the default. Excel's default table styles are a little too colorful for me. Note that this sets the default style only for this workbook.

1.   Click inside the table.

2.   Click: Table Tools→Design→Table Styles→More.

3.   Right-click on the *None* style and click *Set as Default* from the shortcut menu.

Every time we create new tables in this workbook they will now display with the *None* style.

8   Convert the table to a range.

1.   Click anywhere inside the table.

2.   Click: Table Tools→Design→Tools→Convert to Range.

3.   Click Yes.

The table has now been converted back to a range.

9   *Save your work as Inventory-7.*

note

Why it is a good idea to restrict custom style colors to theme colors

If you restrict your color choice to the 60 *Theme Colors*, your worksheet design will be compatible with documents that use other themes.

If you use non-theme colors, your worksheets will not seamlessly integrate (from a design point of view) with PowerPoint presentations, Word documents, and other Office documents that use a different theme.

Example

John creates a worksheet using the default *Office* theme.

Mary wants to use this in her PowerPoint presentation that uses the *Opulent* theme. John e-mails the worksheet to her and then she simply pastes the required cells into her presentation and changes the theme to *Opulent*.

Joe sees the presentation and wants to use the same worksheet in his Word report that uses the *Verve* theme. Mary e-mails the presentation to him and then he simply pastes the required slides into his Word document and changes the theme to *Verve*.

The same worksheet has been used without modification and it blends perfectly into both Joe and Mary's work because John followed best practice and restricted his color choices to theme colors.

Lesson 1-10: Create a custom table style

Perhaps none of the huge selection of styles in the *table styles gallery* is suitable for your requirements. In this case you can create a custom table style from scratch.

Another great feature of a custom table style is that you can set it as the default for this workbook. This saves you from continually reapplying a style every time you create a table.

1 Open *Inventory-7* from your sample files folder (if it isn't already open).

Notice that this range, (created from a table with a total row in: *Lesson 1-9: Format a table using table styles and convert a table into a range*), has totals in row 71.

2 Convert the range into a table.

This was covered in: *Lesson 1-8: Convert a range into a table and add a total row*.

3 Convert the *range total row* to a *table total row*.

If you click Table Tools→Design you will see that the *Total Row* check box is unchecked.

☑ Header Row	☐ First Column
☐ Total Row	☐ Last Column
☑ Banded Rows	☐ Banded Columns

Table Style Options

Why then does the table appear to have a total row in row 71?

	E	F	G
70	9.50	36	342.00
71		3018	69,598.25

The reason is that row 71 is the total row defined in the range and has nothing to do with the total row that is available as a table feature.

1. Check: Table Tools→Design→Table Style Options→ Total Row.

   A second total row appears beneath the first. This is the *table total row*:

	E	F	G
70	9.50	36	342.00
71		3018	69,598.25
72			69,598.25

2. Delete row 71 to remove the range total row.

4 Create a custom table style based upon an existing style.

Inventory-7

1. Click anywhere inside the table.

2. Click: Table Tools→Design→Table Styles→More.

   The *More* button is located on the bottom right hand corner of the Table Styles group:

   The table styles gallery is displayed.

3. Right-click one of the existing styles and then click *Duplicate* from the shortcut menu.

   The *Modify Table Quick Style* dialog is displayed:

4. Name the new table style **TSM**.

   New Table Quick Sty
   Name: TSM
   Table Element:

   Each of the table's elements are listed on the left of the dialog.

   Each element that had been formatted (in the style you chose to duplicate) is shown in bold face type.

   Table Element:
   Preview
   Whole Table
   First Column Stripe
   Second Column Stripe
   First Row Stripe
   Second Row Stripe
   Last Column
   First Column
   Header Row
   Total Row

5. Choose a table element and then click the *Format* button to set the *Font, Border* and *Fill* formatting.

   To follow best practice you should restrict your color and font choices to theme colors and theme fonts (see sidebar on facing page).

6. Customize as many other elements as you wish.

7. Click the OK button.

5 Apply your new custom style to the table.

1. Click: Table Tools→Design→Table Styles→More.

2. Notice the new *Custom* section at the top of the gallery containing your new style.

3. Hover the mouse cursor over your new style and the style name will appear.

4. Click the style to apply it to the worksheet.

5. Change the style back to *None*.

6 Save your work as Inventory-8.

Medium

Custom

TSM

Light

important

Click within the column and not on the column header when you want to sort

If you click on the column header (which selects the entire column) before sorting, Excel will not know whether you want to sort the entire range or the column in isolation.

For this reason, it will present you with a dialog asking if you want to sort the entire range or table (*Expand the selection*) or to simply sort the column, potentially scrambling your data (*Continue with the current selection*).

Because you will very rarely (and probably never) want to sort a column within a range in isolation it is good practice to click any cell in the column, rather than the column header, before sorting.

Lesson 1-11: Sort a range or table by rows

1   Open *Inventory-8* from your sample files folder.

2   Sort the categories from Z-A.

   1.   Click anywhere in the *category* column.

   2.   Click: Data→Sort & Filter→Z-A.

   The categories are now sorted in reverse alphabetical order:

	Category	Unit Price	In Stock
13	Seafood	12.00	95
14	Produce	10.00	4
15	Produce	53.00	20
16	Produce	23.25	35

3   Sort the categories from A-Z.

   1.   Click anywhere in the *category* column.

   2.   Click: Data→Sort & Filter→A-Z.

   The categories are now sorted in alphabetical order:

	Category	Unit Price	In Stock
12	Beverages	18.00	20
13	Condiments	10.00	13
14	Condiments	22.00	53
15	Condiments	15.50	39

4   Sort by both Category and Supplier.

   1.   There's a small problem with the existing sort. It can be seen that one category has many suppliers:

	Supplier	Category
55	Tokyo Traders	Produce
56	G'day, Mate	Produce
57	Mayumi's	Produce
58	Grandma Kelly's Homestead	Produce

   In the above example it would be nice to also have the suppliers listed in alphabetical order. This can be achieved with a two-column sort.

   2.   Click: Data→Sort & Filter→Sort.

   The *Sort* dialog appears:

   3.   Click the *Add Level* button to add a second sort that will list Suppliers from A-Z.

Inventory-8

note

You can also sort from the Home tab

The Home tab also has a *Sort & Filter* menu button in the *Editing* group.

This is one of the unusual cases where a feature is repeated on two different ribbon tabs.

It doesn't matter which you use as the functionality is identical.

	F		G	
1	In Stock ▾		Value ▾	
2		17	⚑	4,479.50
3		69	⚑	1,242.00
4		52	⚑	728.00
5		111	⚑	1,554.00

tip

Sort with a right-click

The fastest sort method of all is to right-click any cell and select *Sort* from the shortcut menu.

The fly-out menu then provides every sort option available from the Ribbon.

⇣	Sort A to Z
⇣	Sort Z to A
	Put Selected Cell Color On Top
	Put Selected Font Color On Top
	Put Selected Cell Icon On Top
⊞	Custom Sort...

Sort dialog box:

Column		Sort On		Order	
Sort by	Category	Values		A to Z	
Then by	Supplier	Values		A to Z	

☑ My data has headers | Add Level | Delete Level | Copy Level | Options...

4. Click the OK button.

The table is now sorted first by *Category* and then by *Supplier*.

	Supplier	Category
55	G'day, Mate	Produce
56	Grandma Kelly's Homestead	Produce
57	Mayumi's	Produce

5 **Select all of the data cells in column G.**

1. Hover the mouse cursor over the top of cell G1 until you see a black down-arrow. Note that you *must* overlap the bottom of the button. If you hover inside the button you'll still see the black arrow but your selection will then include all of the cells in columns G!

G
Value
1,242.00

    The arrow must overlap the bottom of this button!

2. When you see the arrow, click once to select cells G2:G70.

6 **Add a *Three Flags* conditional format icon set to column G.**

Conditional formatting was covered in depth in the *Essential Skills* book in this series.

1. Click: Home→Styles→Conditional Formatting→Icon Sets→ 3 Flags.

    ⚑ ⚑ ⚑

2. Widen column G to make room for the flags.

    Values in column G have red, yellow or green flags added depending upon their value. If you see nearly all red flags it is because you selected G2:G71 by mistake!

7 **Sort by icon so that the green flagged cells appear first, the yellow flagged second and the red flagged last.**

1. Click any value in column G.

2. Click: Data→Sort & Filter→Sort.

3. Click the *Delete Level* button twice to remove existing sort conditions.

4. Add the following three sort conditions to sort by flag.

Column		Sort On		Order			
Sort by	Value	Cell Icon		⚑		On Top	
Then by	Value	Cell Icon		⚑		On Top	
Then by	Value	Cell Icon		⚑		On Top	

5. Click OK

8 **Save your work as *Inventory-9*.**

Lesson 1-12: Sort a range by columns

Students often come to my classes with long "wish lists". Usually by the end of the course they have ticked all of their requirements off and don't have to ask any of the questions they had arrived with.

An item that seems to be on everybody's wish list is a way to sort data by columns. This lesson will teach you a simple technique to achieve this.

Note that this technique will work for ranges but not for tables. If you need to sort a table by columns you'll have to convert it to a range first. That's exactly what we'll do in this lesson.

1   Open *Inventory-9* from your sample files folder.

2   Convert the table into a range.

> This was covered in: *Lesson 1-9: Format a table using table styles and convert a table into a range.*

3   Add a blank row at the top of the range.

4   Add numbers to enable a sort order of: *No, Category, Supplier, Product Name, Price, Stock, Value.*

> The blank row you have just added is a dummy row to set the sort order.
>
> Type numbers into row 1 that numerically describe the desired sorted position for each column:

	A	B	C	D	E	F	G
1	1	4	3	2	5.00	6	7
2	No	Product Name	Supplier	Category	Price	Stock	Value

> Note that the value in cell E1 only appears to be different to the others because it has inherited the two decimal place format from the *Price* field in the table.

5   Sort the range by reference to row one.

> 1.   Click anywhere inside the range.
>
> 2.   Press **<Ctrl>+<A>** to select every cell in the range (including the dummy header row).
>
> 3.   Click: Data→Sort & Filter→Sort.
>
>   Notice that row 1 is no longer included in the selected range. This is because the *My data has headers* box is checked.
>
>   ☑ My data has headers
>
> 4.   Uncheck the *My data has headers* check box.
>
>   ☐ My data has headers
>
> The entire range (including row 1) is now selected.

Inventory-9

5. Remove any existing sort condition(s) by clicking the *Delete Level* button.

6. Click the *Options...* button.

    The *Sort Options* dialog is displayed.

7. Click the *Sort left to right* option button.

Sort Options
☐ Case sensitive
Orientation
○ Sort top to bottom
◉ Sort left to right
OK   Cancel

8. Click the OK button.

9. Click the *Add Level* button. `⟲ Add Level`

10. Set a new sort to sort on *Row 1, Values, Smallest to Largest*.

Sort
Add Level   ✗ Delete Level   Copy Level   ⬆ ⬇   Options...   ☐ My data has headers
Row	Sort On	Order
Sort by Row 1 ▾	Values ▾	Smallest to Largest ▾

11. Click the OK button.

    The worksheet is now sorted in the same order as the dummy sort row.

	A	B	C	D	E	F	G
1	1	2	3	4	5.00	6	7
2	No	Category	Supplier	Product Nai	Price	Stock	Value

6 Delete row 1.

7 Convert the range back into a table.

This was covered in: *Lesson 1-8: Convert a range into a table and add a total* row.

8 Save your work as *Inventory-10*.

Lesson 1-13: Sort a range or table by custom list

Sometimes you need a sort order that is not alphabetical.

For example, you might run a support desk and be given support incidents marked as *Low, Medium, High, Urgent* and *Critical*. You would want to sort such a list in order of priority, but these priorities do not lend themselves to an alphabetic sort.

If you create a custom sort list with each incident listed in order of importance you can then use the list to sort a range or table. This lesson will show you how.

1 Open *Help Desk-1* from your sample files folder.

This worksheet lists several support incidents sent to the help desk and prioritized from *Low* to *Critical*.

	A	B	C	D	E
1	Incident ID	Date Raised	Raised By	Description	Priority
2	10872	27-May-09	George W. Bush	Air conditioning not working	Low
3	10873	27-May-09	Britney Spears	No hot water in staff kitchen	Medium
4	10874	27-May-09	Angelina Jolie	Broken lock on main door	Critical
5	10875	27-May-09	Kofi Anan	Freezer has stopped working	Critical

2 Create a custom list.

1. Click: File→Options→Advanced→General→ Edit Custom Lists.

Add-Ins	ScreenTip style:	Show feature descriptions in ScreenTips	▼
Trust Center	Create lists for use in sorts and fill sequences:		Edit Custom Lists...

The *Custom Lists* dialog is displayed.

2. Type each of the support incidents priority levels followed by the **<Enter>** key into the *List entries* box in the following order :

Custom Lists

Custom Lists

Custom lists:

```
NEW LIST
Mon, Tue, Wed, Thu, Fri, Sat, S
Monday, Tuesday, Wednesday,
Jan, Feb, Mar, Apr, May, Jun, J
January, February, March, April
North, South, East, West
```

List entries:

```
Low
Medium
High
Urgent
Critical
```

3. Click the OK button.

4. Click the OK button.

Help Desk-1

3   Sort the table using the custom list.

1.   Click anywhere in column E.

2.   Click: Data→Sort & Filter→Sort.

The *Sort* dialog appears:

3.   Select *Priority* from the *Sort by* drop down.

4.   Select *Custom List…* for the *Order:*

5.   Click on your newly added custom list and then click the OK button.

6.   Click the OK button.

The worksheet is now sorted in order of priority from lowest to highest.

4   Reverse the sort order to show the higher priority incidents first.

1.   Click anywhere inside the range.

2.   Click: Data→Sort & Filter→Sort.

3.   Click the drop-down arrow next to *Order*. Notice that your custom sort order is shown twice as *low to critical* and as *critical to low*.

Order
Critical, Urgent, High, Medium, Low
A to Z
Z to A
Low, Medium, High, Urgent, Critical
Critical, Urgent, High, Medium, Low
Custom List...

4.   Click *critical to low*.

5.   Click the OK button.

The worksheet is now sorted with higher priority incidents listed first.

D	E
Description	Priority
Broken lock on main door	Critical
Freezer has stopped working	Critical
Burst water main is flooding the basement	Critical
Computer not working	Urgent

5   Save your work as *Help Desk-2*.

Lesson 1-14: Name a table and create an automatic structured table reference

note

If this feature doesn't work for you, somebody may have switched it off

Excel allows structured references to be switched off.

You really wouldn't ever want to do this, as structured references are one of the most useful features of tables.

If you simply want to maintain compatibility with Excel 2003 you can save the workbook in *Excel 97/2003 Workbook* format. The structured reference feature will then be automatically disabled.

You can check that this feature is enabled by clicking:

File→Options→ Formulas→ Working with formulas→ Use table names in Formulas

When the check box is checked the feature is switched on (the default).

One of the key differences between a range and a table is that tables shrink and grow dynamically.

The table's ability to shrink and grow wouldn't be useful without a way to enter a cell reference into a formula that points to all of the rows in a table column (no matter how many rows the table contains).

Consider the following table:

	A	B	C	D	E	F	G
1	Sales						
2							
3	Month	Net	Tax	Total		Total Sales	
4	Jan	15,249.00	2,287.35	17,536.35			
5	Feb	18,320.00	2,748.00	21,068.00			
6	Mar	21,260.00	3,189.00	24,449.00			

To calculate the total sales in cell G3 you could use the formula:

=SUM(D4:D6)

A recurring problem with data ranges is that when you add a new row to the range for April's sales, the SUM formula has to be adjusted (to D4:D7).

In order to exploit the power of dynamic tables the Excel designers had to figure out a whole new way of referencing cell ranges. They needed a cell reference that would mean:

=SUM(All of the cells in Column D that are inside this table)

Because there may be several tables on a single worksheet, the cell reference needs to indicate which table the range is in. This has been solved by adding the ability to name tables. If the table in this example was called *Sales* and the column was called *Total* the formula would be:

=SUM(Sales[Total])

This type of reference is called a structured reference.

In this lesson, we'll use structured references to create some formulas that will always give the correct result, no matter how many rows you add or remove from a table.

1 Open *Sales Summary-1* from your sample files folder.

2 Convert the range into a table.

1. Click anywhere inside the range (A3:D6).

2. Click: Insert→Tables→Table.

   The *Create Table* dialog is displayed

3. Click OK to accept the automatically detected range A3:D6.

Sales Summary-1

3 Set the table name to: *Sales*.

1. Click anywhere inside the table.

   Notice that a *Table Tools* tab has appeared on the ribbon.

2. Click: Table Tools→Design→Properties→Table Name.

3. Type **Sales** into the table name text box).

Table Name:
Sales
⬚ Resize Table
Properties

4. Press the **<Enter>** key.

4 Add a SUM function to cell G3 using a structured reference.

1. Click in cell G3 and type:

   =SUM(

2. Hover the mouse over the top of cell D3 until you see a black down-arrow.

3. When you see the arrow, click once to select cells D4:D7 (all of the data cells in the column).

4. Note the structured reference that has been automatically entered:

E	F	G	H	I
	Total Sales	=SUM(Sales[Total]		
	Average Sales	SUM(**number1**, [number2], ...)		

5. Press the **<Enter>** key.

   There's no need to close the bracket, Excel is clever enough to add this for you automatically.

   The structured reference means:

   The sum of all values in the Total column in the Sales table.

5 Add another row to the Sales table by entering the following values in row 7:

6	Mar	21,260.00	3,189.00	24,449.00
7	Apr	24,400.00	3,660.00	28,060.00

   Note that the total in cell G3 has updated to include April's sales figure. You can now appreciate the power of structured table references.

6 Save your work as *Sales Summary-2.*

Lesson 1-15: Create a manual structured table reference

In the last lesson you created a structured reference automatically by selecting a range in a table with the mouse.

In this lesson you'll appreciate the powerful new tools built into Excel that make the creation of manual structured references very easy and intuitive.

1   Open *Sales Summary-2* from your sample files folder (if it isn't already open).

	A	B	C	D	E	F	G
1	Sales						
2							
3	Month ▾	Net ▾	Tax ▾	Total ▾		**Total Sales**	91113.35
4	Jan	15,249.00	2,287.35	17,536.35			
5	Feb	18,320.00	2,748.00	21,068.00			
6	Mar	21,260.00	3,189.00	24,449.00			
7	Apr	24,400.00	3,660.00	28,060.00			
8							

2   Add a formula to cell G4 that will calculate average sales using a manual structured reference.

1.   Type the words **Average Sales** into cell F4.

2.   Press the **<Tab>** key to move to cell G4.

3.   Type:

=AVERAGE(Sa

	F	G	H	I
3	**Total Sales**	91113.35		
4	**Average Sales**	=Average(Sa		
5		AVERAGE(**number1**, [number2], ...)		
6		▦ Sales		

Notice that a small icon of a table has appeared with the name *Sales*. If there were more than one table on any worksheet in this workbook that began with **Sa** you'd see them all listed here. It doesn't matter whether you type **Sa** or **SA**. Table names are not case sensitive.

4.   Press the **<Tab>** key.

The remaining letters in the table name are entered into the formula.

The table name references all of the data in a table excluding the header and totals row.

In this case and at this time, it will reference cells A4:D7.

As rows are added and removed from the table, the cells referenced by the table name will dynamically adjust to continue to reference all of the data in the table.

Sales Summary-2

5. Open a square bracket after the word *Sales*.

   This time something amazing happens! Excel lists all of the columns in the table:

	F	G	H	I
3	**Total Sales**	91113.35		
4	**Average Sales**	=AVERAGE(Sales[		
5		AVERAGE(**number1**, [number2], ...)		
6				[...] Month
7				[...] Net
8				[...] Tax
9				[...] Total
10				#All
11				#Data
12				#Headers
13				#Totals
				#This Row

6. Use the **<DownArrow>** key to move the highlight to the *Total* field.

7. Press the **<Tab>** key.

8. Close the square bracket.

9. Close the round bracket.

   The formula should now look like this:

Average Sales	=AVERAGE(Sales[Total])

   In a similar way to the table name, the column name will reference all of the data in the Total column excluding the header and total rows.

   In this case and at this time it will reference cells D4:D7.

   As rows are added and removed from the table, the cells referenced by the table name and column name will dynamically adjust to continue to reference all of the data in the column.

10. Press the **<Enter>** key to view the result of the formula.

    Average sales during the period Jan-Apr were 22,778.34.

	A	B	C	D	E	F	G
1	**Sales**						
2							
3	**Month**	**Net**	**Tax**	**Total**		**Total Sales**	91113.35
4	**Jan**	15,249.00	2,287.35	17,536.35		**Average Sales**	22778.34
5	**Feb**	18,320.00	2,748.00	21,068.00			
6	**Mar**	21,260.00	3,189.00	24,449.00			
7	**Apr**	24,400.00	3,660.00	28,060.00			

3 Save your work as *Sales Summary-3*.

note

Automatic name changing in formulas

If you change a table name or a column name, any formulas that reference the table will automatically change.

Unfortunately, this will not be the case if you have macros that reference table names (macros will be covered later in: *Session Eight: Forms and Macros*).

For this reason it is a good idea to name your tables as soon as they are created and to avoid changing table and column names.

Lesson 1-16: Use special items in structured table references

You may have wondered what the items beginning with the hash symbol (#) meant in the last lesson:

◢	F	G	H	I	J
3	**Total Sales**	91113.35			
4	**Average Sales**	=AVERAGE(Sales[			
5		AVERAGE(**number1**, [number2], ...)			
6			{...} Month		
7			{...} Net		
8			{...} Tax		
9			{...} Total		
10			#All		
11			#Data		
12			#Headers		
13			#Totals		
			@ - This Row		

These are called *special items*. They can be used to reference different parts of a table.

The #Data special item is rarely used because it is the default and doesn't have to be explicitly stated. In the last lesson you created the structured reference:

Average Sales	=AVERAGE(Sales[Total])

You could have entered the same formula in a different (and needlessly complex) way by adding the #Data special item like this:

=Average(Sales[[#Data],[Total]])

The #Data special item simply means:

All of the data excluding the header and totals row.

1 Open *Sales Summary-3* from your sample files folder (if it isn't already open).

2 Add a total row to the table.

   This was covered in: *Lesson 1-8: Convert a range into a table and add a total row.*

3 Change the total at the bottom of column D so that it displays the maximum sales in any one month (using the *Max* option).

   1. Click in cell D8.

   2. Click the drop-down arrow next to the cell and select *Max* from the shortcut menu.

4 Type the words: **Max Sales** into cell F5.

Sales Summary-3

	A	B	C	D	E	F	G
3	Month ▾	Net ▾	Tax ▾	Total ▾		Total Sales	91113.35
4	Jan	15,249.00	2,287.35	17,536.35		Average Sales	22778.34
5	Feb	18,320.00	2,748.00	21,068.00		Max Sales	
6	Mar	21,260.00	3,189.00	24,449.00			
7	Apr	24,400.00	3,660.00	28,060.00			
8	Total			28,060.00			

This time we're going to reference the value in cell D8 using the special item: #Totals.

5   Add an automatic structured reference to cell G5 that will reference cell D8.

1.   Click in cell G5.

2.   Press the equals key (=) to start the formula.

3.   Click in cell D8.

An automatic structured reference is created that uses the special item #Totals to point to the Total row.

Max Sales	=Sales[[#Totals],[Total]]

This means:

Reference the value in the Totals row of the Sales table that is at the bottom of the Total column.

4.   Press the <Enter> key to save the formula to the cell.

The *Max Sales* figure is displayed.

6   Apply the comma style to cells G3:G5.

1.   Select G3:G5.

2.   Click: Home→Number→Comma Style.

	A	B	C	D	E	F	G
3	Month ▾	Net ▾	Tax ▾	Total ▾		Total Sales	91,113.35
4	Jan	15,249.00	2,287.35	17,536.35		Average Sales	22,778.34
5	Feb	18,320.00	2,748.00	21,068.00		Max Sales	28,060.00

7   Understand all of the special items.

Here's what the other special items mean:

Special item	What it references
#All	Every cell in the table (this includes the header and total rows).
#Data	The entire contents of the table excluding the header and total rows (this is the default).
#Headers	The header row.
#Totals	The total row.
@ - ThisRow	Covered in the next lesson.

8   Save your work as *Sales Summary-4.*

Lesson 1-17: Understand unqualified structured table references

A qualified structured reference is a reference that includes the table name such as:

=Sum(Sales[Net])

An unqualified structured reference may be used in formulas within the table itself. In this case you do not have to use the table name as well as the field name because it is obvious.

For example, if you wanted to add *Net sales* and *Tax*, you could use the qualified structured reference:

=Sales[Net]+Sales[Tax]

… but it would be easier and more readable to use the unqualified structured reference:

=[Net]+[Tax]

This reference works because the @ (meaning ThisRow) special item is the default when entering structured references into tables.

You could have entered the same formula in a different way by adding the @ (meaning This Row) special item like this:

=[@Net]+[@Tax]

The @ special item is useful when you want to place a formula *alongside* a table and then want to AutoFill the formula to reference each row in the table.

1   Open *Sales Summary-4* from your sample files folder (if it isn't already open).

2   Convert the A1 style references within the table to unqualified structured references.

    1. Double-click in cell C4 and note the existing A1 style reference:

    The formula is calculating sales tax as 15% of the net sales value.

    2. Delete this formula and replace it with the unqualified structured reference:

       =[Net]*0.15

    3. Press the **<Enter>** key.

    4. Double-click in cell D4 and note the existing A1 style reference:

Sales Summary-4

The formula is adding the sales tax to the net value.

5. Delete this formula and replace it with the unqualified structured reference:

=[Net]+[Tax]

6. Press the **<Enter>** key.

7. Select cells C4:D4.

8. Click the AutoFill handle on the bottom right corner of the selected cells (look for the black cross cursor shape).

	B	C	D	E
3	Net	Tax	Total	
4	15,249.00	2,287.35	17,536.35	
5	18,320.00	2,748.00	21,068.00	

9. When you see the black cross cursor shape, drag down to row 7 to AutoFill the formulas to the rest of the table.

10. Click: Formulas→Formula Auditing→Show Formulas to view the formulas in each cell:

	C	D
3	Tax	Total
4	=[Net]*0.15	=[Net]+[Tax]
5	=[Net]*0.15	=[Net]+[Tax]
6	=[Net]*0.15	=[Net]+[Tax]
7	=[Net]*0.15	=[Net]+[Tax]

You don't *have* to convert the old A1 references to unqualified structured references, but it does make the formulas easier to read if you do.

11. Click: Formulas→Formula Auditing→Show Formulas once again to display values.

3 **Convert the table back to an unformatted range.**

1. Click anywhere inside the table.

2. Click: Table Tools→Design→Table Styles→More→None.

The formatting is removed from the table.

3. Click: Table Tools→Design→Tools→Convert To Range.

4. Click the Yes button.

Notice that the filter buttons have now disappeared.

Notice also that the structured references have now changed to (rather verbose) A1 style references.

4 **Convert the range back to a table.**

1. Click anywhere inside the range.

2. Click: Insert→Tables→Table.

3. Click OK to accept the data range A3:D8.

Notice that the filter buttons have now re-appeared. Notice also that A1 style references remain. They are not converted to structured references when you convert a range into a table.

5 **Save your work as** *Sales Summary-5*.

---

tip

You can also convert a table to a range by right-clicking anywhere in the table and then clicking:

Table→Convert To Range

... from the shortcut menu.

The shortcut menu method is much faster than using the Ribbon.

Session 1: Exercise

1 Open *Land Speed Records* from your sample files folder.

2 Convert the range A1:F13 into a table.

3 Name the table *SpeedRecord*.

4 Use a simple filter to only show speed records achieved at Bonneville Salt Flats.

5 Remove the filter to show all speed records.

6 Use an advanced filter to show speed records:

- At Bonneville Salt Flats that are greater than 575 mph.

- Together with all records held by Tom Green (irrespective of location and top speed).

    Another way of expressing this is:

    Where location = Bonneville Salt Flats AND MPH > 575
    OR where Driver = Tom Green.

Here's the result set you should see:

	A	B	C	D	E	F
5	Date	Location	Driver	Vehicle	Power	MPH
7	05-Oct-64	Bonneville Salt Flats	Tom Green	Wingfoot Express	Turbojet	413.199
13	07-Nov-65	Bonneville Salt Flats	Art Arfons	Green Monster	Turbojet	576.553
14	15-Nov-65	Bonneville Salt Flats	Craig Breedlove	Spirit of America - Sonic 1	Turbojet	600.601
15	23-Oct-70	Bonneville Salt Flats	Gary Gabelich	Blue Flame	Rocket	622.407

7 Remove the advanced filter to show all records and remove any rows that you may have added for the advanced filter criteria.

8 Sort the table A-Z, first by *Location* and then by *Driver*.

9 Add a total row to the table and use the MAX function to display the maximum value in column F.

10 Type **Km/h** into cell G1.

11 Use a formula containing a structured reference to show speeds in kilometers per hour in column G.

12 Save your work as *Land Speed Records-2*.

	A	B	C	D	E	F	G
1	Date	Location	Driver	Vehicle	Power	MPH	Km/h
2	15-Oct-97	Black Rock Desert	Andy Green	ThrustSSC	Turbofan	766.000	1232.758
3	04-Oct-83	Black Rock Desert	Richard Noble	Thrust2	Turbojet	633.000	1018.715
4	07-Oct-64	Bonneville Salt Flats	Art Arfons	Green Monster	Turbojet	434.022	698.4907
5	27-Oct-64	Bonneville Salt Flats	Art Arfons	Green Monster	Turbojet	536.710	863.751
6	07-Nov-65	Bonneville Salt Flats	Art Arfons	Green Monster	Turbojet	576.553	927.8721
7	05-Sep-63	Bonneville Salt Flats	Craig Breedlove	Spirit of America	Turbojet	407.447	655.7224
8	13-Oct-64	Bonneville Salt Flats	Craig Breedlove	Spirit of America	Turbojet	468.719	754.3301
9	15-Oct-64	Bonneville Salt Flats	Craig Breedlove	Spirit of America	Turbojet	526.277	846.9607
10	02-Nov-65	Bonneville Salt Flats	Craig Breedlove	Spirit of America - Sonic 1	Turbojet	555.485	893.9665
11	15-Nov-65	Bonneville Salt Flats	Craig Breedlove	Spirit of America - Sonic 1	Turbojet	600.601	966.5736
12	23-Oct-70	Bonneville Salt Flats	Gary Gabelich	Blue Flame	Rocket	622.407	1001.667
13	05-Oct-64	Bonneville Salt Flats	Tom Green	Wingfoot Express	Turbojet	413.199	664.9793
14	Total					766.000	

Land Speed Records

Land Speed Records-1

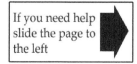

If you need help slide the page to the left

Session 1: Exercise Answers

These are the four questions that students find the most difficult to answer:

Q 11	Q 8	Q 6	Q 2
1. Click in cell G2. 2. Type: = 3. Click on cell F2. 4. Type: / 5. Click on cell B17. 6. Press the **<F4>** key to change the reference to cell B20 into an absolute reference. This was covered in: *Essential Skills Book-Lesson 3 12: Understand absolute and relative cell references available for free download at www.learnmicrosoftexcel.com.* 7. The function should now read: **=[@MPH]]/$B$17** 8. Press the **<Enter>** key. This was covered in: *Lesson 1-14: Name a table and create an automatic structured table reference.*	1. Click anywhere inside the table. 2. Click: Data→ Sort & Filter→Sort. 3. Set *Sort By, Locations, A to Z.* 4. Click *Add Level.* 5. Set *Then by Driver, Values, A to Z.* 6. Click the OK button. This was covered in: *Lesson 1-11: Sort a range or table by rows.*	1. Insert four blank rows at the top of the worksheet. 2. Copy the table headers in row five to row one. 3. In cell F2 type : **>575** 4. In cell B2 type: **Bonneville Salt Flats** 5. In cell C3 type: **Tom Green** 6. Click anywhere inside the table and then click: Data→Sort & Filter→ Advanced. 7. Set the *Criteria Range* to A1:F3. 8. Click the OK button. This was covered in: *Lesson 1-5: Apply an advanced filter with complex criteria.*	1. Click anywhere inside the range. 2. Click: Insert→Tables→Table This was covered in: *Lesson 1-8: Convert a range into a table and add a total row.*

If you have difficulty with the other questions, here are the lessons that cover the relevant skills:

3   Refer to: *Lesson 1-14: Name a table and create an automatic structured table reference.*

4   Refer to: *Lesson 1-2: Apply a simple filter to a range.*

5   Refer to: *Lesson 1-2: Apply a simple filter to a range.*

7   Refer to: *Lesson 1-4: Apply an advanced filter with multiple OR criteria.*

9   Refer to: *Lesson 1-8: Convert a range into a table and add a total row.*

Session Two: Data Integrity, Subtotals and Validations

> The longer I live the more I see that I am never wrong about anything, and that all the pains I have so humbly taken to verify my notions have only wasted my time.
>
> *George Bernard Shaw, Irish dramatist & socialist (1856 - 1950)*

In an ideal world all data entry personnel would be just like George Bernard Shaw and never make any mistakes. Unfortunately, the world is not ideal and we have to give users of our worksheets a little help by validating their input.

In this session, you will learn how to validate cells and entire columns in order to restrict the values that users are able to enter. As well as simple validations, you'll learn several advanced Excel validation techniques.

Excel's ability to automatically add subtotals never fails to elicit a gasp of amazement during my courses. In this lesson, you'll find out why, when you add sophisticated grouped multi-level subtotals with just a few clicks of the mouse.

Session Objectives

By the end of this session you will be able to:

- Keep data atomic using Text to Columns
- Automatically subtotal a range
- Create nested subtotals
- Consolidate data from multiple data ranges
- Use data consolidation to generate quick subtotals from tables
- Validate numerical data
- Create user-friendly messages for validation errors
- Create data entry input messages
- Add a formula-driven date validation and a text length validation
- Add a table-based dynamic list validation
- Use a function-driven custom validation to enforce complex business rules
- Remove duplicate values from a range or table
- Use a custom validation to add a unique constraint to a column

Sales Analysis

Lesson 2-1: Split fixed width data using Text to Columns

Over the years students have brought some very interesting workbooks to my classes from many diverse areas of business and commerce.

Often the workbook has become extremely complex and unmanageable with convoluted formulas that are difficult to audit.

Many times, all of the problems can be traced to the workbook designer breaking one simple golden rule of data table design:

"Keep data atomic"

This is one of Dr Codd's rules for efficient database design (see sidebar) that is equally relevant to Excel tables and ranges. In the same way that the atom is the smallest basic unit we can divide matter into, a column should contain the smallest possible amount of data.

Here's a simple example to illustrate the concept:

	A	B
1	Name	Age
2	Mr John Smith	42
3	Ms Jane Johnson	28

In the example above it wouldn't be easy to sort or filter column A by first name or last name. If you had observed the *keep data atomic* rule you would have split the data into multiple columns like this:

	A	B	C	D
1	Salutation	First Name	Last Name	Age
2	Mr	John	Smith	42
3	Ms	Jane	Johnson	28

The benefits provided by this simple example are obvious. It is not as easy to see the problem when a general ledger code or part number contains many different pieces of data. Here's an example:

	A	B	C	D
1	Part Number	Units	Unit Price	Ext Price
2	GB480Z	2	42.70	85.40
3	EU522S	3	22.50	67.50

The error isn't so easy to see here. In this particular example the *Part Number: GB480Z* is actually made up of three pieces of data:

1. GB: Where the product is made
    (GB=Great Britain, EU = Rest of Europe, US = USA).

2. 480: Product ID.

3. Z: Sales tax rate (Z=Zero rated, S=Standard rated, E=Exempt).

When you see this type of number in your data you should immediately break it up into its constituent parts.

While you could use the MID, LEFT, RIGHT and FIND functions to split the data (you'll learn about these functions later in: *Lesson 3-20: Extract text from fixed width strings using the LEFT, RIGHT and MID functions*), there's a much easier way to do this automatically using the *Text to Columns* tool. In this lesson we'll use this tool to avoid breaking the "keep data atomic" rule.

1 Open *Sales Analysis* from your sample files folder.

The table contains a list of products sold during March, April and May 2009. But there's a problem with this list. Column B contains part numbers that break the atomic data rule.

	A	B	C	D	E
1	Date	Part Number	Units	Unit Price	Ext Price
2	01-Mar-09	EU812Z	3	72.00	216.00
3	01-Mar-09	EU707Z	4	60.00	240.00
4	01-Mar-09	EU522S	3	22.50	67.50

2 Insert two blank columns to the left of column C.

These columns, along with the original column, will receive the new atomic values.

	B	C	D	E
1	Part Number	Column1	Column2	Units
2	EU812Z			3

3 Split column B into atomic data elements.

1. Select all of the values in column B of the table (B2:B54).

2. Click: Data→Data Tools→Text to Columns.

3. Click *Fixed width* (you'll learn about delimited data in *Lesson 2-2: Split delimited data using Text to Columns*).

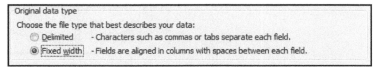

4. Click *Next*.

5. Click in the *Data preview* window to break up each data element within the part number:

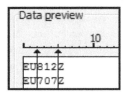

6. Click the *Finish* button.

The part number is split into atomic data:

4 Rename the columns B, C and D as **Region, Part Number** and **Tax**.

	A	B	C	D	
1	Date	Region	Part Number	Tax	U
2	01-Mar-09	EU	812	Z	
3	01-Mar-09	EU	707	Z	

5 Save your work as *Sales Analysis-2*.

Lesson 2-2: Split delimited data using Text to Columns

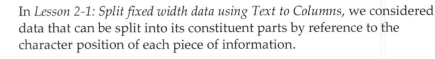

Fixed width data.

In *Lesson 2-1: Split fixed width data using Text to Columns*, we considered data that can be split into its constituent parts by reference to the character position of each piece of information.

Several accounting packages export data in a similar fixed width format:

```
Mr   John      Smith       19-Mar-09  2,220.24  2   4,440.48
Ms   Susan     Phillips    22-Mar-09    125.45  1     125.45
Mrs  Jennifer  Scott       23-Mar-09  1,145.60  2   2,291.20
```

This type of data is easy to recognize because all of the data elements "line up".

Delimited data.

You'll often encounter delimited data. This type of data uses a special character (such as a comma or semicolon) to split each data element. This type of data will be structured like this:

```
Mr;John;Smith;19-Mar-09; 2,220.24; 2; 4,440.48
Ms;Susan;Phillips;22-Mar-09;125.45;1;125.45
Mrs;Jennifer;Scott;23-Mar-09;1,145.60; 2; 2,291.20
```

In the above example the semicolon (;) is used as the delimiter.

1   Open *US Labor Force-1* from your sample files folder.

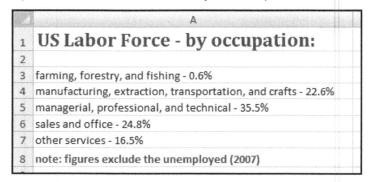

	A
1	**US Labor Force - by occupation:**
2	
3	farming, forestry, and fishing - 0.6%
4	manufacturing, extraction, transportation, and crafts - 22.6%
5	managerial, professional, and technical - 35.5%
6	sales and office - 24.8%
7	other services - 16.5%
8	note: figures exclude the unemployed (2007)

This worksheet contains some data that has been cut and pasted from the *CIA World Factbook* web site.

When you cut and paste information from other documents, (such as web pages), the information usually isn't in a format that is "Excel friendly".

In this lesson you'll split this data into a structured table so that you can display the division of labor as a graph.

2   Split the data in column A into text and percentages.

1.   Select cells A3:A7.

US Labor Force-1

2. Click: Data→Data Tools→Text to Columns.

3. Click *Delimited*.

> Original data type
>
> Choose the file type that best describes your data:
> - ● Delimited   - Characters such as commas or tabs separate each field.
> - ○ Fixed width   - Fields are aligned in columns with spaces between each field.

4. Click the *Next >* button.

5. Set the delimiter to a dash (see sidebar).

> Delimiters
> - ☐ Tab
> - ☐ Semicolon
> - ☐ Comma
> - ☐ Space
> - ☑ Other: -

You can see that there is a dash before each percentage value in column A. By setting this as a delimiter we can extract the percentages.

6. Click *Next >*

7. Click *Finish*.

The percentages are moved to their own column.

	A	B
1	**US Labor Force - by occupation:**	
2		
3	farming, forestry, and fishing	0.60%
4	manufacturing, extraction, transportation, and crafts	22.60%
5	managerial, professional, and technical	35.50%
6	sales and office	24.80%
7	other services	16.50%
8	note: figures exclude the unemployed (2007)	

3 Create a column chart to display the data visually.

1. Select cells A3:B7.

2. Click: Insert→Charts→Column→2D-Column→ Clustered Column.

3. Click: Chart Tools→Design→Data→Switch Row/Column.

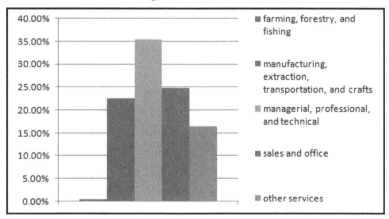

Charting is covered in depth in the *Essential Skills* book in this series.

4 Save your work as *US Labor Force-2*.

Lesson 2-3: Automatically subtotal a range

1 Open *Inventory-10* from your sample files folder.

2 Remove conditional formatting from the table.

1. Click anywhere inside the table.

2. Click: Home→Styles→Conditional Formatting→Clear Rules→ Clear Rules from this Table.

3 Sort the table by *Category* in ascending order.

This was covered in: *Lesson 1-11: Sort a range or table by rows.*

	No	Category	Supplier
11	42	Beverages	Pavlova, Ltd.
12	49	Beverages	Plutzer Lebensmittelgroßmärkte AG
13	57	Condiments	Forêts d'érables
14	18	Condiments	Grandma Kelly's Homestead

4 Convert the table to a range.

This was covered in: *Lesson 1-9: Format a table using table styles and convert a table into a range.*

You must convert the table into a range because you cannot add subtotals to tables.

5 Add subtotals to the *In Stock* and *Value* columns for each category.

1. Click anywhere inside the range.

2. Click: Data→Outline→Subtotal.

The *Subtotal* dialog appears:

3. Tell Excel which column of repeating data you wish to add subtotals to by choosing *Category* in the *At each change in:* drop down.

note

Other subtotal options.

Note the three subtotal options:

> ☑ Replace current subtotals
> ☐ Page break between groups
> ☑ Summary below data

You can use the first option to add different types of subtotal to different columns.

For example, if you wanted to view both the average and the sum at the same time you could add a second subtotal by unchecking this box.

The new subtotal is then shown above the old one:

> **Beverages Average**
> **Beverages Total**

note

Copying subtotals to another location.

A very common request in my courses is:

"How can I copy the subtotals only (ie the level two outline) to another worksheet. When I copy the subtotals and paste I get the detail rows as well – but I just want the subtotals".

The secret here is to only select the visible cells on the worksheet before copying.

Here's how it is done:

1. Display level two subtotals by clicking the [2] button.

2. Click: Home→Editing→ Find & Select→Go To Special→ Visible Cells Only.

OR

Select the range and then press the <Alt>+<;> keys.

3. Click OK.

4. Copy.

5. Paste to the destination cells.

> **At each change in:**
> No
> No
> Category
> Supplier
> Product Name
> Unit Price
> In Stock

4. Make sure that the *Sum* function is selected.

> **Use function:**
> Sum

5. Click the check boxes to add subtotals to the *In Stock* and *Value* columns:

> **Add subtotal to:**
> ☐ Category
> ☐ Supplier
> ☐ Product Name
> ☐ Unit Price
> ☑ In Stock
> ☑ Value

6. Click the OK button.

The worksheet is now subtotalled and Excel has added an outline bar to the left hand side:

1 2 3		A	B	C	D	E	F	G
•	55	64	Grains/Cereals	PB Knäckebröd AB	Tunnbröd	9.00	61	549.00
•	56	68	Grains/Cereals	Plutzer Lebensmitte	Wimmers gute Semme	33.25	22	731.50
−	57		**Grains/Cereals Total**				282	5,230.50
•	58	43	Meat/Poultry	Ma Maison	Pâté chinois	24.00	115	2,760.00
•	59	63	Meat/Poultry	Ma Maison	Tourtière	7.45	21	156.45
−	60		**Meat/Poultry Total**				136	2,916.45

6 **Collapse and expand the entire outline.**

Note the small [1] [2] [3] buttons in the top left corner of the worksheet.

- When you click button 1 only the grand total is shown.
- When you click button 2 each category subtotal is shown.
- When you click button 3 all items are shown.

7 **Collapse and expand categories within the outline.**

Note the [+] and [−] buttons in the left-hand sidebar.

Experiment by clicking them and notice how you can selectively expand and contract any group within the outline.

8 **Remove the subtotals from the range.**

1. Click anywhere within the range.

2. Click: Data→Outline→Subtotal→Remove All.

9 **Save your work as** *Inventory-11*.

Lesson 2-4: Create nested subtotals

Sometimes you'll find a need for more than one level of subtotal.

Consider this data:

	Category	Supplier	Product Name
4	Beverages	Aux joyeux ecclésiastiques	Chartreuse verte
5	Beverages	Bigfoot Breweries	Laughing Lumberjack Lager
6	Beverages	Bigfoot Breweries	Steeleye Stout
7	Beverages	Exotic Liquids	Chai
8	Beverages	Exotic Liquids	Chang

In the example above both *Bigfoot Breweries* and *Exotic Liquids* supply two different products in the *Beverages* category.

As well as wishing to know subtotals for each *category* you may also wish to know subtotals for each *supplier* within each *category*. In other words:

What is the value of Bigfoot Breweries inventory in each category?

By nesting subtotals we can quickly cater for this requirement.

1   Open *Inventory-11* from your sample files folder (if it isn't already open).

2   Apply a two-level sort, first by *Category* and then by *Supplier*.

This was covered in: *Lesson 1-11: Sort a range or table by rows*.

Column		Sort On		Order	
Sort by	Category ▾	Values ▾		A to Z	▾
Then by	Supplier ▾	Values ▾		A to Z	▾

3   At each change in *Category* use the *Sum* function to add subtotals to the *In Stock* and *Value* columns.

Do this in exactly the same way you did in: *Lesson 2-3: Automatically subtotal a range.*

At each change in:

Category ▾

Use function:

Sum ▾

Add subtotal to:

☐ Category
☐ Supplier
☐ Product Name
☐ Unit Price
☑ In Stock
☑ Value

	60		Meat/Poultry Total	
	61	34	Produce	G'day, Mate	Manjimup Dried Apples
	62	65	Produce	Grandma Kelly's Homestead	Uncle Bob's Organic Dried Pears
	63	62	Produce	Mayumi's	Tofu
	64	31	Produce	Tokyo Traders	Longlife Tofu
	65		Produce Total	

Inventory-11

4   Add a nested subtotal to show totals by *Supplier* within each category.

1. Click anywhere within the range.

2. Click: Data→Outline→Subtotal.

3. Uncheck the *Replace current subtotals* check box.

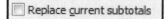

This is the secret when creating nested subtotals. If you didn't uncheck this box, the new subtotal would simply replace the old. By keeping the current subtotal we'll add a nested subtotal.

4. At each change in *Supplier* add a *Sum* function to subtotal the *In Stock* and *Value* columns:

5. Click the OK button.

    Nested subtotals are now shown by category/by supplier:

1 2 3 4		A	B	C	D
·	52	55	Confections	Specialty Biscuits, Ltd.	Sir Rodney's Marmalade
·	53	54	Confections	Specialty Biscuits, Ltd.	Scottish Longbreads
·	54	56	Confections	Specialty Biscuits, Ltd.	Sir Rodney's Scones
·	55	61	Confections	Specialty Biscuits, Ltd.	Teatime Chocolate Biscuits
–	56			**Specialty Biscuits, Ltd. Total**	
·	57	9	Confections	Zaanse Snoepfabriek	Chocolade
·	58	69	Confections	Zaanse Snoepfabriek	Zaanse koeken
–	59			**Zaanse Snoepfabriek Total**	
–	60		**Confections Total**		

    Notice that there's an extra level button too:

    1 2 3 4

    The fourth level is the nested subtotal allowing you to collapse and expand the *Supplier* subtotals.

5   Save your work as *Inventory-12*.

Lesson 2-5: Consolidate data from multiple data ranges

Totaling data from multiple worksheets onto a summary sheet is a very common business requirement. Excel can automatically consolidate data if each worksheet has an identical structure.

If you use this technique, it is a good idea to use templates for each of the worksheets that will be consolidated in order to ensure that they are identical. (Templates are covered in depth in the *Essential Skills* book in this series).

1 Open *Sales and Profit by Employee-1* from your sample files folder.

This worksheet shows each employee's sales, cost and profit data for the first three months in the quarter.

The *January, February, March* and *Summary* worksheets have an identical structure. This makes the consolidation feature very easy to use.

	A	B	C	D	E	F
1	**Sales and Profit By Employee**					
2						
3	Team	First Name	Last Name	Sales	Cost	Profit
4	Blue	Johnny	Caine	16,756	9,431	7,325
5	Blue	George	Marley	19,437	7,412	12,025
6	Blue	Bill	Spears	14,742	7,960	6,782

2 Consolidate data for the first three months into the summary sheet.

1. Click into the destination cell for the consolidated data. This is cell D4 on the *Summary* sheet.

2. Click: Data→Data Tools→Consolidate.

   The *Data Consolidation* dialog appears.

3. Make sure that the *Function* drop-down displays the *Sum* function because we want to add the values in the *January, February* and *March* worksheets:

   Function:
   Sum

4. Click in the *Reference* box.

5. Click the *January* worksheet tab and select cells D4:F17:

   Reference:
   January!$D$4:$F$17

Sales and Profit by Employee-1

6. Click the *Add* button to add the reference to the list of references to be consolidated:

> Reference:
> January!$D$4:$F$17
> All references:
> January!$D$4:$F$17

7. Click the *February* worksheet tab. This time the same range is automatically displayed in the dialog.

8. Click the *Add* button to add the *February* range to the list of references to be consolidated.

9. Repeat the same operation for the *March* range.

   The dialog should now look like this:

> Reference:
> March!$D$4:$F$17
> All references:
> February!$D$4:$F$17
> January!$D$4:$F$17
> March!$D$4:$F$17

10. Click the OK button to display the consolidated totals on the summary sheet:

	Sales and Profit By Employee					
1						
2						
3	Team	First Name	Last Name	Sales	Cost	Profit
4	Blue	Johnny	Caine	52,713	22,243	30,470
5	Blue	George	Marley	46,320	20,824	25,496
6	Blue	Bill	Spears	40,847	20,085	20,762

3 Create a data consolidation that is linked to the source data.

In the previous operation the consolidated values were not linked to the source worksheets. If a value on a source worksheet changes, the summary worksheet will not update.

1. Delete the range D4:F17 on the *Summary* worksheet.

2. Click in cell D4 on the *Summary* worksheet.

3. Click: Data→Data Tools→Consolidate.

4. Check the *Create links to source data* check box:

> ☑ Create links to source data

5. Click the OK button.

This time the data consolidation links to the source data and also displays a grouped outline similar to an automatic subtotal, enabling you to view each of the source data values for the consolidation.

4 Save your work as *Sales and Profit by Employee-2*.

1 2		A	B	C
	3	Team	First Name	Last Name
+	7	Blue	Johnny	Caine
+	11	Blue	George	Marley
+	15	Blue	Bill	Spears
+	19	Blue	Jamie	Oliver
+	23	Blue	Jack	Nicholson

Lesson 2-6: Use data consolidation to generate quick subtotals from tables

In: *Lesson 2-3: Automatically subtotal a range* we used Excel's fantastic *Automatic Subtotal* feature to quickly add subtotals to a range. Unfortunately automatic subtotals do not work with tables.

Another problem with automatic subtotals is that you have little control over the formatting of the subtotal data.

Data consolidation can overcome both of these problems by allowing full control of formatting along with the ability to work with both ranges and tables.

1   Open *Inventory-12* from your sample files folder.

2   Remove subtotals from the range.

   1.   Click anywhere inside the range.

   2.   Click: Data→Outline→Subtotal→Remove All.

3   Convert the range into a table.

This was covered in: *Lesson 1-8: Convert a range into a table and add a total* row.

4   Add quick subtotals by category using data consolidation.

   1.   Click in cell I1.

   2.   Click: Data→Data Tools→Consolidate.

The consolidate dialog is displayed:

   3.   Make sure that *Sum* is shown in the *Function* box. This should be the case as *Sum* is the default.

   4.   Click in the *Reference* box and select the range B1:G70.

A quick way to do this is to click in cell B1,
press **<Ctrl>+<Shift>+<DownArrow>**,
and then press **<Ctrl>+<Shift>+<RightArrow>**.

Inventory-12

Reference:

$B$1:$G$70

5. Check the two check boxes: *Use Labels in Top row, Left column*.

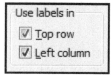

6. Click OK.

Subtotals appear beginning in cell I1 for every column. This is too much information as it is not logical to subtotal columns J:L:

	I	J	K	L	M	N
1		Supplier	Product N	Unit Price	In Stock	Value
2	Beverages			451.25	539	#######
3	Condiments			255.40	507	#######
4	Confections			327.08	386	#######
5	Dairy Products			287.30	393	#######

5 Delete columns J:L.

6 Re-size columns K and I.

Subtotals are now displayed in a useable form:

	I	J	K
1		In Stock	Value
2	Beverages	539	12,390.25
3	Condiments	507	12,023.55
4	Confections	386	10,392.20
5	Dairy Products	393	11,271.20
6	Grains/Cereals	282	5,230.50
7	Meat/Poultry	136	2,916.45
8	Produce	74	2,363.75
9	Seafood	701	13,010.35

7 Add averages alongside totals using the same technique.

1. Click in cell L1.

2. Do exactly the same thing you did for the *Sum* but choose the *Average* function in the consolidate dialog:

3. Click the OK button.

4. Delete columns L:O.

5. Change the label in L1 to: **Average In Stock**.

6. Change the label in M1 to **Average Value**.

7. Change the number of decimal places in column L to zero.

8. Re-size columns L and M.

	I	J	K	L	M
1		In Stock	Value	Average In Stock	Average Value
2	Beverages	539	12,390.25	49	1,126.39
3	Condiments	507	12,023.55	46	1,093.05
4	Confections	386	10,392.20	30	799.40

8 Save your work as *Inventory-13*.

	I	J
2	The Rules	
3		
4	Age	
5	Minimum age	17
6	Maximum age	100
7		
8	Date	
9	today or later	
10		
11	Names	
12	Min length	2
13	Max length	20
14		
15	Price	
16	Minimum	10.00
17	Maximum	100.00
18		
19	Discounts	
20	Minimum price for discount	10.00
21		
22	Valid Groups	
23		
24	Group	
25	Yoga	
26	Aerobics	
27	Weight Training	
28	Aromatherapy	
29	Massage	
30	Aquarobics	

Lesson 2-7: Validate numerical data

In the next lessons, we'll explore the power of Excel's data validation features. You can prevent a huge number of data entry errors by trapping them at source and then politely informing your users that they have made a mistake.

1 Open *Health Club Bookings-1* from your sample files folder.

This worksheet manages all of the treatments sold in a health club.

There are several rules that must not be broken when entering data (see sidebar). These types of rules are often referred to as *business rules* when designing data systems.

At the moment the worksheet doesn't police these rules itself, it relies upon all personnel understanding and applying them.

	A	B	C	D	E	F	G
1	**Health Club Bookings**						
2							
3	Period		From:				
4			To:				
5							
6	Date	Name	Age	Group	Price	Discount	Total
7	05-Apr-09	Depp, Julia	22	Aerobics	22.00	12%	19.36
8	01-Apr-09	Nicholson, Johnny	23	Weight Training	9.00		9.00
9	12-Apr-09	Dickens, Bob	18	Aromatherapy	23.00	10%	20.70
10	15-Apr-09	Oliver, Jamie	38	Weight Training	23.00	15%	19.55

2 Apply the Age rule (see sidebar) to column C.

1. Select all of column C by clicking the column header.

We select the entire column when we want to add data validation to every cell in the column.

2. Click: Data→Data Tools→Data Validation.

The data validation dialog appears.

3. Click the *Settings* tab.

At the moment Excel is allowing *Any value*. This is the default, meaning that the user is free to type anything at all into any cell in column C.

4. Choose *Whole number* from the *Allow* drop-down list.

Whole number will not allow the user to enter decimal values such as 22.8. As ages cannot have decimal places this is a good validation rule for a column containing age data.

Criteria now appear that are relevant to whole numbers.

5. Click in the *Data* box and Select:

between.

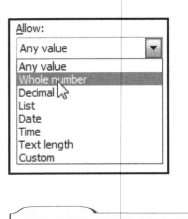

note

Absolute and relative cell references

Absolute and relative cell references are covered in depth in Lesson 3-12 of the *Essential Skills* book in this series.

If you are unsure about how to use absolute and relative cell references you can download this lesson, and watch the matching video, free of charge at our website.

1. Go to:

www.learnmicrosoftexcel.com.

2. Click: *Free Tutorials With Video* (on the top menu bar).

You will then be able to view the video and download the lesson in PDF format.

6. Click in the *Minimum* box and then click on cell J5.

7. Make J5 into an absolute reference (see sidebar).

8. Click in the *Maximum* box and then click on cell J6.

9. Make J6 into an absolute reference.

The dialog should now look like this:

10. Click OK.

3 **Test the data validation.**

Data validation will now ensure that any new values entered into column C are valid. It will not change any existing invalid values in the column.

Enter an invalid value (such as an age of 101 or 15) into any cell in column C.

A rather unfriendly error message appears advising that an error has occurred:

In the next lesson we'll discover how to make this message a little friendlier.

4 **Add another data validation.**

Use the same technique to apply the business rule: *Prices must be between 10.00 and 100.00 (stated in cells I16:J17)* to column E.

5 **Save your work as** *Health Club Bookings-2.*

Lesson 2-8: Create user-friendly messages for validation errors

A very useful design goal when developing computer software is to create a user interface that requires no user training. The interface should be so simple, and the features so obvious, that users can train themselves by experimentation and discovery.

For this reason, a user needs to be provided with an informative error message whenever they do something that is not allowed.

In this lesson, we'll add an error message to the age validation to advise users that ages of less than 17 or more than 100 are not permitted.

1 Open *Health Club Bookings-2* from your sample files folder (if it isn't already open).

2 Add an error message to column C.

    1. Select all of column C.

    2. Click: Data→Data Tools→Data Validation.

    3. Click the *Error Alert* tab.

    4. Type: **Invalid Age** into the *Title* box.

    5. Click in the *Error message* box and type:

       Age must be at least 17 and no more than 100.

       Your dialog should now look like this:

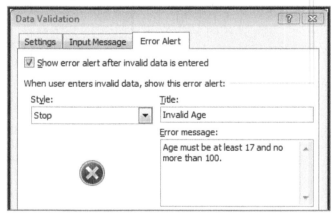

    6. Click the OK button.

3 Test the error message.

    When you enter an invalid age into any cell in column C you will see the error message:

4 **Change the validation from mandatory to advisory.**

This validation is called *mandatory* because there is absolutely no possibility of the user entering an invalid value.

Sometimes this restriction is too strict. You may want to tell the user that an age of over 100 is unusual, but if the user is really sure that the client is over 100 they can still continue.

1. Select all of column C.

2. Click: Data→Data Tools→Data Validation.

3. Change the error message to read: **Age is usually between 17 and 100. Are you sure this is correct?**

4. Change the style of the error message from Stop to Warning.

5. The dialog should now look like this:

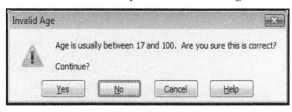

6. Click the OK button.

5 **Test the error message.**

When you enter an invalid age into any cell in column C you will now see a different style of error message:

You then have the opportunity to click the Yes button and override the validation.

6 **Add an informative error message to column E.**

Use the same technique to add an error message to column E.

7 **Save your work as** *Health Club Bookings-3*.

© 2011 The Smart Method® Ltd

81

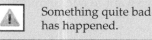

note

The Stop, Warning and Info error alert styles.

Windows users are conditioned to understand the meaning of three different icons.

Stop

 Something terrible has happened!

Warning

Something quite bad has happened.

Information

We just thought you'd like to know.

Each of these styles produces a slightly different error message dialog.

The warning dialog shows four buttons (see text) and the information dialog shows just three buttons: OK, Cancel and Help.

The only important difference between them is that the *Stop* style is mandatory while the *Information* and *Warning* styles are advisory.

Lesson 2-9: Create data entry Input Messages

In the last lesson: *Lesson 2-8: Create user-friendly messages for validation errors,* we discovered how to provide an informative error message whenever the user breaks a business rule.

Users can become frustrated if they can only discover business rules by first making mistakes and then being informed of the error. To make applications more efficient and user-friendly it is better to inform the user of the business rules before they attempt to enter a value.

In this lesson we'll use data entry input messages to provide a better user experience.

1 Open *Health Club Bookings-3* from your sample files folder (if it isn't already open).

2 Add a data validation input message to column C.

In *Lesson 2-7: Validate numerical data,* you added a validation to column C to ensure that ages are entered as whole numbers between 17 and 100.

We will now use the *Input Message* feature to inform the user of this business rule before an attempt is made to enter an age.

1. Select all of column C by clicking the column header.

2. We select the entire column when we want to add an input message to every cell in the column.

2. Click: Data→Data Tools→Data Validation.

The data validation dialog appears.

3. Click the *Input Message* tab.

4. In the *Title* box type: **Age.**

5. In the *Input message* box type: **Ages must be whole numbers in the range 17-100.**

Click the OK button.

3   Test the data validation input message.

Click any cell in column C. The input message is displayed:

	B	C	D
10	Oliver, Jamie	38	Weight Training
11			
12			
13			**Age** Ages must be whole numbers in the range 17-100.
14			
15			
16			

4   Use the same technique to add a data validation input message to column E.

Data Validation

Settings | Input Message | Error Alert

☑ Show input message when cell is selected

When cell is selected, show this input message:

Title:

Price

Input message:

Prices must be a minimum of 10.00 and a maximum of 100.00.

Clear All   OK   Cancel

	D	E	F	G
10	Weight Training	23.00	15%	19.55
11				
12				
13			**Price** Prices must be a minimum of 10.00 and a maximum of 100.00.	
14				
15				
16				

5   Save your work as *Health Club Bookings-4*.

Lesson 2-10: Add a formula-driven date validation and a text length validation

Validation parameters do not have to be simple values. They can also be the result of formulas.

In this lesson we'll use Excel's TODAY function to add a validation that will not allow a date to be entered that is in the past.

1   Open *Health Club Bookings-4* from your sample files folder (if it isn't already open).

2   Add a validation to column A that will not allow dates that are in the past to be entered.

    1.   Select all of column A.

    2.   Click: Data→Data Tools→Data Validation.

    3.   Click the *Settings* tab.

    4.   Set the *Allow:* box to *Date*.

    5.   Set the *Data:* box to *greater than or equal to*.

    6.   Add a TODAY function to the *Start Date* text box by typing:

      =TODAY()

      The TODAY function returns today's date. The TODAY function will be covered later in: *Lesson 3-8: Understand common date functions*.

    7.   Your dialog should now look like this:

3   Add an appropriate error alert message.

    1.   Click the *Error Alert* tab.

    2.   Type: **Date Error** into the *Title* box.

    3.   Type: **Dates cannot be in the past** into the *Error message* box.

    4.   Click OK.

Health Club Bookings-4

4   Test the validation.

Attempt to enter a date that is in the past.

An error message is displayed:

5   Apply a text length validation to enforce the rule: "Minimum name length = 2 characters, Maximum name length = 20 characters" to column B.

The validation dialog will look like this:

6   Add an appropriate Error Alert for this validation.

7   Test the validation.

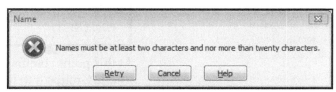

8   Save your work as *Health Club Bookings-5*.

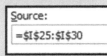

Health Club Bookings-5

Lesson 2-11: Add a table-based dynamic list validation

List validations prevent the user from entering any value into a cell that is not contained within a pre-defined list.

1 Open *Health Club Bookings-5* from your sample files folder (if it isn't already open).

2 Create a table in cells I24:I30 containing a list of the valid groups: *Yoga, Aerobics, Weight Training, Aromatherapy, Massage* and Aquarobics.

   1. Type **Group** into cell I24.

   2. Type the valid group names into cells I25:I30.

   3. Convert cells I24:I30 into a table.

      This was covered in: *Lesson 1-8: Convert a range into a table and add a total row.*

	I
24	Group ▼
25	Yoga
26	Aerobics
27	Weight Traiing
28	Aromatherapy
29	Massage
30	Aquarobics

   Name your new table: **ValidGroups**.

3 Add a validation to column D that will only allow groups defined in the *ValidGroups* table (cells I24:I30) to be added.

   1. Select all of column D.

   2. Click: Data→Data Tools→Data Validation.

   3. Click the *Settings* tab.

   4. In the *Allow* drop down click *List*.

   5. Click in the *Source* box and then select cells I25:I30 with the mouse.

> Allow:
> List ▼   ☑ Ignore blank
> Data: ☑ In-cell dropdown
> between ▼
> Source:
> =$I$25:$I$30 ▦

At this point you may wonder why you don't simply type **=ValidGroups** into the Source box. While this makes total sense, Excel won't allow this. (See the important sidebar for more on this).

6. Add an appropriate Error Alert.

    You learned how to do this in: *Lesson 2-10: Add a formula-driven date validation and a text length* validation.

    > Error message:
    >
    > The group entered is not a valid group. Click the drop-down arrow to view a list of valid choices.

7. Click the OK button.

4   Test the validation.

    1. Click anywhere in column D.

        Notice that a drop down arrow appears on the right-hand side of the cell.

    2. Click the drop-down arrow.

        A list of all valid groups is displayed:

        > Weight Training
        > Yoga
        > Aerobics
        > Weight Training
        > Aromatherapy
        > Massage
        > Aquarobics

    3. Click any of the valid groups.

    The value is displayed in the cell.

5   Add *Circuit Training* as a valid group.

    1. Click in cell I31.

    2. Type: **Circuit Training**.

    3. Press the **<Enter>** key.

        The new item is added to the table.

6   Test the validation again.

    Click on the drop-down arrow to the right of any cell in column D.

    Note that *Circuit Training* is now a valid item in the list.

    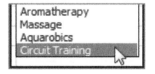

    This has only happened because you converted the source cells I24:I30 into a table. If you hadn't done this, *Circuit Training* would not have been valid. (See the important sidebar on the facing page for more on this).

7   Save your work as *Health Club Bookings-6*.

Lesson 2-12: Use a function-driven custom validation to enforce complex business rules

The simple dialog-driven validations have served all of our requirements up to now.

Sometimes you will have to implement a validation that is too complex for any of the dialog-driven validations to handle. In this case you will have to write a function-driven custom validation.

There is a requirement (listed in the business rules) that states:

Discounts	
Minimum price for discount	10.00

This means that the value in column F will depend upon the value in column E.

	E	F
6	Price	Discount
7	22.00	12%
8	9.00	
9	23.00	10%
10	23.00	15%

In row 8 above it is prohibited to enter a discount because the price is less than 10.00. We'll implement this business rule with a function-driven custom validation.

1   Open *Health Club Bookings-6* from your sample files folder (if it isn't already open).

2   Add a validation to column F that will enforce the business rule: *Minimum price for discount = 10.00*.

   1.   Select all of column F.

   2.   Click: Data→Data Tools→Data Validation.

   3.   Click the *Settings* tab.

   4.   Select *Custom* in the *Allow* drop-down list.

Allow:
Custom ▾

Custom validations require a formula. The validation will only allow a value to be entered if the function returns a value of TRUE.

It is necessary to get a little ahead of ourselves at this point because this validation requires the use of an IF function. The

Health Club Bookings-6

IF function will be thoroughly covered later in: *Lesson 3-5: Use the IF logic function.*

5. Click in the Formula text box and type the following text:

   =IF(E1<10, False, True)

   Don't worry if the function doesn't make too much sense just yet. It will return False if the value in E1 is less than 10, and True if the value in E1 is greater than or equal to 10.

   Note that E1 is a relative cell reference (ie it does not have the dollar prefixes $E$1). This is because we want it to adjust to the current row. For example, when the user enters a percentage into cell F11 we want to check the value in cell E11.

6. Add an appropriate Error Alert:

7. Click the OK button.

3   Test the validation.

1. Enter a discount into cell F8. Because the value in cell E8 is only 9.00 an error alert is displayed:

2. Change the value in cell E8 to 12.00.

3. Enter a discount of 10% in cell F8.

   This time the value is accepted.

	D	E	F	G
6	Group	Price	Discount	Total
7	Aerobics	22.00	12%	19.36
8	Weight Training	12.00	10%	10.80
9	Aromatherapy	23.00	10%	20.70

4   Save your work as *Health Club Bookings-7*.

Lesson 2-13: Remove duplicate values from a range or table

Duplicate entries are a common problem in data systems of all types.

When tables contain duplicate entries they are said to be corrupt. Unfortunately just about every corporate database I've ever worked upon is corrupt! You'll almost certainly have to clean up data sets containing duplicate values at some point in your Excel career.

This lesson will show you how to quickly weed out duplicate entries from ranges and tables.

1   Open *Employees-1* from your sample files folder.

The table contains a list of employees along with their *EmployeeID* – a unique identification number. Every employee should only be listed once but you suspect that the list contains duplicate entries.

	A	B	C
1	EmployeeID ▾	First Name ▾	Last Name ▾
2	362281	Brad	Cruise
3	324794	Ian	Dean
4	998783	Paris	Smith

2   Sort *EmployeeID* from smallest to largest.

If the list was very short you could manually identify duplicate EmployeeID rows by simply sorting column A. This skill was covered in: *Lesson 1-11: Sort a range or table by rows*.

To sort the numeric fields in column A from smallest to largest apply an A-Z sort. Part of the problem is instantly revealed:

	A	B	C
1	EmployeeID ↓1	First Name ▾	Last Name ▾
2	117362	Johnny	Caine
3	117362	Johnny	Caine
4	118657	George	Marley
5	118657	George	Marley
6	128947	Bill	Spears

Johnny Caine and George Marley clearly have duplicate entries in the table.

3   Automatically remove employees with duplicate EmployeeID values.

1.   Click any cell inside the table.

Employees-1

2. Click: Table Tools→Design→Remove Duplicates.

The *Remove Duplicates* dialog is displayed:

Notice that, by default, Excel has selected every field in the table.

3. Click the OK button.

4. All of the duplicate entries are deleted.

	A	B	C
1	EmployeeID	First Name	Last Name
2	117362	Johnny	Caine
3	118657	George	Marley
4	128947	Bill	Spears
5	170292	Jamie	Oliver

This is a very fast method but not very sophisticated as there's no opportunity to review the values that will be deleted.

In: *Lesson 2-14: Use a custom validation to add a unique constraint to a column* we'll discover how to catch duplicate entries at source.

4   Save your work as *Employees-2*.

Lesson 2-14: Use a custom validation to add a unique constraint to a column

You'll often find yourself working with a table or range that contains a column that must have unique values.

For example, consider this list of employees:

	A	B	C
1	EmployeeID	First Name	Last Name
2	117362	Johnny	Caine
3	118657	George	Marley
4	128947	Bill	Spears

The *EmployeeID* column should never contain the same number listed twice. If it does, an error has occurred because no two employees can have the same *EmployeeID*.

In cases such as this, it would be very useful to refuse to let the user add duplicate values to column A. This type of restriction is called a *unique constraint* and is a fundamental feature of database products such as Microsoft Access, SQL Server and Oracle.

Excel doesn't provide an easy way to apply unique constraints directly (hopefully it will in a later version). Fortunately there's an easy way to leverage upon the custom validation feature to add this functionality to Excel 2010 tables.

1 **Open *Employees-2* from your sample files folder (if it isn't already open).**

In this table, each employee should have a unique *EmployeeID*. At the moment the table does not enforce this rule.

2 **Add a duplicate EmployeeID.**

1. Press the **<Ctrl>+<End>** keys to move to the end of the table (cell C120).

2. Press the **<Tab>** key.

   If you press the **<Tab>** key in the last cell of a table a new row is added to the table.

	A	B	C
119	997371	Michal	Marley
120	998783	Paris	Smith
121			

3. Add a duplicate entry for *Paris Smith*.

	A	B	C
119	997371	Michal	Marley
120	998783	Paris	Smith
121	998783	Paris	Smith

   Notice that Excel allows the duplicate entry. In a moment we'll add a unique constraint to make this impossible.

3 **Delete the duplicate EmployeeID (row 121).**

Employees-2

note

The COUNTIF function.

COUNTIF(range, criteria)

The COUNTIF function returns the number of cells in a *range* that meet a specific *criteria*.

In this lesson we defined a range that includes all of the *EmployeeID* values (**A:A** means all of the cells in column A).

We then defined the relative reference A2 as the criteria.

The function compares the value in the current row within column A to every other value in column A. It should always result in finding only one value (the value you are currently entering).

If your entry is unique, the COUNTIF function will return 1. If it is not unique, the function will return a number greater than 1.

As 1=1 is TRUE, the function returns TRUE (passing the validation) when the value is unique and FALSE (failing the validation) when the value is not unique.

The COUNTIF function will be covered in depth later in: *Lesson 3-6: Use the SUMIF and COUNTIF logic functions to create conditional totals.*

4 Add a unique constraint to column A.

1. Select all of the table cells in column A except the header row.

    A quick way to do this is to click in cell A2 and then press **<Ctrl>+<Shift>+<DownArrow>**.

2. Click: Data→Data Tools→Data Validation.

3. Click the *Settings* tab.

4. In the *Allow* drop-down select *Custom*.

5. Type the following function into the Formula box:

    = COUNTIF(A:A,A2)=1

    See sidebar for a discussion of the COUNTIF formula.

6. Add an appropriate error alert.

7. Click the OK button.

5 Test the unique constraint.

Attempt to change the EmployeeID in Row 3 so that it is the same as the EmployeeID in Row 2.

Note that you must type the values in. If you copy and paste the entry is not validated.

Attempt to add a new row at the end of the table with a duplicate ID:

6 Save your work as *Employees-3*.

Session 2: Exercise

1   Open *Sales Performance Analysis-1* from your sample files folder.

	A	B	C	D
3	Salesman	Country	Salary	Sales
4	Alan Shearer	England	60,000	489,817
5	Bobby Charlton	England	34,000	844,935

2   Break the data in the *Salesman* column into two columns: *First Name* and *Last Name*.

Make sure that you also type the column labels **First Name** and **Last Name** into cells A3 and B3.

	A	B	C	D	E
3	First Name	Last Name	Country	Salary	Sales
4	Alan	Shearer	England	60,000	489,817
5	Bobby	Charlton	England	34,000	844,935

3   Automatically subtotal by *Country* showing subtotals for *Salary* and *Sales*.

		C	D	E
	3	Country	Salary	Sales
+	11	**England Total**	364,000	3,657,627
+	26	**France Total**	767,000	7,339,298

4   Remove the subtotals.

5   Add a validation to column C so that the country may only be entered as *England, France* or *Germany*.

	A	B	C	D
3	First Name	Last Name	Country	Salary
4	Alan	Shearer	England ▼	60,000
5	Bobby	Charlton	France / England / Germany	34,000
6	David	Beckham		39,000

6   Add a user-friendly Error Alert to column C.

Country Error   [✕]

❌ Invalid Country. Click the drop-down arrow next to the country to see a list of valid entries.

Retry   Cancel   Help

7   Add an input message to column C to inform users which countries are valid.

	C	D	E
3	Country	Salary	Sales
4	France ▼	60,000	489,817
5	England	00	844,935
6	England	00	766,277
7	England	00	330,707
8	England	00	700,950

Country — Country must be France, England or Germany.

8   Save your work as *Sales Performance Analysis-2*.

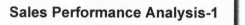

Sales Performance Analysis-1

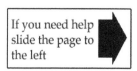

If you need help slide the page to the left ➤

Session 2: Exercise Answers

These are the four questions that students find the most difficult to answer:

Q 6	Q 5	Q 3	Q 2
1. Select all of column C. 2. Click: Data→ Data Tools→ Data Validation. 3. Click the *Error Alert* tab. 4. Enter the text: **Country Error** ...in the *Title* box. 5. Enter the text: **Country must be France, England or Germany** ...in the *Error message* box. 6. Click the OK button. This was covered in: *Lesson 2-8: Create user-friendly messages for validation errors.*	1. In column G3 type the text: **Valid Countries.** 2. type the text: **France, England** and **Germany** into cells G4, G5 and G6 		G
---	---
3	Valid Countries
4	France
5	England
6	Germany | 3. Select all of column C. 4. Click: Data→ Data Tools→ Data Validation. 5. Click the *Settings* tab. 6. Set up the dialog as follows: Allow: List Data: between Source: =$G$4:$G$6 7. Click the OK button. This was covered in: *Lesson 2-11: Add a table-based dynamic list validation.*	1. Click on any of the countries in column C. 2. Click: Data→ Sort & Filter→ A-Z. ...to sort column C in ascending order. 3. Click: Data→Outline→Subtotal 4. Set up the dialog as follows: At each change in: Country Use function: Sum Add subtotal to: First Name Last Name Country ✓ Salary ✓ Sales 5. Click OK. This was covered in: *Lesson 2-3: Automatically subtotal a range.*	1. Enter a column to the left of column B. 2. Select cells A4:A34. 3. Click: Data→ Data Tools→ Text to Columns. 4. Leave the data type as *Delimited* and click the *Next* button. 5. Select *Space* in the *Delimiters* option group. ✓ Space 6. Click *Finish*. 7. Type *First Name* and *Last Name* in cells A3 and B3. This was covered in: *Lesson 2-2: Split delimited data using Text to Columns.*

If you have difficulty with the other questions, here are the lessons that cover the relevant skills:

4   Refer to: *Lesson 2-3: Automatically subtotal a range.*

7   Refer to: *Lesson 2-9: Create data entry Input Messages.*

Session Three: Advanced Functions

> All animals are equal, but some animals are more equal than others.
>
> *George Orwell, "Animal Farm"*
> *English essayist, novelist, & satirist (1903 - 1950)*

There are 348 functions in the Excel function library. This would be a very large book if I tried to cover all of them.

In this session, I'll cover the most important Excel functions and put them into context by demonstrating real-world examples of how they can be used.

With the insights you'll gain from using these functions, you'll be able to confidently explore the vast array of other functions in Excel's huge library should you ever need them.

Session Objectives

- Understand precedence rules and use the Evaluate feature

- Use common functions with Formula AutoComplete

- Use the formula palette and the PMT function

- Use the PV and FV functions to value investments

- Use the IF logic function

- Use the SUMIF and COUNTIF logic functions to create conditional totals

- Understand date serial numbers

- Understand common date functions

- Use the DATEDIF function

- Use date offsets to manage projects using the scheduling equation

- Use the DATE function to offset days, months and years

- Enter time values and perform basic time calculations

- Perform time calculations that span midnight

- Understand common time functions and convert date serial numbers to decimal values

- Use the TIME function to offset hours, minutes and seconds

- Use the AND and OR functions to construct complex Boolean criteria

- Understand calculation options (manual and automatic)

- Concatenate strings using the concatenation operator (&)

- Use the TEXT function to format numerical values as strings

- Extract text from fixed width strings using the LEFT, RIGHT and MID functions

- Extract text from delimited strings using the FIND and LEN functions

- Use a VLOOKUP function for an exact lookup

- Use an IFERROR function to suppress error messages

- Use a VLOOKUP function for an inexact lookup

Lesson 3-1: Understand precedence rules and use the *Evaluate* feature

Here are Excel's precedence rules:

Operator	Description
Parenthesis (brackets)	Any expression in brackets is always evaluated first. **(6+2)*3=24**
Exponent	Exponents are always evaluated next. Exponents tend to be used in engineering/scientific scenarios and are rarely seen in accounting scenarios. **(1+1)*6^2=72**
Multiply and Divide	Multiplication and Division operators have the same precedence and are evaluated from left to right.
Add and Subtract	Addition and Subtraction operators have the same precedence and are evaluated from left to right.

If you only ever work with accounting scenarios, all you really need to remember is:

- Brackets are evaluated first.

- Multiplication and Division are evaluated next.

- Addition and Subtraction are evaluated last.

1 Open *Payroll-1* from your sample files folder.

This worksheet contains some simple formulas required to compute *Net Pay* from *Hours Worked* (see *Payroll Rules* grab on facing page).

Most tax regimes have more complicated rules than those defined in this simple example. Employees are paid the same hourly rate for all hours worked. A different percentage of gross pay is then deducted for Tax, Social Security and Pension contributions.

2 Evaluate the formula in cell B17.

Cell B17 contains the simple formula:

f_x | =B15*B4

There's really not much that can go wrong with such a simple formula, but let's see how it works using Excel's evaluation feature.

1. Click on cell B17.

2. Click: Formulas→Formula Auditing→Evaluate Formula.

	A	B
1	**Payroll**	
2		
3	**Payroll Rules**	
4	Hourly rate	12.00
5	Tax	32%
6	Social Security	8%
7	Pension	5%
8		
9	Day	Hours Worked
10	Monday	10
11	Tuesday	8
12	Wednesday	12
13	Thursday	7
14	Friday	9
15	Total	46
16		
17	Gross	552.00
18	Tax	176.64
19	Social Security	44.16
20	Pension	27.60
21	**Net Pay**	**303.60**
22		
23	**Net Pay**	**303.60**

The *Evaluate Formula* dialog appears. You can see that the first part of the formula that will be evaluated is **B15**. This is indicated by an underline:

```
Evaluation:
=  B15*B4
```

3. Click the *Step In* button. This will show the formula behind cell B15.

```
Reference:                    Evaluation:
Sheet1!$B$17          =   B15*B4
  └ Sheet1!$B$15      =   SUM(B10:B14)
```

4. Click the *Step Out* button.

   The value in cell B15 now replaces the cell reference:

```
Evaluation:
=   46*B4
```

5. Click the *Evaluate* button. The value in cell B4 now replaces the cell reference:

```
Evaluation:
=   46*12
```

6. Click the *Evaluate* button again. You can now see the result of the evaluation:

```
Evaluation:
=   552.00
```

   The *Evaluate* button has now changed its caption to *Restart*. If you wanted, you could click this button to start the evaluation process all over again.

7. Click the *Close* button.

3 **Evaluate the formula in cell B23.**

To better illustrate the Evaluate feature, a formula that uses a rather long winded way of calculating *Net Pay* has been inserted into cell B23:

> f_x =B15*B4-B15*B4*B5-B4*B15*B6-B4*B15*B7

Because of the rules of precedence, the formula works correctly. It could also have been written with parentheses like this:

> f_x =(B15*B4)-(B15*B4*B5)-(B4*B15*B6)-(B4*B15*B7)

The parentheses are not needed because the precedence rules state that multiplication happens before subtraction. I still prefer the formula with redundant parentheses (see sidebar).

4 **Save your work as *Payroll-2*.**

---

tip

Use parentheses to make formulas more readable

I often use parenthesis even when they are not needed.

There are two reasons for this:

1. The formula is easier to read.

2. Errors caused by precedence–related mistakes are eliminated.

---

note

Enabling and disabling AutoComplete

As with so many other features, Microsoft allows you to turn this very useful feature off.

You'd never want to do this, but you may work on a machine that has had *Formula AutoComplete* switched off and you need to turn it on again. To do this click:

File→Options→Formulas

and make sure that the *Formula AutoComplete* box is checked.

The World's Tallest Buildings-1

Lesson 3-2: Use common functions with Formula AutoComplete

The functions most often seen in workbooks are: SUM, AVERAGE, COUNT, MAX and MIN. In this lesson, we'll use Excel's *Formula AutoComplete* feature to add these formulas to a workbook.

1 Open *The World's Tallest Buildings-1* from your sample files folder.

This worksheet contains information about the world's 20 tallest buildings. We'll use the SUM, MAX, MIN, AVERAGE and COUNT functions to populate cells B25:B29.

2 Click into cell B25 and type **=S** into the cell.

	A	B
25	Total number of floors:	=S
26	Height of tallest building (meters):	*fx* SEARCH
27	Height of shortest building (meters):	*fx* SECOND

A list drops down showing every function in the Excel function library beginning with S. This feature (introduced in Excel 2007) is called *Formula AutoComplete*. (If this didn't work for you, see the sidebar).

3 Continue typing: **=SU**

Notice that the list now only shows functions beginning with SU. You can see the SUM function, three down in the list.

4 Press the **<M>** key.

The SUM function is highlighted. There are two methods for selecting the SUM function:

- Press the **<Down Arrow>** key twice.

- Click the function name with the mouse.

The SUM function now displays a tip telling you what the function does:

	A	B
25	Total number of floors:	=SUM
26	Height [Adds all the numbers in a range of cells]	*fx* SUM
27	Height of shortest building (meters):	*fx* SUMIF
28	Average number of floors:	*fx* SUMIFS

5 Display detailed help for the SUM function.

The tip tells you a little about the SUM function but to get the full story press the **<F1>** key while *SUM* is still highlighted in the dropdown list.

The Excel help system opens showing detailed help for the SUM function.

note

The syntax box

The Syntax box tells you which arguments (sometimes called parameters) the function needs.

In the case of the SUM function, the first argument does not have square brackets, meaning that you can't leave it out. Arguments in square brackets are optional.

For such a simple function as SUM, the syntax box is hardly needed, but later we'll discover functions that require several arguments and then the syntax box will be invaluable.

trivia

How the foot got shorter in 1959

This workbook uses the foot-to-meter conversion factor of 0.3048. Before 1959, a foot was slightly longer at 0.3048006096012 meters!

In 1893, the US Office of Weights and Measures (now the National Bureau of Standards) fixed the value of the US foot at 0.3048006096012 Meters. Unfortunately, the rest of the world used a slightly different factor.

Because this caused problems, an international agreement was reached in 1959 to re-define the standard conversion factor at exactly 0.3048 meters – making a post-1959 foot slightly shorter than a pre-1959 foot!

Because the new standard upset existing survey data, it was further agreed that, for geodetic purposes only, the old conversion factor would remain good. To avoid confusion, survey data is now defined in a new unit called the *US Survey Foot*.

Read the help text if you are interested and then close the help window.

Complete the formula so that you see: **SUM(**

=SUM(

SUM(**number1**, [number2], ...)

Notice that a little box has appeared beneath the function call. This is the *Syntax box* (see sidebar for more information).

6   Select the cells that you need to sum (cells F4:F23) with the mouse or keyboard.

You can select the cells with the keyboard using the following technique:

1. Press the **<Up Arrow>** and **<Right Arrow>** keys until you reach cell F4.

2. Press **<Ctrl>+<Shift>+<Down Arrow>** to select cells F4:F23.

7   Press the **<Enter>** key to finish the formula.

There's no need to type the closing bracket as Excel is clever enough to enter it for you. The total number of floors in all 20 buildings is now displayed in cell B25.

8   Use the same technique to add a MAX function to cell B26.

1. Click in cell B26.

2. Type = **MA**

3. Press the **<Down Arrow>** key once to move the cursor over the MAX function.

4. Press the **<Tab>** key to automatically enter the MAX function into cell B26.

5. Select the range D4:D23 using either the mouse or the keyboard.

    The formula should now be: **=MAX(D4:D23**

6. Press the **<Enter>** key.

    There's no need to type the closing bracket as, once again, Excel helps you out by entering it automatically.

9   Use the same technique to add MIN, AVERAGE and COUNT functions to cells B27:B29.

	A	B
25	Total number of floors:	=SUM(F4:F23)
26	Height of tallest building (meters):	=MAX(D4:D23)
27	Height of shortest building (meters):	=MIN(D4:D23)
28	Average number of floors:	=AVERAGE(F4:F23)
29	Number of buildings in the list:	=COUNT(D4:D23)

10 Save your work as *The World's Tallest Buildings-2*.

Lesson 3-3: Use the formula palette and the PMT function

In this lesson, we'll use a complex function with five parameters that will calculate the repayments on a mortgage loan.

1 Open *Mortgage Repayments-1* from your sample files folder.

This worksheet contains details of mortgages for loans from 50,000 to 300,000 with a 25 year term and an interest rate of 6.7%. We will use the PMT function to calculate the monthly repayments.

	A	B	C	D
			Interest	Monthly
3	Price	Term (Years)	(APR)	Repayment
4	50,000	25	6.70%	
5	100,000	25	6.70%	

2 Calculate the monthly repayments using the PMT function and the formula palette.

1. Click in cell D4.

2. Click the *Insert Function* button at the left of the formula bar:

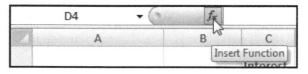

The formula palette appears:

3. Type **Loan** into the *Search for a function* text box and then click the *Go* button:

A list of functions is shown in the *Select a function* list. Excel's best guess is the PMT function. Look at the help text below the list. You can see what the PMT function is used for:

> **PMT(rate,nper,pv,fv,type)**
> Calculates the payment for a loan based on constant payments and a constant interest rate.

While the help lets you know what the function does, it is unclear (at this stage) what the arguments mean.

Note also that there is a hyperlink pointing to the help page for this function.

Help on this function

The help page provides detailed information about each argument. It is, however, more convenient to obtain interactive help as each argument is entered.

4. Click the OK button.

Mortgage Repayments-1

note

What are the Fv and Type arguments used for?

FV

FV is the Future Value. It is an amount that will still be owed, or a cash bonus that will be paid to the borrower, at the end of the loan. This is sometimes called a balloon payment.

If a positive amount is entered into the Fv box then this amount will be paid to the borrower at the end of the loan.

If a negative amount is entered, it will represent an amount still owed at the end of the loan.

This type of loan is common in vehicle loan agreements and can also be used to model *interest only* mortgages.

Example:

A car is sold for 10,000 across three years. At the end of the three years, the borrower is able to buy the car for 3,000 or to hand it back to the dealer.

To model this loan, the Pv would be 10,000 and the Fv would be -3000.

Type

Most loans require the repayment to be made at the end of the period (in this example, at the end of each month). Some insurance-backed loans require the repayment to be made at the beginning of the period.

Payments for this type of loan can be calculated by setting the *Type* argument to 1.

	C	D
3	Interest (APR)	Monthly Repayment
4	6.70%	£343.88
5	6.70%	£687.76
6	6.70%	£1,031.64
7	6.70%	£1,375.51
8	6.70%	£1,719.39
9	6.70%	£2,063.27

The *Function Arguments* dialog is displayed.

Rate		= number
Nper		= number
Pv		= number
Fv		= number
Type		= number

The arguments shown in bold face are required (**Rate, Nper** and **Pv**). The last two arguments are optional (Fv and Type). We won't be using the Fv and Type arguments, but if you are interested in their purpose see the sidebar for more information.

5. Click in the first box (Rate). Notice that help is provided at the bottom of the dialog:

> **Rate** is the interest rate per period for the loan. For example, use 6%/4 for quarterly payments at 6% APR.

6. Click in cell C4 and then type **/12.** We divide the annual interest rate by twelve to calculate the monthly interest rate.

7. Complete the next two arguments by studying the help text for each. Your dialog should now look like this:

Rate	C4/12	= 0.005583333
Nper	B4*12	= 300
Pv	A4	= 50000

8. Click the OK button.

The monthly repayment is now shown in cell D4 but the amount shown is negative. The number is shown as negative because it represents money going out of our account (a negative cash flow).

The PMT function automatically formats the repayment with a currency prefix matching the currency locale on your computer. Because my computer had a currency locale of pounds sterling the value is prefixed by a GBP (£) symbol.

9. Click on cell D4 and add a minus operator to the front of the formula:

> *fx* =-PMT(C4/12,B4*12,A4)

10. Press the **<Enter>** key.

This will display the value as a positive number, which is more visually pleasing:

	A	B	C	D
3	Price	Term (Years)	Interest (APR)	Monthly Repayment
4	50,000	25	6.70%	£343.88

11. AutoFill the formula to the end of the list to show monthly repayments for all six loan amounts.

3 Save your work as *Mortgage Repayments-2*.

Lesson 3-4: Use the PV and FV functions to value investments

Present Value

Present Value is the total amount that a series of future payments is worth now.

Present Value can be used to value an existing loan. This would be useful if you wanted to sell the loan to another party.

In this lesson, we explore the following scenario:

I have loaned my friend John $20,000 to buy a car. John has agreed to repay $1,000 per month for two years (making me $4,000 in interest on the deal). I want to sell the loan on to my other friend Bill. Bill says he is happy to buy it from me but he needs a return of 12% on his investment. I can use the PV function to work out what the loan is worth today based upon Bill's requirement for a 12% return.

Future Value

Future value is used to work out how much capital will accumulate if a fixed amount is saved each month at a specified compound interest rate.

In this lesson, we explore the following scenario:

I save $100 each month towards my retirement fund. If I save for 25 years and the interest rate during this time will be 4%, how much money will I have in my fund upon retirement?

1   Open *Investments-1* from your sample files folder.

This worksheet contains details of the retirement fund and car loan scenarios described above:

	A	B
1	**Retirement Fund**	
2		
3	Monthly Savings	100.00
4	Number of years	25
5	Interest Rate	4%
6		
7	**Value upon retirement**	
8		
9	**Car Loan**	
10		
11	Monthly repayment	1,000.00
12	Number of years	2
13	Interest rate	12%
14		
15	**Value of investment**	

2   Use the FV function to calculate the retirement fund value.

In the last lesson, you discovered how to use the *Insert Function* button [*fx*] to access functions in Excel's vast function library.

Investments-1

You can also access the library by using the Function Library buttons on the Ribbon.

1. Click in cell B7.

2. Click: Formulas→Function Library→Financial→FV.

   Notice the tip showing a short description of the function:

   FV

   FVS
   FV(rate,nper,pmt,pv,type)
   INT
   Returns the future value of an
   IPM   investment based on periodic,
          constant payments and a constant
   IRR   interest rate.
   ISP ⓘ Press F1 for more help.
   MDURATION

3. Add the correct values to the Function Arguments dialog:

Rate	B5/12		= 0.003333333
Nper	B4*12		= 300
Pmt	B3		= 100
Pv			= number
Type			= number

4. Click the OK button.

The retirement fund is shown as a negative number (-$51,412.95). This is shown as negative because it represents money leaving our account. Add a minus sign in front of *FV* in the formula bar to convert it to a more visually pleasing positive value:

fx =-FV(B5/12,B4*12,B3)

	A	B
1	**Retirement Fund**	
2		
3	Monthly Savings	100.00
4	Number of years	25
5	Interest Rate	4%
6		
7	Value upon retireme	51,412.95
8		
9	**Car Loan**	
10		
11	Monthly repayment	1,000.00
12	Number of years	2
13	Interest rate	12%
14		
15	Value of investment	21,243.39

3 Use the PV function to calculate the value of the car loan.

1. Click in cell B15.

2. Click: Formulas→Function Library→Financial→PV.

3. Add the correct values to the *Function Arguments* dialog:

Rate	B13/12		= 0.01
Nper	B12*12		= 24
Pmt	B11		= 1000
Fv			= number
Type			= number

4. Add a minus sign in front of *PV* in the formula bar to convert it to a positive value:

fx =-PV(B13/12,B12*12,B11)

5. Click OK. The result is $21,243.39 so you turned a profit on the deal!

   (The Fv and Type arguments are discussed in: *Lesson 3-3: Use the formula palette and the PMT function*).

4 Save your work as *Investments-2*.

Lesson 3-5: Use the IF logic function

The IF function is one of Excel's most widely used and useful functions. It is also a function that often confuses my students, so I'll begin this lesson by explaining the concept of the logical test. Later, we'll construct a worksheet containing three examples of the IF function at work.

The IF function requires a *logical test* and then performs one action if the test returns TRUE and a different action if the test returns FALSE.

Here are some examples of logical tests:

Expression	Returns	Why?
6=2	False	Because six does not equal two.
100<90	False	Because 100 is not less than 90.
6+2 = 4+4	True	Because eight does equal eight.

In this lesson, we'll use three different logical tests in order to calculate several employees' earnings during a week.

1   Open *Earnings Summary-1* from your sample files folder.

Notice the *Payroll Rules* section:

	A	B	C	D	E	F
3	**Payroll Rules:**					
4	All hours up to 35 hours per week paid at hourly rate					
5	All hours over 35 hours per week paid at time and a half (150% of hourly rate)					
6	Bonus of 5% paid on all sales above target					

Logical tests will be constructed to calculate *Standard Pay, Overtime Pay* and *Bonus*:

	A	B	C	D	E	F	G	H	I
8	Name	Sales	Target	Hourly Rate	Hours Worked	Standard Pay	Overtime Pay	Bonus	Total
9	Brad Cruise	22,000	10,000	15.00	40				

In the case of *Standard Pay*, the logical test will be:

"Did this employee work more than 35 hours this week?"

The formula for the logical test is: **E9<=35** (Cell E9 is less than or equal to 35).

If this returns **TRUE,** then standard pay will be:

Hours Worked * Hourly Rate, (E9*D9)

…because the employee worked for 35 hours or less.

If this returns **FALSE,** then standard pay will be:

35*Hourly Rate, (35*D9)

… because the employee worked more than 35 hours.

tip

Avoid nesting IF functions

My students often bring their own workbooks to my courses in order to find a solution to their real-world problems.

Some hideously complex and completely unfathomable workbooks turn up at my courses!

A common theme to many of these difficult-to-use workbooks is the use of nested IF functions.

Here's an example of a two-level nested IF function:

=IF(A31="Apples",10%,IF(A31="Lemons",20%,0))

This would return 10% if the value in A31 was *Apples*, 20% if the value was *Lemons* and zero if the value was anything else. Note that the words *Apples* and *Lemons* are enclosed in quotation marks. You must refer to text in this way within Excel formulas.

Whenever I see nested IF functions, I know that there's almost surely a better, less complex, and more understandable solution. In the above example, a VLOOKUP would provide a better solution (VLOOKUP functions will be covered in: *Lesson 3-22: Use a VLOOKUP function for an exact lookup.*)

In pre-2007 versions of Excel, you could nest IF functions seven deep, (which was six too many). Excel 2007/2010 have now increased this to 64!

2 Use an IF function to calculate standard pay.

1. Click in cell F9.

2. Click: Formulas→Logical→IF.

    The *Function Arguments* dialog appears.

3. Complete the dialog as follows:

Logical_test	E9<=35	=	FALSE
Value_if_true	E9*D9	=	600
Value_if_false	35*D9	=	525

If you do not completely understand why the above formulas are used, read the introduction to this lesson again.

4. Click the OK button.

    Standard Pay is correctly displayed in cell F9 (525.00).

3 Use an IF function to calculate overtime pay.

It should now be clear to you why the correct arguments for the IF function, this time, are:

Logical_test	E9<=35	=	FALSE
Value_if_true	0	=	0
Value_if_false	(E9-35)*D9*1.5	=	112.5

4 Use the IF function to calculate bonus.

Once again, it should be clear to you why the correct arguments for the IF function this time are:

Logical_test	B9>C9	=	TRUE
Value_if_true	(B9-C9)*5%	=	600
Value_if_false	0	=	0

5 Add a formula to cell I9 to calculate total pay.

The correct formula could be either of the following:

=F9+G9+H9
=SUM(F9:H9)

6 AutoFill the formulas in cells F9:I9 to cells F10:I17.

The payroll worksheet is now complete.

	A	B	C	D	E	F	G	H	I
8	Name	Sales	Target	Hourly Rate	Hours Worked	Standard Pay	Overtime Pay	Bonus	Total
9	Brad Cruise	22,000	10,000	15.00	40	525.00	112.50	600.00	1,237.50
10	Ian Dean	9,000	8,000	13.00	35	455.00	-	50.00	505.00
11	Paris Smith	10,000	12,000	15.00	42	525.00	157.50	-	682.50

7 Save your work as *Earnings Summary-2*.

Lesson 3-6: Use the SUMIF and COUNTIF logic functions to create conditional totals

In the previous lesson, you used the IF conditional function to return different values based upon a logical test that returned TRUE or FALSE.

SUMIF and COUNTIF are similar functions but are used to sum or count values within a range based upon a similar logical test.

This session's sample workbook lists all of an organization's employees along with their gender and department:

	A	B	C	D
3	Name	Sex	Salary	Department
4	Johnny Caine	M	37,864	Sales
5	George Marley	M	26,148	Purchasing
6	Betty Anan	F	26,345	Logistics
7	Paris Winfrey	F	23,562	Sales

We'll use the SUMIF and COUNTIF functions to list the total salary and headcount for each department, along with the total salary and headcount for each gender.

1   Open *Headcount & Salaries-1* from your sample files folder.

2   Use the SUMIF function to calculate the total salary for each department.

1.   Click in cell B21.

2.   Click: Formulas→Math & Trig→SUMIF.

The *Function Arguments* dialog appears.

There are three arguments for the SUMIF function.

The *Range* argument defines the range in which to look for the department name (in this case *Sales*). This will be D4:D17.

The *Criteria* argument is the thing to look for within the stated range. In this case, it is the word "Sales" contained in cell A21.

The *Sum-range* argument is the range containing numerical data that needs to be added up when the criteria is true. In this case, it is the range C4:C17.

3.   Complete the dialog with the following arguments:

Range	$D$4:$D$17
Criteria	A21
Sum_range	$C$4:$C$17

Note the use of absolute references for each range. This will allow you to AutoFill the function for the *Purchasing* and *Logistics* totals. See sidebar for more on Absolute references,

4.   Click the OK button.

note

Absolute and relative cell references

Absolute and relative cell references are covered in depth in Lesson 3-12 of the *Essential Skills* book in this series.

If you are unsure about how to use absolute and relative cell references you can download this lesson, and watch the matching video, free of charge at our website.

1. Go to:

www.learnmicrosoftexcel.com.

2. Click: *Free Tutorials With Video* (on the top menu bar).

You will then be able to view the video and download the lesson in PDF format.

Headcount & Salaries-1

note

Using wildcards in logical criteria

Sometimes you will only have a partial idea of what you need to find.

In this case, you can use the wildcard characters – the asterisk (*) and the question mark (?).

It is easiest to explain how wildcards work with a few examples:

C*g   Finds **Containing**
       Finds **Citing**
       Finds **Changing**

S?d   Finds **Sid**
       Finds **Sad**
       Finds **Syd**
       Finds **Sud**

In the above examples, you can see that the first search finds all words that begin with C and end with g.

The second example only finds three letter words that begin with S and end with d.

Later in this session, in: *Lesson 3-18: Concatenate strings using the concatenation operator (&)*, you'll learn about concatenating strings. After this lesson, you will understand the following examples:

Imagine you have a range containing the values:

22 Cherry Walk
144 Cherry Road
Cherry Tree House
Cherry Tree Lodge

... and you want to construct a COUNTIF or SUMIF based upon the partial string contained in cell A1 (for this example, let's imagine that the word *Cherry* is in cell A1).

The criteria would be:

"*" & A1 & "*"

This would find all four values.

To find values that begin with the word *Cherry*, you would use the criteria:

A1 & "*"

This would find two values.

5. AutoFill cell B21 to cells B22:B23 to display the total salary for the *Purchasing* and *Logistics* departments.

3   **Use the COUNTIF function to calculate the headcount for each department.**

COUNTIF works in exactly the same way as SUMIF but returns a count of all cells that match the criteria.

1. Click in cell C21.

2. Click: Formulas→More Functions→Statistical→COUNTIF.

3. Complete the dialog with the following arguments:

Range	$D$4:$D$17
Criteria	A21

4. Click the OK button.

5. AutoFill cell C21 to cells C22:C23 to display the headcount for the *Purchasing* and *Logistics* departments.

4   **Use a SUMIF and COUNTIF function to calculate the salary and headcount for male and female employees in cells B27:C28.**

Use exactly the same technique as you did for *Salary* and *Headcount by Department*. The correct arguments for cells B27 and C27 are:

SUMIF

Range	$B$4:$B$17
Criteria	A27
Sum_range	$C$4:$C$17

And:

COUNTIF

Range	$B$4:$B$17
Criteria	A27

	A	B	C
20	Department	Salary	Headcount
21	Sales	179,898	6
22	Purchasing	137,557	5
23	Logistics	73,601	3
24	**Total:**	**391,056**	**14**
25			
26	Gender	Salary	Headcount
27	M	253,587	9
28	F	137,469	5
29	**Total:**	**391,056**	**14**

5   Save your work as *Headcount & Salaries-2*.

Lesson 3-7: Understand date serial numbers

This lesson was also included in the *Essential Skills* book in this series but is also included in this book as a recap. A full understanding of the date serial number concept is essential in order to understand the date and time functions that will be introduced in later lessons.

How Excel stores dates

Dates are stored as simple numbers called *date serial numbers*. The serial number contains the number of days that have elapsed since 1st January 1900 (where 1st January 1900 is represented by 1).

The world began in 1900

An interesting shortcoming of Excel is its inability to easily work with dates before 1900. Excel simply doesn't acknowledge that there were any dates before this time. If you work with older dates, you will have to work-around this limitation.

In Excel, every time is a date, and every date is a time

This one is an eye opener! We've already realized that 5th January 1900 is stored as the number 5. What would the number 5.5 mean? It would mean midday on 5th January 1900.

It is possible to format a date to show only the date, only the time, or both a time and a date.

When you enter a pure time into a cell, the time is stored as a number less than one. Excel regards this as having the non-existent date of 00 January 1900!

When you enter a pure date into a cell, the time is stored as midnight at the beginning of that day.

1   Create a new blank workbook and put the numbers 1 to 5 in cells A1-A5.

2   Type the formula **=A1** into cell B1 followed by the **<Enter>** key, and then AutoFill the formula to the end of the list.

	A	B
1	1	1
2	2	2
3	3	3
4	4	4
5	5	5

3   Apply a date format to column A that will show a four digit year.

	A	B
1	01 January 1900	1
2	02 January 1900	2

This reveals that the numbers 1 to 5 represent the dates 1-Jan-1900 to 05-Jan-1900.

4 Set a custom format of **dd/mm/yyyy hh:mm** for the dates in column A (to show both dates and times).

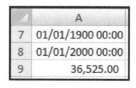

Notice that when you enter a date without a time, the time is set to midnight at the beginning of that day.

	A	B
1	01/01/1900 00:00	1
2	02/01/1900 00:00	2

5 Change the time in cell A2 to 12:00.

Notice that the number in cell B2 has altered to 2.5 showing that times are stored by Excel as the decimal part of a number.

	A	B
1	01/01/1900 00:00	1
2	02/01/1900 12:00	2.5

6 Compute the number of days that occurred between 01/01/1900 and 01/01/2000.

Now that you have a good grasp of Excel's serial numbers, this task is easy.

1. Enter the two dates in cells A7 and A8, one beneath the other.

2. Apply the comma style to cell A9.

3. Subtract one date from the other by entering the formula: **=A8-A7** into cell A9.

	A
7	01/01/1900 00:00
8	01/01/2000 00:00
9	36,525.00

You now know that 36,525 days occurred during the last millennium (actually 36,524 due to the Lotus 1-2-3 bug – see sidebar).

7 Close the workbook without saving.

Lesson 3-8: Understand common date functions

Excel's primary date functions are TODAY, DAY, MONTH and YEAR. In the previous lesson, you gained an understanding of how Excel stores dates as serial numbers. You can now use this knowledge in conjunction with the above date functions to create some very useful date related formulas.

1 Open *Resources-1* from your sample files folder.

This worksheet contains a list of Employees along with their dates of birth.

	A	B	C	D	E	F
3	First Name	Last Name	Date of Birth	Year Born	Day Born	Month Born
4	Brad	Cruise	15-Apr-65			
5	Ian	Dean	22-May-67			
6	Paris	Smith	16-Jul-72			

2 Use the YEAR function to calculate the year in which each employee was born.

1. Click in cell D4.

2. Click Formulas→Date & Time→Year.

The Function Arguments dialog is displayed.

Function Arguments	
YEAR	
Serial_number	= number
	=

Returns the year of a date, an integer in the range 1900 - 9999.

Serial_number is a number in the date-time code used by Microsoft Office Excel.

3. Click cell C4.

Because you know that all dates are represented by a serial number, and because cell C4 contains a date, this reference will cause the YEAR function to return 1965 (the year Brad Cruise was born).

Notice that the dialog previews the result as = *1965* and also lets you know that the date serial number for 15th April 1965 is *23,847*.

YEAR	
Serial_number	C4 = 23847
	= 1965

4. Click the OK button.

The year in which Brad Cruise was born is now displayed in cell D4.

	A	B	C	D
3	First Name	Last Name	Date of Birth	Year Born
4	Brad	Cruise	15-Apr-65	1965

Resources-1

3   Use the DAY function to place the day upon which Brad Cruise was born into cell E4.

4   Use the MONTH function to calculate the month upon which Brad Cruise was born into cell F4.

	D	E	F
3	Year Born	Day Born	Month Born
4	=YEAR(C4)	=DAY(C4)	=MONTH(C4)

	A	B	C	D	E	F
3	First Name	Last Name	Date of Birth	Year Born	Day Born	Month Born
4	Brad	Cruise	15-Apr-65	1965	15	4

5   Use the TODAY function to place a volatile current date into cell G4.

	G
3	Today
4	=TODAY()

	G
3	Today
4	03-Jul-09

The TODAY function returns the current date. The date is volatile, this means that if you were to open this worksheet again tomorrow, you would see tomorrow's date in cell G4.

6   Use the YEAR function to place the current year into cell H4.

By using the value in cell G4 as the argument for the YEAR function, it is possible to insert the current year into cell H4.

Because the value in cell G4 is volatile, the value in H4 is also volatile. This means that if you were to open this worksheet again in the year 2010, you would see the value 2010 in cell H4.

	H
3	Current Year
4	=YEAR(G4)

	H
3	Current Year
4	2009

7   Add a formula to cell I4 to calculate the employee's maximum age this year.

Calculating the employee's current age from date of birth using the YEAR, MONTH and DAY functions is quite a feat (although it can be done). We'll discover an easy way to do this in the next lesson using a different technique.

In this lesson, we'll simply calculate what the employee's maximum age will be this year with a simple subtraction of the current year from the year born.

	D	E	F	G	H	I
3	Year Born	Day Born	Month Born	Today	Current Year	Max Age This Year
4	1965	15	4	04/06/2009	2009	=H4-D4

8   Autofill cells D4:I4 down to row 12.

9   Save your work as *Resources-2*.

note

Why calculating age from date of birth is so difficult without DATEDIF.

I've seen some weird and wonderful attempts to calculate age from date of birth in my student's worksheets.

At first, it doesn't seem such a big deal. The first solution that occurs is to simply convert each date to days and then divide by 365. Like this:

(TODAY() – BirthDate)/365

If it wasn't for leap years, this would work. To overcome the leap year issue, I've seen solutions based upon the assumption that a year is, on average, 365.25 days long. So why won't this work?

(TODAY() – BirthDate)/365.25

There are two reasons why.

The first reason is that the date may belong to a child who has not yet lived through a leap year.

The second reason is caused by the Gregorian leap year rule that skips a leap year in centurial years (see: *Lesson 3-7: Understand date serial numbers* sidebar).

So is there any Excel based solution at all without DATEDIF?

Well yes, there is, but it is hideously complicated, involves nested IF functions and doesn't bear thinking about!

Aren't you pleased that you know about the secret DATEDIF function?

Lesson 3-9: Use the DATEDIF function

Three may keep a secret, if two of them are dead.

Benjamin Franklin (1706 - 1790)

One of the most useful date-related functions available in Excel is the DATEDIF function. For some reason, this is a secret and you'll find nothing about this wonderful function anywhere in the Excel 2010 documentation. Some have speculated that this may be for legal reasons as the function was originally included for compatibility with Lotus 1-2-3.

Microsoft documented the function in Excel 2000 so, in their spirit of backward compatibility, they continue to support it in Excel 2010 and can be expected to also support it in all future Excel versions.

DATEDIF is able to calculate the difference between two dates for several intervals. In this lesson, we'll use it to calculate an age from a date of birth. This is hugely complex without the DATEDIF function (see sidebar).

Because you probably don't have a copy of Excel 2000, here is the syntax for the function:

=DATEDIF(StartDate, EndDate, Interval)

StartDate: The first date.

EndDate: The second date.

Interval: The interval to return, such as the number of months or years between the two dates.

The interval arguments are:

"m"   Months between two dates.

"d"   Days between two dates.

"y"   Years between two dates.

"ym"   Months between two dates, ignoring the year (ie as if both dates were the same year).

"yd"   Days between two dates, ignoring the year.

"md"   Days between two dates, ignoring the months and years.

1   Open *Resources-2* from your sample files folder (if it isn't already open).

2   Change the text in cell I3 to **Age (Years).**

Resources-2

3   Delete cells I4:I12.

	C	D	E	F	G	H	I
3	Date of Birth	Year Born	Day Born	Month Born	Today	Current Year	Age (Years)
4	15-Apr-65	1965	15	4	21-Sep-11	2011	
5	22-May-67	1967	22	5	21-Sep-11	2011	
6	16-Jul-72	1972	16	7	21-Sep-11	2011	

4   Add the following formula to cell I4:

=DATEDIF(C4,TODAY(),"y")

Notice that *Formula AutoComplete* doesn't even want to admit that this function exists!

The function works by comparing the date of birth (in cell C4) with today's date (returned by the TODAY function) and returns the interval in years.

5   Calculate each resource's precise age in years, months and days.

This requirement illustrates the use of the "ym" and "md" intervals.

1.   Type the text **Age (Months)** into cell J3.

2.   Type the text **Age (Days)** into cell K3.

3.   Match the formatting of cells J3 and K3 to that in cell I3.

(Formatting is an elementary skill covered in the *Essential Skills* book in this series).

	H	I	J	K
3	Current Year	Age (Years)	Age (Months)	Age (Days)
4	2011	46		

(You may see a different age depending upon whatever today's date is at the time you read this book).

4.   Add the following formula to cell J4:

=DATEDIF(C4,TODAY(),"ym")

5.   Add the following formula to cell K4:

=DATEDIF(C4,TODAY(),"md")

6.   Autofill cells I4:K4 to the end of the range.

	A	B	C	D	I	J	K
3	First Name	Last Name	Date of Birth	Year Born	Age (Years)	Age (Months)	Age (Days)
4	Brad	Cruise	15-Apr-65	1965	46	5	6
5	Ian	Dean	22-May-67	1967	44	3	30

The above was calculated on 21st Sept 2011. They'll all be a little older by the time you complete this exercise!

6   Save your work as Resources-3.

note

Project Management and Excel

Excel is often misused to manage projects.

Project Management involves scheduling tasks and assigning resources to complete each task. For example, to build a house you would have tasks such as *lay bricks* and *fit windows*.

Each task has a start and end date and one or more dependencies (for example you cannot fit the windows until you have laid the bricks).

Each task also has one or more resources assigned to it (for example you may assign Bill and Bob to lay the bricks and Colin to fit the windows).

The best way to illustrate a project plan is the Gantt chart named after Henry Gantt (1861–1919). It is quite easy to produce a primitive Gantt chart using Excel (but not a true Gantt chart showing inter-task dependencies).

Now that you understand Excel's date functions, you might think that Excel is a great tool for managing projects – but there's a far, far better way.

Microsoft Project is a tool designed specifically to manage projects and produce excellent Gantt charts.

If you have complex workbooks that seek to manage the type of scenario described above you really should check out Microsoft Project – it is a superb tool.

Many students that attend my Project Management courses have first tried hard and failed using Excel!

Lesson 3-10: Use date offsets to manage projects using the scheduling equation

In this lesson, we'll use date offsets in conjunction with the scheduling equation to create a worksheet that will manage a small project.

In order to understand project management, you need to first understand the scheduling equation:

Time = Work/Units

Let's pose the age-old primary school math problem:

"If it takes one man ten days to dig a hole, how long will it take two men to dig the same hole"?

The answer is, of course, five days (in mathematics, if not in reality)!

To use the scheduling equation, we describe each unit as being a man and define the work in days.

In the first example:

10 days = 10 days/1 Man

In the second example:

5 days = 10 days/2 Men

If you increase your estimate of 10 days work, then the time will increase. If you add more men to the task, then the time will decrease as the equation will always balance.

In this lesson, you'll learn how to create formulas that will enable task lengths to dynamically re-scale as you add more resources to each task, or revise your estimate for the amount of work needed to complete each task.

1 Open *Project-1* from your sample files folder.

The worksheet contains a simple project plan consisting of four linked tasks:

	A	B	C	D	E
3	Task Name	Start date	Work (Man-Days)	Units	End Date
4	Dig Foundations	15-Jun-09	3	3	
5	Pour Footings		2	1	
6	Lay Bricks to DPC		8	4	
7	Pour floor slab		2	1	

Each task has a *start to finish dependency*. This means that each task must complete before the following task can begin.

2 Calculate the *End Date* for the first task.

Enter the formula: **=B4+C4/D4-1** into cell E4.

Note that, because of the rules of precedence, this is the equivalent of **=B4+(C4/D4)-1**

Project-1

(Precedence was covered in: *Lesson 3-1: Understand precedence rules and use the Evaluate feature*).

We subtract one day so that a job of one day's duration will begin and end on the same day. The formula calculates the *End Date* using the scheduling equation discussed at the beginning of this lesson.

	A	B	C	D	E
			Work		
3	Task Name	Start date	(Man-Days)	Units	End Date
4	Dig Foundations	15-Jun-09	3	3	15-Jun-09

The *End Date* is 15-Jun-09 because we have assigned three men to the task which has three man-day's work. The task thus takes one day to complete and so begins and ends on the same day.

3   Test the scheduling equation.

If you were to take two men off the job the single remaining man would take three days to complete the task.

1.   Change the value in cell D4 to 1.

Notice that the task now takes three days to complete.

	A	B	C	D	E
			Work		
3	Task Name	Start date	(Man-Days)	Units	End Date
4	Dig Foundations	15-Jun-09	3	1	17-Jun-09

2.   Revise your estimate of the work to 6 Man-Days and assign two men to the task.

This time, the task takes three days to complete.

	A	B	C	D	E
			Work		
3	Task Name	Start date	(Man-Days)	Units	End Date
4	Dig Foundations	15-Jun-09	6	2	17-Jun-09

4   Add a formula to show the start date for the *Pour Footings* task.

The start date of the *Pour Footings* task will be the day after the End Date of the *Dig Foundations* task.

Enter the formula: **=E4+1** into cell B5.

5   AutoFill cells B5 and E4 to the end of the range.

You now have a dynamic project plan that will adjust the end date of the project based upon your work estimates and the number of resources that you assign to each task.

	A	B	C	D	E
			Work		
3	Task Name	Start date	(Man-Days)	Units	End Date
4	Dig Foundations	15-Jun-09	6	2	17-Jun-09
5	Pour Footings	18-Jun-09	2	1	19-Jun-09

6   Save your work as *Project-2*.

Lesson 3-11: Use the DATE function to offset days, months and years

Now that you understand the TODAY, DAY, MONTH and YEAR functions, we can introduce the DATE function to dynamically manage more sophisticated date offsets.

1 Open *Service Schedule-1* from your sample files folder.

In this example, the service schedule requires that vehicles are inspected 20 days after first supply, 3 months after the 20 day inspection, and then every year thereafter.

	A	B	C	D	E
1	**Service Schedule**				
2					
3	Vehicle Supplied On	20 Day Inspection	3 month Inspection	12 Month Services Thereafter...	
4	16-Jan-08				
5	18-Feb-09				
6	16-Mar-09				

2 Put a formula in cell B4 that will calculate the date for the 20 day inspection based upon the date in cell A4.

1. Type **=D** into cell B4.

The DATE function is the first in the drop-down list:

	A	B	
3	Vehicle Supplied On	20 Day Inspection	3 mor Inspe
4	16-Jan-08	=D	
5	18-Feb-09	*fx* DATE	
6	16-Mar-09	*fx* DATEVALUE	
7		*fx* DAVERAGE	

2. Press the **<Tab>** key to enter the formula into the cell.

3. Click the *Insert Function* button on the left of the formula bar:

=DATE(

The *Function Arguments* dialog is displayed.

The DATE function demands three numerical arguments: *Year, Month* and *Day.* For example:

=DATE(2011,9,20)

... would return 20th September 2011.

Because the DATE function requires numerical arguments, we need to use the YEAR, MONTH and DAY functions to convert each part of the date into numbers.

Service Schedule-1

4. Complete the dialog as follows:

DATE			
Year	YEAR(A4)		= 2008
Month	MONTH(A4)		= 1
Day	DAY(A4)+20		= 36

Note that in the case of the Day argument, we have added the number 20 to create a date that is 20 days later than that in cell A4.

5. Click the OK button.

A date is shown that is 20 days after 16th January 2008:

	A	B
3	Vehicle Supplied On	20 Day Inspection
4	16-Jan-08	05-Feb-08

3   Put a formula in cell C4 that will calculate a date that is three months later than the 20 day inspection date.

This time your dialog should look like this:

DATE			
Year	YEAR(B4)		= 2008
Month	MONTH(B4)+3		= 5
Day	DAY(B4)		= 5

4   Put a formula in cell D4 that will calculate a date that is twelve months later than the 3 month inspection date.

This time your dialog should look like this:

DATE			
Year	YEAR(C4)+1		= 2009
Month	MONTH(C4)		= 5
Day	DAY(C4)		= 5

5   AutoFill the formula in cell D4 to cells E4:G4.

6   AutoFill the formulas in cells B4:G4 to the end of the range.

	A	B	C	D
3	Vehicle Supplied On	20 Day Inspection	3 month Inspection	12 Month S
4	16-Jan-08	05-Feb-08	05-May-08	05-May-09
5	18-Feb-09	10-Mar-09	10-Jun-09	10-Jun-10

7   Save your work as *Service Schedule-2*.

Lesson 3-12: Enter time values and perform basic time calculations

Serial number recap

In *Lesson 3-7: Understand date serial numbers*, we discussed how Excel combines time and date information in a single date serial number.

Excel represents dates by counting from 1st January 1900 to the present day. For example, the date serial number 2.0 represents midnight (00:00) on 2nd January 1900.

Excel represents time using the decimal part of the serial number. For example, the date serial number 3.5 represents midday on 3rd January 1900.

Excel also allows you to work with pure time values (times that do not have an associated date). In this case, the mythical date of 0 Jan 1900 is used. For example, the date serial number 0.3333 represents the time 08:00 but does not represent any date at all.

In this lesson, we'll focus on entering time values into a worksheet without any associated date and explain how to avoid the mistakes commonly made when working with time values.

1   Open *Time Sheet-1* from your sample files folder.

This worksheet contains details of the hours worked by an employee during a single week.

2   Add a start time of 08:00 and finish time 17:00 for Monday.

24-hour notation is the best way to enter times as it is the least error prone and easiest to read.

Type **08:00** into cell B8 and **17:00** into cell C8.

	A	B	C
7	Day	Start	Finish
8	Monday	08:00	17:00

3   Add a start time of 10:00 AM and finish time 6:00 PM for Tuesday.

AM/PM notation is preferred by some users, but is more error prone than the recommended 24-hour notation.

Type **10:00 AM** into cell B9 and **6:00 PM** into cell C9. Make sure that you leave a space after the time otherwise Excel will interpret the value as text rather than time.

	A	B	C
9	Tuesday	10:00 AM	6:00 PM

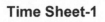

Time Sheet-1

4 Complete the rest of the time sheet as follows:

	A	B	C
7	Day	Start	Finish
8	Monday	08:00	17:00
9	Tuesday	10:00 AM	6:00 PM
10	Wednesday	21:00	03:00
11	Thursday	10:00 PM	4:00 AM
12	Friday	08:00	17:00

Depending upon which country you are in, your dates and times may display differently to those shown above. See the sidebar on the facing page for more information about how your regional settings affect the default format of dates and times.

5 Examine the date serial numbers in cells B8:C12.

1. Select cells B8:C12.

2. Right-click the selected cells and click *Format Cells...* on the shortcut menu.

3. Click *General* in the *Category* list.

4. Click the OK button.

Notice that all time values begin with zero. This is because no date is associated with them. Understanding this is very important when creating time formulas.

Notice that the time in cell B8 is 0.333333. This is because at 08:00 33.333333% of the day has elapsed, as eight hours is 33.333333% of 24.

6 Add a formula to cell D8 that will calculate the number of hours worked.

1. Add the formula **=C8-B8** to cell D8.

	A	B	C	D
7	Day	Start	Finish	Hours Worked
8	Monday	0.333333	0.708333	0.375

The result shows that Frank worked for 37.5% of the day on Monday.

7 Format cells B8:D12 to show times in the 24-hour format.

1. Select cells B8:D12.

2. Right-click the selected cells and click *Format Cells...* from the shortcut list.

3. From the *Custom* category set the format to **hh:mm**.

4. Click the OK button.

The number of hours and minutes worked is now shown in cell D8.

	A	B	C	D	E
7	Day	Start	Finish	Hours Worked	Earnings
8	Monday	08:00	17:00	09:00	
9	Tuesday	10:00	18:00		

8 Save your work as *Time Sheet-2*.

---

tip

You can also return to *General* format using the shortcut key:

<Ctrl>+<Shift>+<~>

(Control + Shift + Tilde).

---

tip

Converting time serial numbers to decimal values

In this lesson, we subtracted 08:00 from 17:00 giving a result of 0.375 representing 8 hours as 37.5% of one 24-hour day.

Sometimes, it is convenient to express times as simple decimal numbers (in this case as 9.0). In order to convert a time serial number to a numeric value representing hours, you simply multiply the serial number by 24:

24*37.5% = 9.0 hours

---

tip

You can also open the *Format Cells* dialog using the shortcut key:

<Ctrl>+<1>

Type:
hh:mm

	A	B	C
7	Day	Start	Finish
8	Monday	08:00	17:00
9	Tuesday	10:00	18:00
10	Wednesday	21:00	03:00
11	Thursday	22:00	04:00
12	Friday	08:00	17:00

Lesson 3-13: Perform time calculations that span midnight

1 Open *Time Sheet-2* from your sample files folder (if it isn't already open).

2 AutoFill the formula in cell D8 to cells D9:D12.

	A	B	C	D
7	Day	Start	Finish	Hours Worked
8	Monday	08:00	17:00	09:00
9	Tuesday	10:00	18:00	08:00
10	Wednesday	21:00	03:00	#############
11	Thursday	22:00	04:00	#############
12	Friday	08:00	17:00	09:00
13	Total:			

A problem is now revealed. On Wednesday and Thursday, Frank's working times spanned midnight. Unfortunately, Excel doesn't know this. A row of hashes is shown to signify an error as Excel cannot display a time of minus 18 hours.

3 Correct the formulas in cells D8:D12 so that time is correctly calculated, even when the times span midnight.

Fortunately, it is very easy to correct the formula using the IF logic function covered in: *Lesson 3-5: Use the IF logic function.*

1. Change the formula in cell D8 to the following:

   =IF(C8>B8, C8-B8, C8+1-B8)

   The formula works by adding the number one (representing one day) to the finish time when the finish time is less than the start time.

2. AutoFill the formula from cell D8 to cells D9:D12.

   The times are now correctly calculated:

	A	B	C	D
7	Day	Start	Finish	Hours Worked
8	Monday	08:00	17:00	09:00
9	Tuesday	10:00	18:00	08:00
10	Wednesday	21:00	03:00	06:00
11	Thursday	22:00	04:00	06:00
12	Friday	08:00	17:00	09:00
13	Total:			

4 Add a formula to show the total hours worked this week in cell D13.

Add a SUM function to cell D13 to sum the values in cells D8:D12.

	D
13	=SUM(D8:D12)

The formula doesn't return an error but it seems to produce the wrong answer:

IF

Logical_test	C8>B8
Value_if_true	C8-B8
Value_if_false	C8+1-B8

Time Sheet-2

	A	B	C	D
7	Day	Start	Finish	Hours Worked
8	Monday	08:00	17:00	09:00
9	Tuesday	10:00	18:00	08:00
10	Wednesday	21:00	03:00	06:00
11	Thursday	22:00	04:00	06:00
12	Friday	08:00	17:00	09:00
13	Total:			14:00

The answer is actually correct. The problem lies in the way in which cell D13 is formatted.

Remember that the date serial numbers in cells D8:D12 contain the percentage of each 24 hour day that was worked. When they are added together they will add up to more than one. Because cell D13 is formatted to show times, it will ignore the whole number part of the date/time serial number, believing that this represents a date.

The actual value in cell D13 is 1.583333 and that represents 14:00 on 1st January 1900.

5 **Display the value in cell D13 correctly by adjusting the format.**

There are two ways to solve this problem. We'll solve it using a custom format. The other potential method is discussed in the sidebar.

Because adding time values is a common requirement, Excel provides a special custom format to display times that exceed 24 hours.

1. Click on cell D13.

2. Click: Home→Number→Dialog Launcher.

   The *Format Cells* dialog appears.

3. Click the *Custom* category.

   Notice that the current format is **hh:mm.**

4. Manually type in the new custom format: **[h]:mm.**

   The brackets around the [h] means that where there is a whole number in the date serial number it should be regarded as time data.

   For example, the date serial number **2.0** will be interpreted as meaning 48 hours and not midnight on 2nd January 1900. The serial number 1.5 will be interpreted as 36 hours and not midday on 1st January 1900.

5. Click OK.

6. The worksheet now displays correctly:

	A	B	C	D
11	Thursday	22:00	04:00	06:00
12	Friday	08:00	17:00	09:00
13	Total:			38:00

6 **Save your work as** *Time Sheet-3*.

Lesson 3-14: Understand common time functions and convert date serial numbers to decimal values

Excel's primary time functions are NOW, HOUR, MINUTE and SECOND. In this lesson, you'll learn how to use all of them along with some important techniques when performing calculations with time values.

1 Open *Time Sheet-3* from your sample files folder (if it isn't already open).

2 Add formulas to cells E8:E12 to calculate earnings.

This isn't as straightforward as it first seems.

The actual values in cells D8:D12 represent the percentage of each day that was worked. For example, cell D9 actually contains the value 0.333333 as eight hours are 33.3333% of one 24 hour day.

In order to calculate the correct earnings figure, it is necessary to multiply the date serial number in column D by 24 to convert the date serial number to a decimal value.

1. Type the formula: **=D8*24*$B$5** into cell E8.

   Note the absolute reference for cell B5. This will enable the formula to be AutoFilled to the cells below.

2. AutoFill the formula to cells E9:E12.

3. Select cells E8:E13.

4. Click: Home→Number→Comma Style to show two decimal places.

5. Use a SUM function to show total earnings for the week in cell E13.

   The correct earnings figure is now shown in every case.

	E
7	**Earnings**
8	135
9	120
10	90
11	90
12	135
13	

	A	B	C	D	E
5	Hourly Rate:	15.00			
6					
7	Day	Start	Finish	Hours Worked	Earnings
8	Monday	08:00	17:00	09:00	135.00
9	Tuesday	10:00	18:00	08:00	120.00
10	Wednesday	21:00	03:00	06:00	90.00
11	Thursday	22:00	04:00	06:00	90.00
12	Friday	08:00	17:00	09:00	135.00
13	Total:			38:00	570.00

3 Add a NOW function to cell B15 to display the current date and time.

1. Type **Current Date and Time** into cell A15.

2. Click on cell B15.

Time Sheet-3

3. Type **=NOW**

	B	C	D	E	F	G	H
15	=NOW						
16	𝑓x NOW	Returns the current date and time formatted as a date and time					

The tip advises that this function returns the current date and time. This is a little like the TODAY function encountered in *Lesson 3-8: Understand common date functions* except that it returns the current date *and* time rather than midnight on the current date.

The current date and time is the time that the worksheet was last recalculated (we'll learn how to recalculate the worksheet later in this lesson).

4. Press the **<Tab>** key twice.

5. If necessary, widen columns A and B so that they are wide enough to see all of their contents.

	A	B
15	**Current Date and Time**	21/09/2011 16:02

4 Add a TIME function to cell B16 to display the current time.

The TIME function works in a similar way to the DATE function encountered in: *Lesson 3-10: Use date offsets to manage projects using the scheduling equation.*

1. Type **Current Time** into cell A16.

2. Click in cell B16.

3. Click: Formulas→Function Library→Date&Time→TIME.

    The *Function Arguments* dialog is displayed.

4. Enter the following values for each argument:

TIME		
Hour	HOUR(NOW())	= Volatile
Minute	MINUTE(NOW())	= Volatile
Second	SECOND(NOW())	= Volatile

5. Click the OK button.

    The current time appears in cell B16.

	A	B
15	**Current Date and Time**	21/09/2011 16:05
16	**Current Time**	4:05 PM

5 Re-calculate the worksheet to update the current time.

Click: Formulas→Calculation→Calculate Sheet.

Provided that at least a minute has passed since you created the NOW and TIME functions, you will see the time update to the current time.

6 Save your work as *Time Sheet-4*.

Lesson 3-15: Use the TIME function to offset hours, minutes and seconds

In this lesson, we will use the TIME function in conjunction with the HOUR, MINUTE and SECOND functions to offset time data.

We'll construct a train timetable that will run a service every 10 minutes before 09:00 and every hour thereafter.

1   Open *Train Timetable-1* from your sample files folder.

The formulas in this worksheet will be constructed so that it can be automatically updated by simply changing the *First Train* times in column B.

This will work because all of the subsequent journeys will be defined as offsets from the first train's arrival time using the TIME function.

	A	B	C	D	E	F	G
3	Trains run every 10 minutes before 09:00 and every hour at other times.						
4							
5	Route	First Train	Further trains at...				
6	Northern	08:30					
7	Jubilee	08:20					

2   Put a formula in cells C6:K6 that will calculate the arrival times of subsequent trains on the Northern line.

We know that trains arrive every 10 minutes before 09:00 so would expect trains at 08:40, 08:50 and 09:00. After that, we would expect trains each hour at 10:00, 11:00, 12:00…

1.   Click in cell C6.

2.   Click: Formulas→Function Library→Date & Time→Time.

The *Function Arguments* dialog appears.

3.   Enter the following values for each argument:

TIME			
Hour	HOUR(B6)		= 8
Minute	MINUTE(B6)+10		= 40
Second	SECOND(B6)		= 0

4.   Click the OK button.

The correct time of the next train appears in cell C6.

	A	B	C	D
5	Route	First Train	Further trains at...	
6	Northern	08:30	8:40 AM	

5.   AutoFill the formula in cell C6 to cells D6:K6.

Unsurprisingly, the formula applies an offset of 10 minutes to each cell:

Train Timetable-1

	A	B	C	D	E	F
5	Route	First Train	Further trains at...			
6	Northern	08:30	8:40 AM	8:50 AM	9:00 AM	9:10 AM

Unfortunately, that isn't what we wanted. After the 09:00 train there shouldn't be another until 10:00.

To fix the formula, we need to add an IF function that will check the time of the previous train. If the time is later than or equal to 09:00, the increment should be one hour and not 10 minutes. (The IF function was covered in: *Lesson 3-5: Use the IF logic function*).

6. Copy the function from cell C6 *excluding the = sign* by clicking in cell C6, selecting the function in the formula bar (but not the = sign) and then copying (by pressing **<Ctrl>+<C>** or by right-clicking and then selecting *Copy* from the shortcut menu).

fx =TIME(HOUR(B6),MINUTE(B6)+10,SECOND(B6))

7. Press the **<ESCAPE>** key to exit cell edit mode.

8. Click cell C6 again and then press the **<Delete>** key to remove the existing formula from the cell.

9. Click: Formulas→Function Library→Logical→IF.

The Function arguments dialog is displayed.

10. Paste the function (previously copied) into the **Value_if_true** and **Value_if_false** text boxes.

The dialog should now look like this:

Logical_test	
Value_if_true	TIME(HOUR(B6),MINUTE(B6)+10,
Value_if_false	TIME(HOUR(B6),MINUTE(B6)+10,

11. Set the Logical_test argument to:

HOUR(B6)>=9

12. Edit the **Value_if_true** argument so that it offsets the previous train time by one hour rather than ten minutes:

TIME(HOUR(B6)+1,MINUTE(B6),SECOND(B6))

13. Click the OK button.

14. AutoFill cell C6 to cells D6:K6.

3 AutoFill the formulas to the remaining cells to complete the timetable.

AutoFill cells C6:K6 to cells C10:K10.

The timetable is now complete and correct:

	A	B	C	D	E	F	G
5	Route	First Train	Further trains at...				
6	Northern	08:30	08:40	08:50	09:00	10:00	11:00

4 Save your work as *Train Timetable-2*.

Note

The NOT logical function

"He was a brilliant talker, and when he was arguing some difficult point he had a way of skipping from side to side and whisking his tail which was somehow very persuasive. The others said of Squealer that he could turn black into white".

George Orwell, Animal Farm

This session introduces the Excel logical functions:

AND, OR

There's another logical function that can sometimes make your formulas easier to read (though it is never actually necessary).

This is the NOT function that will invert a logical result.

In other words, it will change TRUE to FALSE and FALSE to TRUE. (Squealer would have loved it)!

The rule:

If Sales > Target AND Years Service >2

OR

Years Service >5

Could also be written as:

If Sales > Target AND NOT Years Service <2

OR

Years Service NOT <5

Lesson 3-16: Use the AND and OR functions to construct complex Boolean criteria

When using logical functions such as IF, COUNTIF and SUMIF, you need to construct a logical test (sometimes also called criteria) that will return TRUE or FALSE.

We've already used simple Boolean criteria such as:

E9<=35

This Boolean expression returns TRUE if the value in cell E9 is less than or equal to 35, otherwise it returns FALSE.

In this lesson, we'll use the Logical functions AND and OR to create more complex Boolean criteria.

The sample file for this lesson computes bonuses for employees, based upon the following rules:

A bonus of 2% of sales will be paid to employees who meet the following criteria:
1/ Sales are above target.
2/ Have worked for the company for more than two years.

Note: *Employees with more than five years service will receive the bonus even if sales are below target.*

Here are the bonus figures for the first three employees:

	A	B	C	D	E
9	Name	Years service	Sales	Target	Bonus
10	Johnny Caine	2	11,000	9,000	-
11	George Marley	7	7,000	9,000	140
12	Betty Anan	3	13,000	5,000	260

- You can see that Johnny Caine exceeded his target but received no bonus because he only has two years' service.

- George Marley has over five years' service and thus receives bonus even though he didn't reach his sales target.

- Betty Annan has three years service and she has also exceeded her sales target, so she receives her bonus.

Another way of expressing the logical test that governs when bonus will be paid is:

If Sales > Target AND Years Service >2

OR

Years Service >5

A logical expression can be created to implement the rules using Excel's AND and OR functions.

Bonus Calculator-1

Here's how we can use the AND function to test that Johnny Caine's sales are above target AND that he has more than two years' service

=AND(C10>D10, B10>2)

The AND function will return True only if both expressions evaluate True. In Johnny's case, it will return False because Johnny only has two years' service.

We also need to check whether the employee has over five years' service. Here's how we can use the OR function to do this:

=OR(B10>5, AND(C10>D10, B10>2)**)**

The OR function will return true if either of the arguments return true. In Johnny's case, this will still return false as he also has less than five years' service, but in George's case, it would return true since George has seven years' service.

Now that you understand how to construct the logical test for the bonus calculation, we can create the IF function for the sample file.

1   Open *Bonus Calculator-1* from your sample files folder.

    1. Click in cell E10.

    2. Click: Formulas→Function Library→Logical→IF.

    3. Enter the following values into the dialog (see text above for explanation):

Logical_test	OR(B10>5,AND(C10>D10,B10>2))
Value_if_true	C10*0.02
Value_if_false	0

    4. Click the OK button.

    5. AutoFill the formula from cell E10 to the end of the range.

	A	B	C	D	E
9	Name	Years service	Sales	Target	Bonus
10	Johnny Caine	2	11,000	9,000	-
11	George Marley	7	7,000	9,000	140
12	Betty Anan	3	13,000	5,000	260
13	Paris Winfrey	1	11,000	10,000	-
14	Ozzy Dickens	5	9,000	9,000	-
15	Johnny Roberts	2	6,000	7,000	-
16	Charles Monroe	8	10,000	5,000	200

2   Save your work as Bonus Calculator-2.

note

Gross profit and mark up

Newcomers to the retail business often confuse mark up with gross profit. The phrase: "I make a 50% profit" is meaningless without clarifying whether the profit is a gross profit or mark up.

In general business, gross profit is the more widely accepted metric when discussing profits.

Here's an example of mark up:

Bob buys a watch for $500 and marks it up by 50%. This means that he adds 50% to the cost price and sells it for $750. In this case, the formula is:

Selling Price = Cost Price * (1+MarkUp)

$750 = $500 * 1.5

Here's an example of gross profit:

Bill buys a hard disk for $100. His company needs to make 50% gross profit on all goods sold. This means that they need to sell the hard drive for $200 making 50% of the selling price ($100) in profit. In this case, the formula is:

Selling Price = Cost Price/ (1-Gross Profit%)

$200 = $100/(1-0.5)

You can see from the above example that a gross profit of 50% is the same as a mark up of 100%.

Terminology

I use the terms *Gross Profit* when discussing both cash amounts and percentages.

There's a lot of controversy about correct terminology. Some purists would argue that the correct terms are *Gross Margin* (or simply *Margin*) for % values, and *Gross Profit* for cash values.

Classic Watches-1

Lesson 3-17: Understand calculation options (manual and automatic)

It is possible to change the calculation mode used by Excel at workbook level. The three modes available are:

1. *Automatic:* Whenever you change the value in a cell, all values that reference that cell are automatically recalculated. This is the default.

2. *Automatic except for data tables:* This is similar to Automatic, but tables will only be recalculated when one of the values within a table is changed.

3. *Manual:* Calculation will only take place when the **<F9>** key is pressed.

Most users are unaware that the calculation options exist and leave Excel set to the default *Automatic* at all times.

So why would you ever need the other two options? The answer is that Excel worksheets can be very big indeed (over a million rows and over 16,500 columns). A worksheet could contain many millions (or even many billions) of formulas. Such a worksheet is very unusual, but could take a substantial amount of time to recalculate. You wouldn't want to have to pause for recalculation every time you edited such a worksheet, so you would switch to one of the other two calculation modes under those circumstances.

1 Open *Classic Watches-1* from your sample files folder.

This worksheet calculates the selling prices for a classic watch dealer.

	A	B	C	D	E
5			Gross Profit	33%	
7	Description	Date	Cost price	Selling Price	Profit
8	Breitling Duograph 18K	1948	11,500.00	17,164.18	5,664.18
9	Cartier Tank 18K	1974	3,200.00	4,776.12	1,576.12
10	Rolex Tudor Oyster	1966	300.00	447.76	147.76

The dealer makes 33% Gross Profit (sometimes also called *Margin, Gross Margin* or *Gross Profit Margin*) on all watch sales (see sidebar for a discussion of the difference between gross profit and mark up).

The formula in column D:

=C8/(1-$D$5)

... calculates the selling price based upon the gross profit stated in cell D5.

2 Change the gross profit to 25%.

When the value in cell D5 is changed to 25%, the worksheet recalculates to show the new selling prices.

	A	B	C	D	E
5			Gross Profit	25%	
7	Description	Date	Cost price	Selling Price	Profit
8	Breitling Duograph 18K	1948	11,500.00	15,333.33	3,833.33
9	Cartier Tank 18K	1974	3,200.00	4,266.67	1,066.67
10	Rolex Tudor Oyster	1966	300.00	400.00	100.00

This is exactly what you would expect because this workbook has the default *automatic* calculation mode.

3 **Change the calculation mode to manual.**

Click: Formulas→Calculation→
Calculation Options→Manual.

4 **Change the gross profit to 30%.**

This time nothing happens because the worksheet will only recalculate when you explicitly request a recalculation.

	A	B	C	D	E
5			Gross Profit	30%	
7	Description	Date	Cost price	Selling Price	Profit
8	Breitling Duograph 18K	1948	11,500.00	15,333.33	3,833.33
9	Cartier Tank 18K	1974	3,200.00	4,266.67	1,066.67
10	Rolex Tudor Oyster	1966	300.00	400.00	100.00

5 **Manually recalculate the workbook.**

EITHER

Press the **<F9>** key.

OR

Click: Formulas→Calculation→Calculate Now.

The workbook recalculates to show the new selling prices at 30% gross profit.

	A	B	C	D	E
5			Gross Profit	30%	
7	Description	Date	Cost price	Selling Price	Profit
8	Breitling Duograph 18K	1948	11,500.00	16,428.57	4,928.57
9	Cartier Tank 18K	1974	3,200.00	4,571.43	1,371.43
10	Rolex Tudor Oyster	1966	300.00	428.57	128.57

Note that you can also click:

Formulas→Calculation→Calculate Sheet

You would use this option to save calculation time when other worksheets in the workbook contained large numbers of formulas. In the case of this simple worksheet, the calculation appears instantaneous.

6 **Change the calculation mode back to automatic.**

Click: Formulas→Calculation→
Calculation Options→Automatic.

7 **Save your work as *Classic Watches-2*.**

important

Calculation mode is set at application level

It would be quite reasonable to assume that the calculation mode could be set for a specific worksheet or workbook. Unfortunately, Excel doesn't work in this way, causing great confusion amongst users who begin to believe that Excel is randomly changing the calculation mode!

You can't set the calculation mode for a single worksheet or workbook. When you change the calculation mode, it also changes for all other worksheets and all other open workbooks!

Consider the following scenario:

1/ You create a workbook and set the calculation mode to *Manual*.

2/ You then open another workbook without closing the first one. The second workbook is also in manual calculation mode because only one calculation mode can exist for all open workbooks.

Things become even more confusing because the calculation mode is saved with the workbook.

Suppose that you had two workbooks called *Manual* and *Automatic*. The first was saved in manual calculation mode and the second saved in automatic calculation mode.

If you open the *Manual* workbook followed by the *Automatic* workbook, then both workbooks will be set to *Manual* calculation mode, as this was the mode of the first workbook opened.

If you open the *Automatic* workbook followed by the *Manual* workbook then both workbooks will be set to *Automatic* calculation mode.

Lesson 3-18: Concatenate strings using the concatenation operator (&)

About strings

In the world of computers; letters, numbers, spaces, punctuation marks and other symbols are referred to as *characters*.

When several characters are grouped together (perhaps to spell out words), they are referred to as a *string*.

Here are some examples of strings:

Abc123

John Smith

Strings may be of any length, from a single character to thousands of words.

The concatenation operator (&)

When numbers are added together, the addition operator (+) is used to return the sum of the numbers. For example:

4+2=6

The concatenation operator joins two strings together. For example:

4 & 2 = 42

Concatenation is rarely used with numbers. It is more likely that you may wish to concatenate *Salutation*, *First Name* and *Last Name* cells to produce full name. For example:

= "Mr" & "John" & "Smith" = "MrJohnSmith".

Note the use of double quotation marks to indicate that each value is a string.

In this example, it would be nice to have spaces between each of the words. To do this, we would concatenate a string containing only a space between each word. Here's how it's done:

= "Mr" & " " & "John" & " " & "Smith" = "Mr John Smith"

1   Open *Classic Watches-2* from your sample files folder (if it isn't already open).

Classic Watches-2

2   Type **Classified Ad** into cell F7 and apply the *Heading 3* style.

To apply the *Heading 3* style, select cell F7 and then click:

Home→Styles→Style Gallery→Titles and Headings→Heading 3

Cell styles were covered in depth in Session 4 of the *Essential Skills* book in this series.

Cells F8:F17 will contain text to be included in a classified ad listing in the local newspaper. We want to show the description of the watch, the year of manufacture and the selling price.

	A	B	C	D	E	F
7	Description	Date	Cost price	Selling Price	Profit	Classified Ad
8	Breitling Duograph 18K	1948	11,500.00	16,428.57	4,928.57	

3   Round the values in cells D8:D17 to the nearest five dollars.

The Breitling Duograph is priced at $16,428.57. It would be cleaner to round all of the prices up (or down) to the nearest five dollars. This can easily be achieved using the MROUND (multiple round) function.

1. Change the formula in cell D8 from:

=C8/(1-$D$5)

TO

=MROUND(C8/(1-$D$5),5)

2. AutoFill the function to the end of the range.

4   Use the concatenation operator to place the classified ad into cell F8 in the format:
Breitling Duograph 18K (1948) - $16,430.

As described in the introduction to this lesson, this can easily be achieved using the concatenation operator. The correct formula is:

    f_x =A8 & " (" & B8 & ") - $" & D8

This very nearly provides the required result:

	F	G	H	I
7	Classified Ad			
8	Breitling Duograph 18K (1948) - $16430			

The only thing we have a problem with is the comma in the cash price of the watch ($16430 should be $16,430). In the next lesson, we'll discover how to solve this problem using the TEXT function.

5   AutoFill the formula in cell F8 to cells F9:F17.

	F	G	H	I
7	Classified Ad			
8	Breitling Duograph 18K (1948) - $16430			
9	Cartier Tank 18K (1974) - $4570			
10	Rolex Tudor Oyster (1966) - $430			

6   Save your work as Classic Watches-3.

Lesson 3-19: Use the TEXT function to format numerical values as strings

Custom format strings recap

The TEXT function allows numbers to be explicitly formatted as strings. The *Essential Skills* book in this series extensively covers the (rather cryptic) formatting codes available in Excel.

Zeroes are used in formatting codes to define the number of decimal places that are required, along with leading and trailing zeroes. Here are some examples (reproduced from the *Essential Skills* book).

Custom Format String	Value	Display
0	1234.56	1235
0.0	1234.56 1234.5	1234.6 1234.5
0.00	1234.56 1234.5	1234.56 1234.50
00.000	4.56	04.560
0.000	1234.56	1234.560

The hash symbol (#) is mainly used to add comma separators to thousands and millions. Here are some examples (once again, reproduced from the *Essential Skills* book).

Custom Format String	Value	Display
#	123.4500	123
#.##	123.45 123.50	123.45 123.5
#,#	1234.56	1,234
#,#.##	1234.56 1234.50 12341234.56	1,234.56 1,234.5 12,341,234.56

Because the hash symbol can be used in conjunction with zeroes, it is also possible to indicate that you want both thousand separators *and* a specific number of leading or trailing zeroes.

Custom Format String	Value	Display
#,#0.00	12341234.5	12,341,234.50

1   Open *Classic Watches-3* from your sample files folder (if it isn't already open).

2   Delete the contents of cells F8:F17.

3   Use the CONCATENATE function to place the classified ad into cell F8 in the format:
Breitling Duograph 18K (1948) - $16,430.

The concatenation operation (&) used in the last lesson provides a quick and easy way to concatenate text:

> f_x =A8 & " (" & B8 & ") - $" & D8

It would be possible to use the TEXT function in conjunction with the concatenation operator (&) to construct the formula but this approach would result in the formula:

> f_x =A8 & " (" & B8 & ") " & TEXT(D8, "$#,#0")

... which is difficult to read and prone to error. Instead, we'll use the CONCATENATE function.

1.   Click in cell F8.

2.   Click: Formulas→Function Library→Text→Concatenate.

3.   Populate the dialog as follows:

Text1	A8		=	"Breitling Duograph 18K"
Text2	" ("		=	" ("
Text3	B8		=	"1948"
Text4	") "		=	") "
Text5	TEXT(D8,"$#,#0")		=	"$16,430"

Note that each string is enclosed in double quotation marks to denote text.

Note also the use of the TEXT function with a reference to cell D8 followed by the custom format string:

"$#,#0"

This format string means "show a leading dollar sign, show a comma after thousands and show only whole numbers (no decimal places)".

4.   Click the OK button.

The text is displayed as specified:

	F	G	H	I
7	Classified Ad			
8	Breitling Duograph 18K (1948) $16,430			

4   Autofill cell F8 to the end of the range (cells F9:F17).

	F	G	H	I
7	Classified Ad			
8	Breitling Duograph 18K (1948) $16,430			
9	Cartier Tank 18K (1974) $4,570			

5   Save your work as *Classic Watches-4.*

---

note

Why can I only see Text1 and Text2?

The CONCATENATE function accepts up to 255 arguments.

When the dialog is first shown you will only see two arguments (Text1 and Text2):

Text1	
Text2	

When you add an argument to the Text2 box, a Text3 box magically appears:

Text1	A8
Text2	" ("
Text3	

The dialog then continues to expand as you add each argument until the maximum of 255 is reached.

Lesson 3-20: Extract text from fixed width strings using the LEFT, RIGHT and MID functions

In *Lesson 2-1: Split fixed width data using Text to Columns*, you learned how to extract fixed width data using Excel's *Text to Columns* feature. While this works well, you'll often need to extract data dynamically using a formula. In this lesson, we'll use the LEFT, RIGHT and MID functions to do just that.

1   Open *Best Selling Books-1* from your sample files folder.

This worksheet lists some of the bestselling fiction books of all time:

	A	B	C	D	E
3	Title	Author	Year	Copies (millions)	ISBN-13
4	A Tale of Two Cities	Charles Dickens	1859	200	978-0141439600
5	The Lord of the Rings	J.R.R. Tolkein	1954	150	978-0618640157
6	And Then There Were None	Agatha Christie	1939	100	978-0312330873

For this lesson, the interesting data is in column E; the *International Standard Book Number* (ISBN-13).

ISBN numbers are a good example of fixed width strings. At first they simply seem to be a jumble of numbers but they actually contain four discrete pieces of data:

	A	B	C	D	E
17	Anatomy of an ISBN Number				
18	Digits 1-3	EAN (European Article Number)			
19	Digit 4	Group Identifier (country or language code)			
20	Digits 5-12	publisher prefix and title identifier			
21	Digit 13	Check digit (proves accuracy)			

2   Use a LEFT function to extract the EAN from the ISBN code.

We know that the leftmost three digits represent the EAN. The LEFT function extracts a given number of digits from the left part of a string.

1.   Click in cell F4.

2.   Click: Formulas→Function Library→Text→Left.

3.   Complete the dialog as follows:

Text	E4	=	"978-0141439600"
Num_chars	3	=	3

4.   Click the OK button.

The EAN is extracted into cell F4.

3 Use a RIGHT function to extract the Check Digit from the ISBN code.

We know that the rightmost single digit represents the Check Digit. The RIGHT function extracts a given number of digits from the right part of a string.

1. Click in cell I4.

2. Click: Formulas→Function Library→Text→Right.

3. Complete the dialog as follows:

Text	E4		= "978-0141439600"
Num_chars	1|		= 1

4. Click the OK button.

The Check Digit is extracted into cell I4.

4 Use a MID function to extract the Group from the ISBN code.

The MID function extracts text from within a string. We know that digit 4 is the *Group Identifier* and will tell us the language that the book is written in. Because the ISBN has a dash between the third and fourth digits, we'll have to extract a single character from position five in the string.

1. Click in cell G4.

2. Click: Formulas→Function Library→Text→Mid.

3. Complete the dialog as follows:

Text	E4		= "978-0141439600"
Start_num	5		= 5
Num_chars	1		= 1

4. Click the OK button.

The Group is extracted into cell G4:

5 Use a MID function to extract the *Publisher and Title* code from the ISBN code.

This time, the correct arguments for the dialog will be:

Text	E4		= "978-0141439600"
Start_num	6		= 6
Num_chars	8		= 8

6 Autofill the formulas in cells F4:I4 to cells F15:I15.

You can now see from the Group (country or language code) that *Le Petit Prince* was published in French and *Heidis Lehr- und Wanderj* was published in German.

7 Save your work as *Best Selling Books-2.*

Lesson 3-21: Extract text from delimited strings using the FIND and LEN functions

Here are two examples of international telephone numbers.

+44 (0)113-4960227 (a UK telephone number)
+356 (0)2138-3393 (a Maltese telephone number)

The *country code* (or international dialling code) is shown as a + symbol followed by one or more numbers. The *NDD* (National Direct Dialling prefix) is shown in brackets. This is the access code used to make a call within the relevant country but is omitted when calling from outside the country. The *Area Code* consists of the numbers after the closing bracket but before the hyphen.

In this lesson, we'll use the FIND and LEN functions in combination with the MID function to extract the country code, NDD and phone number from an international telephone number.

1   Open *Phone Book-1* from your sample files folder.

2   Insert a FIND function into cell C4 to find the first occurrence of an opening bracket within the telephone number.

1.   Click in cell C4.

2.   Click Formulas→Text→Find.

The FIND function demands three arguments. The first is the character to find (in this case the opening bracket), the second is the text to search within (in this case the telephone number in cell B4). There's also an optional argument that allows you to begin the search at a specified position within the string.

3.   Complete the dialog as follows:

Find_text	"("		=	"("
Within_text	B4		=	"+44 (0)113-4960227"
Start_num			=	number

Note that you don't have to manually type the quotation marks around the text in the Find_text argument. Excel will helpfully add them for you automatically.

4.   Click the OK button.

The number 5 is shown in cell C4. This is because the opening bracket is positioned five characters from the left of the string **+44 (**. Note that the space before the opening bracket is counted as a character.

3   Insert a FIND function into cell D4 to find the first occurrence of a closing bracket within the telephone number.

Repeat *Step 2*, but use a closing bracket for the Find_text argument.

4   Insert a FIND function into cell E4 to find the first occurrence of a hyphen within the telephone number.

Phone Book-1

note

Avoid leading and trailing spaces with the TRIM function

In *Step 6* you extracted the country code using the LEFT function.

This could result in strings with a trailing space such as:

"+44 "
"+356 "

Because you can't see the trailing space this doesn't seem to matter.

Trailing spaces cause many problems when comparing data because strings that appear to be the same visually are, in fact, different:

="+44 " = "+44"
(returns FALSE)

="+44" = "+44"
(returns TRUE)

For this reason it is good practice to always remove leading and trailing spaces using the TRIM function.

You could have used the TRIM function in *Step 6* like this:

=TRIM(LEFT(B4,C4-1))

If this seems a little too complex, you could also have placed the trimmed country code in a different column and then used the untrimmed result as an argument like this:

=TRIM(G4)

Repeat *Step 2*, but use a hyphen ("-") for the Find_text argument.

5   Insert a LEN function into cell F4 to find the total number of characters in the telephone number.

1.   Click in cell F4.

2.   Click: Formulas→Text→Len.

3.   Click Cell B4 for the single argument for this function.

4.   Click the OK button.

The length of the telephone number string (18 characters) is displayed in cell F4.

6   Insert a LEFT function into cell G4 to extract the country code.

The correct arguments are:

Text	B4	= "+44 (0)113-4960227"
Num_chars	C4-1	= 4

Note that C4-1 is used for the number of characters to avoid returning the opening bracket. This could result in a trailing space (see sidebar for a way to remove trailing spaces).

7   Insert a MID function into cell H4 to extract the area code.

The MID function was covered in: *Lesson 3-20: Extract text from fixed width strings using the LEFT, RIGHT and MID functions.*

The correct arguments are:

Text	B4	= "+44 (0)113-4960227"
Start_num	D4+1	= 8
Num_chars	E4-D4-1	= 3

8   Insert a MID function into cell I4 to extract the phone number.

The correct arguments are:

Text	B4	= "+44 (0)113-4960227"
Start_num	E4+1	= 12
Num_chars	F4-E4	= 7

9   AutoFill cells C4:I4 into cells C5:I18.

	A	B	C	D	E	F	G	H	I
			Position of opening bracket (	Position of closing bracket)	Position of Hyphen	Length of entire string	Country Code	Area Code	Phone Number
3	Company	Telephone							
4	Books A Million	+44 (0)113-4960227	5	7	11	18	+44	113	4960227
5	Maltese Books	+356 (0)2138-3393	6	8	13	17	+356	2138	3393

10   Hide columns C:F.

Select columns C:F, right click the mouse and then click *Hide* on the shortcut menu.

11   Save your work as *Phone Book-2.*

Lesson 3-22: Use a VLOOKUP function for an exact lookup

Consider the following worksheet:

	A	B	C	D	E
5	Code	Description	Date	Cost price	Selling Price
6	BR48	Breitling Duograph 18K	1948	11,500.00	16,430.00
7	CA74	Cartier Tank 18K	1974	3,200.00	4,570.00
8	RO66	Rolex Tudor Oyster	1966	300.00	430.00

The retailer has created a stock code to save time when creating invoices. The code is made up of the first two letters of the watch description, along with the two last numbers of the date of manufacture.

When provided with a stock code, the VLOOKUP function can scan all of the codes in column A until a match is found and then return a value from the same row for any of the other columns.

In this lesson, we will create a VLOOKUP that will automatically return the *Description* of any watch, into column B when the user enters a stock code into column A.

1   Open *Invoice-1* from your sample files folder.

	A	B	C
5	Code	Description	Price
6	CA74		
7			
8			
9		Total:	-

2   Convert the range A5:G15 on the *Stock* worksheet into a table named *Stock*.

This was covered in: *Lesson 1-8: Convert a range into a table and add a total row* and *Lesson 1-14: Name a table and create an automatic structured table reference.*

When working with the VLOOKUP function in Excel 2010 it is best practice to use a table for the *Table_array* argument (see sidebar on facing page).

Using a table will make the data dynamic. In other words, the VLOOKUP will still work correctly if you add and remove rows from the Stock table.

3   AutoSize all columns so that each column is wide enough to display all data.

4   Insert a VLOOKUP function into cell B6 on the *Invoice* worksheet to find the description to match the *Code* in cell A6.

1.   Click in cell B6.

2.   Click: Formulas→Function Library→ Lookup & Reference→VLOOKUP.

Invoice-1

important

It is best practice to use tables with your VLOOKUP functions

In this lesson I've shown you how to construct a VLOOKUP that uses a table for the *Table_array* argument.

This is best practice in Excel 2007/2010, but it wasn't possible in Excel 2003 as the (fantastically useful) table feature wasn't available.

In worksheets constructed using pre 2007 versions of Excel it is common to see absolute range references for *Table_array* arguments like this:

Table_array	$A$5:$G$15

More sophisticated users of pre 2007 Excel versions learned how to use *Range Names*. (You'll learn all about Range Names in: *Session Four: Using Names and the Formula Auditing Tools*).

When you see a *Range Name* reference it looks the same as a table reference. This example shows the use of a *Range Name* also called *Stock*:

Table_array	Stock

While *Range Names* were best practice in pre 2007 Excel versions, they have a fatal flaw as they are not truly dynamic.

Users of earlier versions had to resort to a complex work-around to make their Range Names dynamic. You'll learn about this work-around in: *Lesson 4-6: Create dynamic formula-based range names using the OFFSET function*.

This information is provided so that you will understand any older Excel worksheets you may inherit, (or worksheets that were created by users that haven't yet learned how to use tables)!

The VLOOKUP Function Arguments dialog appears. It can be seen that the VLOOKUP function has three required arguments (shown in bold face) and one optional argument:

Lookup_value		📄	= any
Table_array		📄	= number
Col_index_num		📄	= number
Range_lookup		📄	= logical

5 Add the *Lookup_value* argument.

This is the cell on the *Invoice* worksheet that provides the value to be searched for in Column A of the *Stock* worksheet. We want to look up the description for the watch that has the code *CA74*. This is contained in cell A6.

Lookup_value	A6	📄	= "CA74"

6 Add the *Table_array* argument.

The table array is the *range, table or name* (see sidebar) we will search for a match to the value in cell A6. VLOOKUP always searches the left-most column of the *range, table or name*.

1. Type **Stock** into the *Table_array* text box.

Table_array	Stock	📄

It is best practice to use a table for the *Table_array* argument (see sidebar).

7 Add the *Col_index_num* argument.

	A	B	C	D	E
5	Code	Description	Date	Cost price	Selling Price
6	BR48	Breitling Duograph 18K	1948	11,500.00	16,430.00

Counting from left to right, the *Col_index_num* argument is the column that contains the value we want to return. In this case, it is the *Description* column, so we want to return column 2.

Col_index_num	2	📄	= 2

8 Add the *Range_lookup* argument.

Beginners often overlook this vital argument because it is optional.

If it is left blank, VLOOKUP will return an inexact match. Later, in *Lesson 3-24: Use a VLOOKUP function for an inexact lookup*, we'll find why that might be useful, but in this case we want an error to be returned if the stock code is not found, so it is vital to set this argument to FALSE.

Range_lookup	FALSE	📄

9 Click the OK button.

The description of the *Cartier Tank* is returned to cell B6.

	A	B
6	CA74	Cartier Tank 18K

10 Save your work as *Invoice-2*.

Lesson 3-23: Use an IFERROR function to suppress error messages

1   Open *Invoice-2* from your sample files folder (if it isn't already open).

2   Add a VLOOKUP to cell C6 to return the price that corresponds to the *Code* in cell A6.

You learned how to add a VLOOKUP in *Lesson 3-22: Use a VLOOKUP function for an exact lookup*. This time, the correct arguments are:

Lookup_value	A6
Table_array	Stock
Col_index_num	5
Range_lookup	FALSE

3   AutoFill cells B6:C6 to cells B7:C8.

	A	B	C
5	Code	Description	Price
6	CA74	Cartier Tank 18K	4,570.00
7		#N/A	#N/A
8		#N/A	#N/A
9		Total:	#N/A

This is nearly what is needed. The invoice will work just fine when all three lines are populated:

	A	B	C
5	Code	Description	Price
6	CA74	Cartier Tank 18K	4,570.00
7	RO66	Rolex Tudor Oyster	430.00
8	BR43	Breitling Chronomat 18K	3,070.00
9		Total:	8,070.00

But we need to cater for customers that only wish to purchase one watch. To make this work, we need to suppress the error messages when some invoice lines have no stock code.

Fortunately, the IFERROR function is designed precisely for this purpose.

4   Wrap each VLOOKUP function with an IFERROR function to return a blank space when an error is encountered.

The IFERROR function can return the value of your choice whenever a formula returns an error.

1.   Click in cell B6.

Look at the formula in the formula bar.

Invoice-2

This is the VLOOKUP that returns the description. We're going to use this formula as the *value* argument for the IFERROR function. When one function is used inside another function in this way, we sometimes refer to the outside function as a *wrapper.*

2. Click just to the right of the equals sign in the formula bar.

3. Type **IFERROR(**

> =IFERROR(VLOOKUP(A6,Stock
>
> IFERROR(**value**, value_if_error)

Notice the tip that has appeared. The entire VLOOKUP function is now being used as the *value* argument for the IFERROR function.

4. Click to the extreme right of the formula in the formula bar and add a comma:

fx =IFERROR(VLOOKUP(A6,Stock,2,FALSE),

You are now ready to add the second argument for the IFERROR function. This argument defines what will be displayed if the VLOOKUP function returns an error.

5. Add an empty string to the IFERROR function.

Type "". This is an empty string and tells Excel to keep the cell blank when an error is returned.

fx =IFERROR(VLOOKUP(A6,Stock,2,FALSE), ""

6. Close the bracket to complete the formula.

fx =IFERROR(VLOOKUP(A6,Stock,2,FALSE), "")

7. Press the **<Enter>** key.

8. Do the same thing for the *Price* formula in cell C6.

fx =IFERROR(VLOOKUP(A6,Stock,5,FALSE), "")

5   AutoFill the formulas in cells B6:C6 to cells B8:C8.

The invoice now works fine, even when some stock codes are left blank.

	A	B	C
5	Code	Description	Price
6	CA74	Cartier Tank 18K	4,570.00
7			
8	PA83	Patek Phillipe Jumbo Nautilus	20,355.00
9		Total:	24,925.00

6   Save your work as *Invoice-3.*

---

tip

AutoFill a range of cells in one operation

I've noticed in my classes that many students will respond to the instruction:

"AutoFill the formulas in cells B6:C6 to cells B8:C8"

... by performing two AutoFill operations:

1. Select cell B6.

2. AutoFill cell B6 down to row 8.

3. Select cell C6.

2. AutoFill cell C6 down to row 8.

A quicker way to do this is to AutoFill both cells at the same time:

1. Select cells B6:C6.

2. AutoFill both cells down to row 8.

Lesson 3-24: Use a VLOOKUP function for an inexact lookup

In: *Lesson 3-22: Use a VLOOKUP function for an exact lookup,* we set the fourth argument of the VLOOKUP to FALSE in order to achieve an *exact* lookup. Most of the time, that's exactly what you want to do.

Sometimes you don't want to search for an exact match but are interested in the nearest match. This is called an *inexact* lookup. Consider the following exam grades:

	E	F
3	Percentage	Grade
4	0%	Fail
5	60%	C
6	70%	B
7	80%	A
8	90%	A*

If we were to perform an *exact* lookup on a mark of 80%, it would correctly return a grade of A. A student with a mark of 77% would result in an error because there is no exact value of 77% in column E.

If we ask VLOOKUP to perform an *inexact* lookup, it will return an exact match if one is found. If an exact match is not found, it will return the largest value *that is less than* the lookup value.

For VLOOKUP to work with inexact matches, it is vital that the lookup column is sorted in ascending order (from the lowest to the highest value).

In the above example, a search for 68% would find row 5 (a C grade) because 60% is the largest value that is less than 68%.

1   Open *Grades-1* from your sample files folder.

	A	B	C	D	E	F
1	**Exam Results**					
2						
3	Name	Percentage	Grade		Percentage	Grade
4	Johnny Caine	70%			0%	Fail
5	George Marley	68%			60%	C
6	Betty Anan	86%			70%	B
7	Paris Winfrey	80%			80%	A
8	Ozzy Dickens	95%			90%	A*
9	Johnny Roberts	84%				

2   Convert cells E3:F8 to a table named *Grade*.

This was covered in: *Lesson 1-8: Convert a range into a table and add a total row* and *Lesson 1-14: Name a table and create an automatic structured table reference.*

Grades-1

When working with the VLOOKUP function in Excel 2010 it is best practice to use a table for the *Table_array* argument.

This will make the data dynamic. In other words, the VLOOKUP will still work correctly if you add and remove grades from the *Grade* table.

3   Add an inexact VLOOKUP to cell C4 to return the grade that corresponds to the percentage mark in cell B4.

You learned how to add an exact VLOOKUP in *Lesson 3-22: Use a VLOOKUP function for an exact lookup*. An inexact lookup is done in exactly the same way, except that the *Range_lookup* argument is set to TRUE (or omitted, as the default is TRUE).

This time, the correct arguments are therefore:

Lookup_value	B4	
Table_array	Grade	
Col_index_num	2	
Range_lookup	TRUE	

4   AutoFill cell C4 to cells C5:C17.

The correct grades are now shown for each student.

	A	B	C
3	Name	Percentage	Grade
4	Johnny Caine	70%	B
5	George Marley	68%	C
6	Betty Anan	86%	A
7	Paris Winfrey	80%	A
8	Ozzy Dickens	95%	A*
9	Johnny Roberts	84%	A
10	Charles Monroe	55%	Fail
11	Ronnie Bush	58%	Fail
12	Michal Jolie	69%	C
13	JK Spears	77%	B
14	Ozzy Rowling	84%	A
15	Oprah Hilton	60%	C
16	Bill Biggs	58%	Fail
17	Angelina Osbourne	30%	Fail

5   Save your work as *Grades-2*.

Session 3: Exercise

1   Open *Employee Summary-1* from your sample files folder.

	A	B	C	D	E	F	G
					Date	Year	
3	Full Name	Last Name	First Name	Department	Started	Started	Bonus
4	Johnny Caine				16-Jan-98		
5	George Marley				18-Feb-02		

2   Using the RIGHT, LEFT, LEN and FIND functions, split the *Full Name* in column A into *Last Name* and *First Name* in columns B and C.

	A	B	C
3	Full Name	Last Name	First Name
4	Johnny Caine	Caine	Johnny

3   Use an exact VLOOKUP to return the *Department* for each employee (departments are listed on the *Departments* worksheet).

	A	B	C	D
3	Full Name	Last Name	First Name	Department
4	Johnny Caine	Caine	Johnny	Sales

4   Use a COUNTIF function to return the headcount for each department in cells B20:B22.

	A	B
19	Department	Headcount
20	Sales	6
21	Purchasing	5
22	Logistics	3

5   Use the YEAR function to populate column F with the year each employee started.

	A	B	C	D	E	F
					Date	Year
3	Full Name	Last Name	First Name	Department	Started	Started
4	Johnny Caine	Caine	Johnny	Sales	16-Jan-98	1998
5	George Marley	Marley	George	Purchasing	18-Feb-02	2002

6   Each employee in the *Sales* department receives a 10% bonus while all other employees receive a 5% bonus. Use an IF function to populate column G with the correct bonus percentage.

	A	B	C	D	E	F	G
					Date	Year	
3	Full Name	Last Name	First Name	Department	Started	Started	Bonus
4	Johnny Caine	Caine	Johnny	Sales	16-Jan-98	1998	10%
5	George Marley	Marley	George	Purchasing	18-Feb-02	2002	5%

7   Save your work as *Employee Summary-2*.

Employee Summary-1

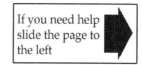

If you need help slide the page to the left

Session 3: Exercise Answers

These are the four questions that students find the most difficult to answer:

Q 6	Q 4	Q 3	Q 2
1. Click in cell G4. 2. Click: Formulas→ Function Library→ Logical→ IF. 3. Add the following arguments: **Logical_test** `D4="Sales"` **Value_if_true** `10%` **Value_if_false** `5%` 4. Click the OK button. 5. AutoFill the formula in cell G4 to cells G5:G17. *This was covered in: Lesson 3-5: Use the IF logic function.*	1. Click in cell B20. 2. Click: Formulas→ Function Library→ MoreFunctions→ Statistical→ COUNTIF. 3. Add the following arguments: **Range** `$D$4:$D$17` **Criteria** `A20` 4. Click the OK button. 5. AutoFill the formula in cell B20 to cells B21:B22. *This was covered in: Lesson 3-6: Use the SUMIF and COUNTIF logic functions to create conditional totals.*	1. Select the *Departments* worksheet. 2. Convert the range A3:B17 into a table named: *Department*. 3. Select the *Employees* worksheet. 4. Click in cell D4. 5. Click: Formulas→ Function Library→ Formulas & Reference→ VLOOKUP. 6. Add the following arguments: *Lookup_value:* **A4** *Table_array:* **Deparment** *Col_index_num:* **2** *Range_lookup:* **FALSE** 7. Click the OK button. 8. AutoFill the formula in cell D4 to cells D5:D17. *This was covered in: Lesson 3-22: Use a VLOOKUP function for an exact lookup.*	The easiest way to do this is to use the LEFT and RIGHT functions to return a given number of characters from the left and right hand side of the *Full Name* string. The formula for the *First Name* (in cell C4) is quite easy. We simply use the FIND function to find the first space and return that number of characters from the left hand side of the string: **=LEFT(A4, FIND(" ",A4)-1)** The *Last Name* is a little more involved. We also need to use the LEN function to return the total number of characters in the string: **=RIGHT(A4,LEN(A4)-FIND(" ",A4))** *This was covered in: Lesson 3-21: Extract text from delimited strings using the FIND and LEN functions.*

If you have difficulty with the other questions, here are the lessons that cover the relevant skills:

5   Refer to: *Lesson 3-8: Understand common date functions.*

4

Session Four: Using Names and the Formula Auditing Tools

> To make no mistakes is not in the power of man; but from their errors and mistakes, the wise and good learn wisdom for the future.
>
> *Plutarch (46 AD - 120 AD)*

This session introduces Excel's ability to apply a name to a range of cells, a single cell, a formula, a constant or a table. Some problems are almost impossible to solve without names. In this lesson, you'll use name-based techniques to address several common business scenarios.

This session also introduces Excel's superb auditing tools. These will allow you to check your work for mistakes or track down errors when you know that something is wrong. As Plutarch asserts, you *will* make errors when working with Excel (assuming that you are human of course).

By the end of this session, you'll be able to use all of the auditing tools to track down and repair workbook errors.

Session Objectives

By the end of this session you will be able to:

- Automatically create single-cell range names
- Manually create single cell range names and named constants
- Use range names to make formulas more readable
- Automatically create range names in two dimensions
- Use intersection range names and the INDIRECT function
- Create dynamic formula-based range names using the OFFSET function
- Create table based dynamic range names
- Create two linked drop-down lists using range names
- Understand the #NUM!, #DIV/0! and #NAME? Error Values
- Understand the #VALUE!, #REF! and #NULL! Error Values
- Understand background error checking and error checking rules
- Manually check a worksheet for errors
- Audit a formula by tracing precedents
- Audit a formula by tracing dependents
- Use the watch window to monitor cell values
- Use Speak Cells to eliminate data entry errors

Lesson 4-1: Automatically create single-cell range names

The sample worksheet for this lesson contains prices that need to be expressed in different currencies. When you have this type of data, a separate exchange rate worksheet makes the exchange rates easy to maintain.

Here's how the exchange rates will be defined:

	A	B
3	USD/GBP	1.6155
4	USD/EUR	1.3958
5	USD/JPY	0.01053

A range name will then be automatically created for each of the values in column B. Excel will choose range names for column B based upon the values in column A. For the exchange rate in cell B3, it will automatically create the range name:

USD_GBP

You can then use the range name to make your formulas more readable.

	A	B	C	D
3	Description	Year	US Dollars	British Pounds
4	Chateau Lafite	1787	$160,000.00	=C4/USD_GBP

note

About range names

A Name can be applied to a range of cells, a single cell, a formula, a constant or a table.

When a name has been applied, it can be referred to within a formula in place of the item that it represents. For example, if the range A5:A45 was given the name *Sales*, the formulas:

=SUM(A5:A45)

And

=SUM(Sales)

Would produce exactly the same result.

tip

You can also bring up the *Create Names from Selection* dialog using the keyboard shortcut:

<Ctrl>+<Shift>+<F3>

Vintage Wines-1

1   Open *Vintage Wines-1* from your sample files folder.

2   Automatically create a range name for each of the exchange rates.

1.   Click the *ExchangeRates* worksheet tab.

2.   Select the range A3:B5.

	A	B
3	USD/GBP	1.6155
4	USD/EUR	1.3958
5	USD/JPY	0.01053

3.   Click: Formulas→Defined Names→Create from Selection.

The *Create Names from Selection* dialog appears:

Create Names from Selection

Create names from values in the:

- [ ] Top row
- [x] Left column
- [ ] Bottom row
- [ ] Right column

OK   Cancel

Notice that Excel has correctly guessed that the labels for each exchange rate are in the left column.

4. Click the OK button.

   Nothing seems to have happened but Excel has actually created a range name for each of the values in cells B3:B5.

3 Click the drop-down arrow on the right of the *Name* box to view the range names.

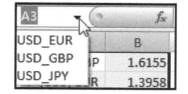

Notice that Excel hasn't used the names shown in column A, but has changed each forward slash to an underscore. This is because a forward slash isn't valid syntax for a range name (see sidebar for more on range name syntax).

4 Use a formula containing a range name to calculate prices in Great Britain Pounds, Euros and Japanese Yen.

1. Click the *Prices* worksheet tab.

2. Click in cell D4.

3. Type =**C4/** to begin the formula.

4. Click: Formulas→Defined Names→Use In Formula.

   A drop-down list appears containing all defined range names.

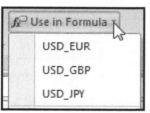

5. Click USD_GBP to insert the range name.

	C	D	
3	US Dollars	British Pounds	
4	$160,000.00	=C4/USD_GBP	

6. Press the **<Enter>** Key.

7. Use the same technique to enter a formula to calculate the Euro and Japanese Yen prices in cells E4 and F4.

5 AutoFill the formulas in cells D4:F4 to cells D11:F11.

	C	D	E	F
3	US Dollars	British Pounds	Euros	Japanese Yen
4	$160,000.00	£ 99,040.54	€ 114,629.60	¥15,194,681.86
5	$ 43,500.00	£ 26,926.65	€ 31,164.92	¥4,131,054.13

6 Save your work as *Vintage Wines-2*.

note

Range Name scope

Scope means the places in your workbook where the *unqualified* range name may be used. There are two possible scopes:

Workbook Scope – The name may be used within any of the worksheets in the workbook.

Worksheet Scope – The name may only be used within a specified worksheet.

Qualified and Unqualified range name references

An unqualified reference means that the range name is used on its own. For example:

=C4*KilometerToMile

Qualified references state the worksheet name, then an exclamation mark, and then the *range name*. For example:

ConversionFactors! KilometerToMile

If the *KilometerToMile* name had been created in this way with the worksheet scope: *ConversionFactors* a formula such as:

=C4*KilometerToMile

... would only work in the *ConversionFactors* worksheet.

To use it in another worksheet, you would need to use the *qualified* name within the formula like this:

=C4*ConversionFactors! KilometerToMile

Scope mayhem

Excel confusingly allows a *workbook scope* and a *worksheet scope* range name to share the same name. If this is done, the *worksheet scope* name takes precedence within the specified worksheet and the *workbook scope* name has precedence everywhere else!

Distances-1

Lesson 4-2: Manually create single cell range names and named constants

1   Open *Distances-1* from your sample files folder.

2   Manually create a range name for the *Kilometer to Mile* conversion factor using the *Name* box.

   1.   Click the *ConversionFactors* worksheet.

	A	B	C
3	From	To	Multiply By
4	Kilometer	Mile	0.621371192
5	Meter	Foot	3.28083

   This time we are unable to automatically create range names because the values in column B are not descriptive enough to easily identify each conversion factor.

   2.   Click cell C4.

   3.   Type **KilometerToMile** into the Name box.

KilometerToMile			f_x	0.621371192	
	A	B	C	D	E
3	From	To	Multiply By		
4	Kilometer	Mile	0.621371192		

   4.   Press the **<Enter>** key.

3   Manually create a range name for the Meter to Foot conversion factor using the *Define Name* dialog.

   This is an alternative method of defining range names.

   1.   Click cell C5.

   2.   Click: Formulas→Defined Names→Define Name.

   The *New Name* dialog appears.

   3.   Type the name **MeterToFoot** into the *Name* box:

   Leave the scope as *Workbook* (see sidebar for an explanation of scope).

   4.   Click the OK button.

4   Use formulas containing range names to calculate distances in miles on the *Distances* worksheet.

	A	B	C	D
3	From	To	Km	Miles
4	London	Paris	343	

   1.   Click cell D4 in the *Distances* worksheet.

   2.   Type **= C4***

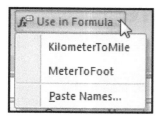

tip

You can also use the **<F3>** shortcut key to display a list of all currently defined names.

This is very useful when creating formulas that incorporate names.

note

When to use constants rather than range names.

You should use single-cell range names when a value may possibly change in the future. This was the case in: *Lesson 4-1: Automatically create single-cell range names* because we were dealing with currency exchange rates that fluctuate.

Constants are more appropriate when a value is never expected to change. For this reason, constants would be more appropriate for the conversion factors used in this lesson.

We now want to insert the conversion factor to convert Kilometers to Miles.

3. Click: Formulas→Defined Names→Use In Formula.

    A drop-down list appears showing all currently defined range names:

4. Click *KilometerToMile*.

5. Press the **<Enter>** key.

5   AutoFill cell D4 to cells D5:D11.

	A	B	C	D
3	From	To	Km	Miles
4	London	Paris	343	213
5	New York	Sydney	15,989	9,935

6   Given that one Kilometer = 0.539956803 Nautical Miles, create a named constant that will convert Kilometers into Nautical Miles.

Constants are used for values that will rarely change. Named constants are useful because they are difficult to change and are thus less likely to be changed accidentally.

When you create a named constant, there is no cell on the worksheet that contains the constant value.

1. Click: Formulas→Defined Names→Define Name.

2. Type **KilometerToNauticalMile** into the *Name* box:

    Name: | KilometerToNauticalMile

3. Type: **=0.539956803** into the *Refers to* box.

    Refers to: | =0.539956803

4. Click the OK button.

7   Use the *KilometerToNauticalMile* named constant to add a formula to cell E4 that will calculate the distance from London to Paris in nautical miles.

1. Click in cell E4.

2. Type **=C4*** to start the formula.

3. Click: Formulas→Defined Names→Use in Formula to see the list of defined names.

4. Click *KilometerToNauticalMile* in the drop down list.

    f_x =C4*KilometerToNauticalMile

5. Press the **<Enter>** Key.

8   AutoFill cell E4 to cells E5:E11.

9   Save your work as *Distances-2.*

Lesson 4-3: Use range names to make formulas more readable

1 Open *Sales and Profit-1* from your sample files folder.

	A	B
3	Sales	10,000.00
4	Cost	8,000.00
5	Gross Profit	2,000.00
6	Commission	100.00
7	Tax	200.00
8	Net Profit	1,700.00

2 Show formulas instead of values within the worksheet.

Click: Formulas→Formula Auditing→Show Formulas.

	A	B
3	Sales	10000
4	Cost	8000
5	Gross Profit	=B3-B4
6	Commission	=B5*5%
7	Tax	=B5*10%
8	Net Profit	=B5-B6-B7

It is reasonably clear from the formulas that:

Gross Profit = Sales - Cost

... and that five percent commission and ten percent tax are being deducted.

We can make the formulas a lot easier to read using range names.

3 Create automatic range names for all of the values in cells B3:B8.

This was covered in depth in : *Lesson 4-1: Automatically create single-cell range name.*

1. Select cells A3:B8.

2. Click: Formulas→Defined Names→Create from Selection.

3. Click OK.

4 View the range names created by Excel.

The easiest way to view the range names is to click the drop-down arrow to the right of the *Name* box:

Sales and Profit-1

5 **Apply the new range names to the existing formulas.**

1. Click: Formulas→Defined Names→Define Name→Apply Names…

   The *Apply Names* dialog appears:

2. Click the OK button.

   The formulas now show range names instead of cell references making them a lot easier to read:

	A	B
3	Sales	10000
4	Cost	8000
5	Gross Profit	=Sales-Cost
6	Commission	=Gross_Profit*5%
7	Tax	=Gross_Profit*10%
8	Net Profit	=Gross_Profit-Commission-Tax

6 **Correct a possible Excel 2010 bug.**

In Excel 2007 the range names would display as shown in the screen grab above. Due to a bug introduced in Excel 2010 (which may have been repaired by the time you read this book) you may see the incorrect formula:

	A	B
8	Net Profit	=Gross_Profit Commission

If this is the case manually change it to:

	A	B
8	Net Profit	=Gross_Profit-Commission-Tax

7 **Show values instead of formulas within the worksheet.**

Click: Formulas→Formula Auditing→Show Formulas.

Values are now displayed rather than formulas:

	A	B
3	Sales	10,000.00
4	Cost	8,000.00
5	Gross Profit	2,000.00
6	Commission	100.00
7	Tax	200.00
8	Net Profit	1,700.00

8 **Save your work as *Sales and Profit-2*.**

Lesson 4-4: Automatically create range names in two dimensions

1   Open *Earnings Summary-2* from your sample files folder.

	A	B	C	D	E	F	G	H	I
8	Name	Sales	Target	Hourly Rate	Hours Worked	Standard Pay	Overtime Pay	Bonus	Total
9	Brad Cruise	22,000	10,000	15.00	40	525.00	112.50	600.00	1,237.50
10	Ian Dean	9,000	8,000	13.00	35	455.00	-	50.00	505.00
11	Paris Smith	10,000	12,000	15.00	42	525.00	157.50	-	682.50
12	Gordon Ramsay	12,000	14,000	17.00	45	595.00	255.00	-	850.00
13	Barack Brown	15,000	9,000	13.00	35	455.00	-	300.00	755.00
14	Johnny Nicholson	18,000	14,000	17.00	40	595.00	127.50	200.00	922.50
15	Tony Blair	9,000	10,000	15.00	42	525.00	157.50	-	682.50
16	Jack Nicholson	10,000	9,000	13.00	30	390.00	-	50.00	440.00
17	Bob Clinton	9,000	11,000	15.00	35	525.00	-	-	525.00
18	Totals:	114,000	97,000		344	4,590.00	810.00	1,200.00	6,600.00

This worksheet was previously created in Session 3.

2   Create automatic range names based upon the labels in column A and row 8.

1. Select the range A8:I17.

2. Click: Formulas→Defined Names→Create from Selection.

   Excel correctly guesses that the labels are in the *Top row* and *Left column*.

3. Click the OK button.

3   View the range names created using the *Name Manager*.

1. Click: Formulas→Defined Names→Name Manager.

   The *Name Manager* appears.

The *Name Manager* is fantastically useful when working with names. It lists all currently defined names and allows you to edit them. Note the *Filter* drop-down that allows you to show a subset of names. This is useful when working with workbooks that contain large numbers of names.

You can see that we have created a range name for each employee (named in column A) and for each of the columns (named in row 8).

tip

You can also bring up the Name Manager using the keyboard shortcut:

<Ctrl>+<F3>

Earnings Summary-2

2. Click the *Close* button.

4 Type **Average Sales** into cell A20.

5 Type **Average Bonus** into cell A21.

6 Add a formula to cell B20 that uses a range name to calculate the average sales.

This time, we'll use Excel's *formula AutoComplete* feature to insert the range name into an AVERAGE formula.

1. Click in cell B20 and type:

=AVERAGE(S

Notice that *Formula AutoComplete* shows all defined names beginning with S at the top of a drop-down list:

Average Sales	=AVERAGE(S	
Average Bonus	AVERAGE(**number1**, [number2], ...)	
	▤ Sales	▲
	(*fx*) SEARCH	
	(*fx*) SECOND	

2. Press the **<Tab>** key to insert the *Sales* range name.

	A	B	C
21	Average Sales	=AVERAGE(Sales	

3. Press the **<Enter>** key (the closing bracket is automatically entered).

7 Add a formula to cell B21 that uses a range name to calculate the average bonus.

The correct formula is:

	A	B	C
20	Average Sales	12,666.67	
21	Average Bonus	=AVERAGE(Bonus)	

8 Apply the *comma style* to cells B20:B21.

9 Widen column B slightly so that both values are visible.

10 Copy cells A20:B21 to cells A1:B2 on the *Sheet2* worksheet.

	A	B
1	Average Sales	12,666.67
2	Average Bonus	133.33

You can now appreciate one of the great advantages of range names. The formula on *Sheet2* is exactly the same as that on *Sheet1* and still works fine.

Without the use of range names, it wouldn't have been possible to copy and paste the formulas between worksheets. You would have had to re-write the formula as:

=AVERAGE(Sheet1!B9:B17)

11 Save your work as *Earnings Summary-3.*

Lesson 4-5: Use intersection range names and the INDIRECT function

1 Open *Distance Chart-1* from your sample files folder.

	A	B	C	D	E	F	G	H	I
3		York	Southampton	Sheffield	Portsmouth	Oxford	Nottingham	Norwich	Newcastle
4	Aberdeen_	307	538	347	552	473	379	480	228
5	Aberystwyth_	195	198	156	218	157	156	271	259
6	Birmingham_	129	128	76	141	63	49	161	204

The chart allows you to quickly find the distance between two UK locations. For example, it is clear that the distance from Birmingham to Oxford is 63 miles.

2 Create automatic range names based upon the labels in column A and row 3.

1. Select the range A3:X26.

2. Click: Formulas→Defined Names→Create from Selection.

   Excel correctly guesses that the labels are in the *Top row* and *Left column*.

3. Click the OK button.

3 View the range names created using the *Name Manager*.

1. Click: Formulas→Defined Names→Name Manager.

   The *Name Manager* dialog appears.

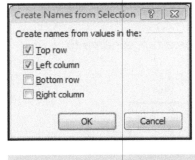

It is now clear why trailing underscores were used for the labels in column A. Without them, there would have been a naming conflict as each place name appears for both a row and a column.

2. Click the *Close* button.

4 Type **From** into cell A30.

5 Type **To** into cell A31.

6 Type **Miles** into cell A32.

7 Merge cells B30:E30, B31:E31 and B32:E32 (see facing page sidebar if you are unable to do this).

Distance Chart-1

Note

Merging cells

Merging cells is a basic skill covered in depth in Lesson 4-6 of the *Essential Skills* book in this series.

To merge the cells:

1. Select cells B30:E30.

2. Click:

Home→Alignment→
Merge & Center→
Merge Across

8   Add a list validation to cell B30 that will restrict the cell to the items appearing in cells A4:A26.

This was covered in: *Lesson 2-11: Add a table-based dynamic list validation.*

9   Add a list validation to cell B31 that will restrict the cell to the items appearing in cells B3:X3.

10   Click in cell B30 and choose *Birmingham_* from the drop down list.

11   Click in cell B31 and choose *Oxford* from the drop down list.

Your worksheet should now look like this:

	A	B	C	D	E	F
30	From	Birmingham_				
31	To	Oxford				
32	Miles					

12   Use the intersection operator to create a formula in cell B32 that will show the distance from Birmingham to Oxford.

1.   Click in cell B32.

2.   Type the formula:

=Birmingham_ Oxford

Note that there is a space between the words *Birmingham_* and *Oxford*.

3.   Press the **<Enter>** key.

The space is the intersection operator. Amazingly, the correct answer is displayed in cell B32.

13   Use the INDIRECT function and the intersection operator (space) to show the correct distance in cell B32 based upon the values in cells B30 and B31.

This is more difficult than it first seems.

You could be forgiven for thinking that the formula:

=B30 B31

…would work.

Unfortunately, you can't refer to range names in this way. Excel provides the INDIRECT function to solve this problem.

1.   Type the following formula into cell B32:

fx   =INDIRECT(B30) INDIRECT(B31)

Note that there is a space between *=INDIRECT(B30)* and *INDIRECT(B31)*.

2.   Press the **<Enter>** key.

The correct mileage is now shown in cell B32 for any journey that you select in cells B30 and B31.

	A	B	C	D	E
30	From	Derby_			
31	To	Manchester			
32	Miles				59

14   Save your work as Distance Chart-2.

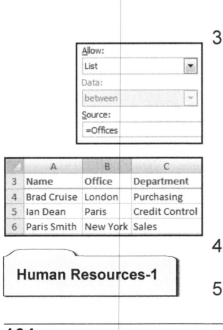

Lesson 4-6: Create dynamic formula-based range names using the OFFSET function

The technique shown in this lesson is a work-around that is rarely needed in Excel 2010 due to the introduction of the table feature. Feel free to skip it if you feel that it is not relevant to you (see sidebar).

The range referred to by a range name is already dynamic to a point. If the range has rows or columns added or removed *inside the range,* the range name will automatically adjust. Problems occur when a new value is added to a blank row immediately below a range. In this case, the range name does not automatically adjust.

1   Open *Human Resources-1* from your sample files folder.

This is a simple worksheet with two tabs. One tab lists employees and the other lists all of the company's current offices and departments.

2   Create automatic range names for cells A4:A6 and C4:C7 on the *Validations* worksheet.

1.   Select the *Validations* worksheet.

2.   Select cells A3:A6 (to include the range header).

3.   Click: Formulas→Defined Names→Create From Selection.

Note that the actual range name will be A4:A6. Cell A3 was only included in order to define the automatic name: *Offices.*

4.   Click the OK button.

5.   Repeat for the range C3:C7.

3   Create list validations for columns B and C on the *Employees* worksheet.

1.   Select all of the cells in column B on the *Employees* worksheet.

2.   Click: Data→Data Tools→Data Validation.

3.   Select *List* in the *Allow* drop-down list.

4.   Type **=Offices** into the source box.

5.   Click the OK button.

6.   Use the same technique to add a list validation for *Departments* to column C.

4   Use the drop-down lists to add some random *Offices* and *Departments* for Brad Cruise, Ian Dean and Paris Smith.

5   Type **Rome** into cell A7on the *Validations* worksheet.

6 Select the *Employees* worksheet.

7 Add an office for Gordon Ramsay.

Notice that the new *Rome* office can't be added. That's because the range does not adjust itself when a new value is added to a blank row immediately below a range.

8 Convert the *Offices* range name into a formula-based name that will enable the name to automatically re-size.

To do this we need to use the OFFSET function. This returns a range reference that is a given number of rows or columns from a specified cell, or from an offset from a specified cell.

In this case, the specified cell will be A4 (on the *Validations* worksheet) as this contains the first *Office*, but how can we automatically detect how many offices there are?

The answer is to use the COUNTA function to return the number of cells in column A that are not empty. COUNTA needs a range to examine for non-blank cells. We'll use the range A4:A200 on the basis that we're unlikely to ever have more than 197 offices.

=COUNTA(Validations!$A$4:$A$200) will thus return 4, the current number of offices in the range.

To convert the *Offices* range name into a formula-based range name, we will need to use the *Name Manager*.

1. Click: Formulas→Defined Names→Name Manager.

2. Click the *Offices* range name.

3. Click the *Edit* button.

   Note that this name currently refers to the range:

   Refers to: `=Validations!$A$4:$A$6`

4. Type the following formula into the *Refers to* box:

   Refers to: `=OFFSET(Validations!$A$4,0,0,COUNTA(Validations!$A$4:$A$200))`

   The four arguments specify where the range will begin, the number of rows to offset the start of the range, the number of columns to offset the start of the range, and the number of rows in the range.

9 Convert the *Department* range name into a formula-based range name that will enable the range name to automatically re-size.

Do this in exactly the same way as for the *Offices* range. This time, the formula will be:

Refers to: `=OFFSET(Validations!$C$4,0,0,COUNTA(Validations!$C$4:$C$200))`

10 Test the validation by adding *Offices* and *Departments*.

When you add a new *Office* or *Department*, the range names now dynamically expand to include the new item.

11 *Save your work as Human Resources-2.*

Lesson 4-7: Create table-based dynamic range names

In the last lesson: *Lesson 4-6: Create dynamic formula-based range names using the OFFSET function,* you used a complex method based on the OFFSET and COUNTA functions to implement a dynamic formula-based range name.

You'll be pleased to know that there is a much simpler way to achieve the same thing using a table-based range name.

You won't be able to use this technique if you need to create workbooks that are compatible with pre-2007 versions of Excel. If you are sure that the workbook will only ever be used with Excel 2007/2010 (or a later version), the technique described in this lesson is simpler, more elegant and less prone to error.

1   Open *Human Resources-2 from* your sample files folder (if it isn't already open).

	A	B	C
3	Name	Office	Department
4	Brad Cruise	Paris	Sales
5	Ian Dean	Paris	Purchasing

I◄ ◄ ► ►I   **Employees**   Validations

	A	B	C
3	Offices		Departments
4	London		Sales
5	Paris		Purchasing
6	New York		Credit Control
7	Rome		R&D

I◄ ◄ ► ►I   Employees   **Validations**

This is a simple worksheet with two tabs. One tab lists employees and the other lists all of the company's current offices and departments.

2   Delete the existing range names for *Departments* and *Offices.*

1.   Click: Formulas→Defined Names→Name Manager.

2.   Select *Departments* and *Offices* and then click the *Delete* button.

3.   Click the *Close* button to close the *Name Manager.*

3   Convert the ranges A3:A7 and C3:C7 on the Validation worksheet into tables.

This was covered in depth in: *Lesson 1-8: Convert a range into a table and add a total row.*

1.   Click anywhere in the range A3:A7 on the *Validation* worksheet.

2.   Click: Insert→Tables→Table.

3.   Click OK.

4.   Do exactly the same thing for the *Departments* range.

4   Name the two new tables *Office* and *Department.*

1.   Click anywhere inside the range A3:A7.

2.   Click Table Tools→Design→Properties→Table Name.

3.   Type **Office** into the text box.

	A	B	C
3	Offices ▼		Departments ▼
4	London		Sales
5	Paris		Purchasing
6	New York		Credit Control
7	Rome		R&D

Table Name:

Office

⊞ Resize Table

Properties

Human Resources-2

4. Do exactly the same thing to name the *Department* table.

5 Create range names called *OfficeTable* and *DepartmentTable* based upon the two new tables.

Unfortunately, Excel doesn't accept a table name for a list validation. Fortunately, it is happy to accept a range name associated with a table.

1. Select all of the values in the *Office* table (cells A4:A7); be careful not to include the header row.

2. Click: Formulas→Defined Names→Define Name.

   The *New Name* dialog appears.

3. Type **OfficeTable** in the *Name* text box.

Name:	OfficeTable

   Note that the *Refers to* box now contains the range name:

Refers to:	=Office[Offices]

   This means that it refers to everything in the *Office* table. In other words, it is a dynamic named range that will shrink and grow with the *Office* table.

4. Click the OK button.

5. Create the *DepartmentTable* range name in exactly the same way.

6 Edit the list validation on columns B and C in the *Employees* worksheet to reference the *OfficeTable* and *DepartmentTable* range names.

1. Select column B on the *Employees* worksheet.

2. Click: Data→Data Tools→Data Validation.

3. Delete *=Offices* from the *Source* text box.

4. Press the **<F3>** key to bring up a list of range names. Select *OfficeTable* and then click the OK button.

   This is the fastest way to bring up the *Paste Name* dialog. The slower Ribbon method is to click:

   Formulas→Defined Names→Use In Formula→Paste Names

5. Click the OK button on the *Data Validation* dialog.

6. Use the same method to edit the list validation for column C.

7 Test the validations.

As items are added and deleted from the tables in the *Validations* worksheet, the changes are reflected in the contents of the drop-down validation lists on the *Employees* worksheet.

8 *Save your work as Human Resources-3.*

Lesson 4-8: Create two linked drop-down lists using range names

In this lesson, we're going to push Excel's validation feature into bold new territory by addressing a common business requirement.

Here's the sample worksheet for this session:

	A	B
3	Make	Model
4	Jaguar	X-Type

We want to add a validation to the *Make* and *Model* columns.

The *Make* validation is easy to implement as a simple list validation.

The *Model* validation is not so simple. The values that are valid depend upon the selected *Make*.

Here's what we want to see:

- When the Make is *Ford,* valid models are *Fiesta, Focus* and *Mondeo.*

- When the Make is *Fiat,* valid models are *500, Panda* and *Bravo.*

This lesson provides a solution to the problem by dynamically selecting the *Model* range name depending upon the selected *Make*.

1 Open *New Car Model Range-1* from your sample files folder.

2 Create an automatic range name for the *Make* table on the *Model Range* worksheet.

   1. Select the *Model Range* worksheet.

   2. Select cells A5:A8.

   3. Click: Formulas→Defined Names→Create From Selection.

   4. Click the OK button.

3 Create automatic range names for each *Model* on the *Model Range* worksheet.

   1. Select cells A12:C15.

   2. Click Formulas→Defined Names→Create From Selection.

   3. De-select the *Left column* check box because we only want the range names to use the labels from the *Top row*.

   4. Click the OK button.

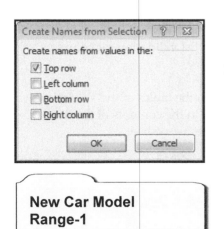

New Car Model Range-1

4   Apply a list validation to column A of the *Cars* worksheet that uses the *Make* range name as its source.

   1.   Select column A on the *Cars* worksheet.

   2.   Click: Data→Data Tools→Data Validation.

   3.   Enter the following values into the dialog:

> Allow:
> List ▼
> Data:
> between ▼
> Source:
> =Make

   4.   Click the OK button.

5   Use the drop-down list to select a car make in cell A4.

6   Apply a list validation to B4 that will display a list of models based upon the make displayed in cell A4.

   1.   Click in cell B4.

   2.   Click: Data→Data Tools→Data Validation.

   3.   Enter the following values into the dialog:

> Allow:
> List ▼
> Data:
> between ▼
> Source:
> =INDIRECT(A4)

It is very important that the reference to cell A4 is relative (A4) and not absolute ($A$4) because we are going to copy the validation to the other cells in column B in a moment.

   4.   Click OK.

7   Copy and paste the validation to all of the cells in column B.

   1.   Copy the contents of cell B4.

   2.   Select all of column B.

   3.   Right-click inside the selected range and click on *Paste Special…* from the shortcut menu.

   4.   Select *Validation* from the *Paste Special* dialog.

8   Test the validation.

The valid choices for *Model* now change based upon the *Make* selected in column A.

	A	B
3	Make	Model
4	Ford	Mondeo ▼
5		Fiesta
6		Focus
		Mondeo

	A	B
3	Make	Model
4	Fiat	500 ▼
5		500
6		Panda
		Bravo

9   Save your work as *New Car Model Range-2*.

---

tip

Removing validation from the label row

It is quick and convenient to add validation to an entire column because you are never sure how many entries will ultimately be added to the range.

An unfortunate side-effect of this is that the validation drop-down arrows also appear when you click in the header and label rows (in this example rows 1 to 3).

To solve this problem:

1/ Click on any empty cell in the worksheet *that contains no validation constraint.*

2/ Copy.

3/ Select the cells that you want to remove validation from, and then Paste Special→Validation to clear the validation.

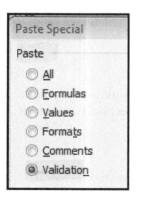

> Paste Special
>
> Paste
> ○ All
> ○ Formulas
> ○ Values
> ○ Formats
> ○ Comments
> ◉ Validation

Lesson 4-9: Understand the #NUM!, #DIV/0! and #NAME? Error Values

note

The #N/A error value

Sometimes Excel can't figure out exactly why an error has occurred.

In this case it displays the "I don't know" error value.

#N/A

So why call it #N/A?

The official explanation is that this error displays when a value is *not available* to a function or formula.

Excel has six specific error values that it is able to display in cells containing formulas. It's important that you understand the type of problem that causes Excel to display each of these errors.

The error values are:

#DIV/0!, #NAME?, #NULL!, #NUM!, #REF! and **#VALUE!**

There's also a nonspecific error value called **#N/A** (see sidebar).

The sample worksheet for this lesson has faulty formulas that produce all six errors.

1   Open *Errors-1* from your sample files folder.

This worksheet has a lot of problems. You can see each of the six error messages appearing in different cells.

2   Diagnose and solve the problem causing the #NUM! error in cell D4.

	A	B	C	D
3		Sales	Target	Above/Below Target
4	Jan	$ 5,210.00	$3,500.00	#NUM!
5	Feb	$ 5,650.00	$ -	$ 5,650.00

The #NUM! error is usually caused by a formula that returns a number that is too large, or too small for Excel to handle.

Another possible cause is a non-numeric value entered as an argument for a function that expects a numeric value.

1. Examine the formula in cell D4:

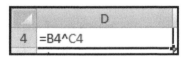

	D
4	=B4^C4

Here lies the problem. Excel is trying to calculate B4 *exponent* C4, which results in a huge number that Excel isn't capable of handling.

2. Correct the formula:

As we need to calculate how far sales are above or below target you will need to correct the formula to:

f_x =B4-C4

The problem then vanishes. Notice that the formula in cell D10 now also displays correctly as it was simply inheriting the #NUM! error from cell D4.

Errors-1

3 Diagnose and solve the problem causing the #DIV/0! error in cell E5.

	A	B	C	D	E
3	Month	Sales	Target	Above/Below Target	% of Target
4	Jan	$ 5,210.00	$ 3,500.00	$ 1,710.00	149%
5	Feb	$ 5,650.00	$ -	$ 5,650.00	#DIV/0!
6	Mar	$ 6,092.00	$ 4,000.00	$ 2,092.00	152%

Dividing by zero results in an infinite number causing Excel's "Divide by Zero" error to be displayed.

1. Examine the formula in cell E5.

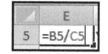

You know that the zero value must be in cell C5. Sure enough, no sales target was entered for February.

2. Enter a sales target of **3,250** for February.

The problem is solved.

If you didn't know the target for February and wanted to suppress the error message you could use the IFERROR function as described in: *Lesson 3-23: Use an IFERROR function to suppress error messages.*

4 Diagnose and solve the problem causing the #NAME? error in cell C10.

	A	B	C	D
9	Jun	$ 7,130.00	$4,750.00	$ 2,380.00
10	Totals:	$ 34,292.00	#NAME?	$ 10,042.00

The #NAME? error means that Excel has encountered a name it doesn't understand. The most likely cause is that you've used a range name that doesn't exist.

1. Examine the formula in cell C10.

	C	
10	=SUM(Target)	

Because there was a #NAME? error you know that there is no range name called *Target.*

2. Select cells C3:C9.

3. Click: Formulas→Defined Names→Create from Selection.

4. Click the OK button.

The problem is then solved.

5 Save your work as *Errors-2.*

Lesson 4-10: Understand the #VALUE!, #REF! and #NULL! Error Values

1 Open *Errors-2 from* your sample files folder (if it isn't already open).

2 Diagnose and solve the problem causing the #VALUE! error in cell F8.

	A	B	C	D	E	F
3		Sales	Target	Above/Below Target	% of Target	Exceeded Target?
4	Jan	$ 5,210.00	$ 3,500.00	$ 1,710.00	149%	Yes
5	Feb	$ 5,650.00	$ 3,250.00	$ 2,400.00	174%	Yes
6	Mar	$ 6,092.00	$ 4,000.00	$ 2,092.00	152%	Yes
7	Apr	$ 3,955.00	$ 4,250.00	$ -295.00	93%	No
8	May	$ 6,255.00	$ 4,500.00	$ 1,755.00	139%	#VALUE!

The #VALUE! error means that a function contains an invalid argument.

1. Examine the formula in cell F8.

> *fx* =IF("B8>C8", "Yes", "No")

The IF function was covered in: *Lesson 3-5: Use the IF logic function.*

The first argument of an IF function demands a logical expression that evaluates TRUE or FALSE.

There's nothing wrong with the expression: **B8>C8**. The problem is caused by the quotation marks that cause Excel to interpret it as text.

2. Correct the formula in cell F8 by removing the quotation marks from the expression **B8>C8** (the IF function's first argument).

> *fx* =IF(B8>C8, "Yes", "No")

The problem is solved.

3 Diagnose and solve the problem causing the #REF! error in cell B11.

	A	B	C
10	Totals:	$ 34,292.00	$ 24,250.00
11	GBP Totals:	#REF!	

The #REF! error means that a formula refers to a cell that isn't valid. This happens when you reference a cell from a formula and then delete the row or column that used to contain the referenced cell.

Errors-2

1. Examine the formula in cell B11

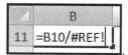

Because this cell needs to convert the dollar sales figure in cell B10 to Great Britain Pounds (GBP), the missing reference is the USD/GBP exchange rate.

2. Replace the #REF! part of the formula with **1.62** (the USD/GBP exchange rate when this lesson was written).

fx =B10/1.62

3. Press the **<Enter>** key.

The problem is solved.

4 Diagnose and cure the problem causing the #NULL! error in cell B16.

	A	B
15	Period	Sales
16	1st Quarter	#NULL!
17	2nd Quarter	17,340

The #NULL! error occurred because Excel is confused by the use of the intersection (space) operator. It usually simply means that you've incorrectly typed one of the arguments.

1. Examine the formula in cell B16.

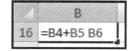

It is clear that there is a missing addition (+) operator between B5 and B6.

Excel has interpreted the missing operator as an attempt to reference the intersection of cells B5 and B6. It is, of course, impossible to have an intersection between two single cell references.

The intersection operator was covered in: *Lesson 4-5: Use intersection range names and the INDIRECT function.*

2. Correct the formula in cell B16 by adding the missing addition operator.

fx =B4+B5+B6

3. Press the **<Enter>** key.

The problem is solved.

5 Save your work as *Errors-3*.

Lesson 4-11: Understand background error checking and error checking rules

Excel is constantly working in the background, automatically checking for errors. Whenever Excel thinks you've made a mistake, it will politely let you know. Of course, Excel isn't always correct. It can only guess that you've made a mistake and it is often wrong.

1   Open *Daily Profit Report-1 from* your sample files folder.

This workbook contains two errors. Excel has automatically detected them and indicates each by a small green triangle in the top left hand corner of each cell containing a suspected error.

If you don't see the green triangles on your computer, somebody has switched automatic error checking off. See the sidebar for instructions on how to switch it back on.

	A	B	C	D
3	Date	Sales	Costs	Profit
4	18-Sep-08	20,000	12,000	8,000
5	19-Sep-08	21,000	12,500	8,500
6	20-Sep-08	22,800	12,600	35,400
7	21-Sep-08	23,500	13,000	10,500
8	Total:	87,300	50,100	62,400

2   Understand error checking rules.

    1.   Click: File→Options→Formulas.

       Note that Excel monitors for eight different error conditions by default. There's a ninth that is switched off by default but can be enabled if required:

> ☑ Cells containing formulas that result in an error ⓘ
> ☑ Inconsistent calculated column formula in tables ⓘ
> ☑ Cells containing years represented as 2 digits ⓘ
> ☑ Numbers formatted as text or preceded by an apostrophe ⓘ
> ☑ Formulas inconsistent with other formulas in the region ⓘ

> ☑ Formulas which omit cells in a region ⓘ
> ☑ Unlocked cells containing formulas ⓘ
> ☐ Formulas referring to empty cells ⓘ
> ☑ Data entered in a table is invalid ⓘ

    2.   Click the *Cancel* button.

3   Remove the error warning from cell A5.

    1.   Click on cell A5. Notice that an *Error Smart Tag* has appeared to the right of the cell.

    2.   Hover the mouse cursor over the *Smart Tag*.

Daily Profit Report-1

A tip appears showing the rule that Excel believes has been violated:

3. Click the down arrow on the Smart Tag.

Excel is worried because the date (unlike the other dates in the column) has been entered as text value with two digits. This is a throw-back to the problems caused in the year 2000 when such dates were predicted to bring about the end of the world (see sidebar).

A date can be entered in this way by preceding the date by an apostrophe to indicate that the entry is a textual value:

'19-Sep-08

Notice that two of the options in the *Smart Tag list* offer to convert the date to 2008 or to 1908.

4. Click *Ignore Error*.

The green triangle vanishes.

4 Correct the error in cell D6.

1. Click on cell D6 and hover the mouse cursor over the *Smart Tag*.

This time Excel has found a real error. It has noticed that the formula in cell D6 is inconsistent with the other formulas in column D. The formula is adding costs to sales when it should be subtracting them.

2. Click the down arrow on the *Smart Tag* and click *Copy Formula From Above* on the shortcut menu.

The error is corrected.

5 Save your work as *Daily Profit Report-2*.

Lesson 4-12: Manually check a worksheet for errors

Sometimes those little green triangles can be annoying. Excel often picks up "errors" that are not really errors at all.

Some Excel users would prefer to switch off background error checking and instead, run a manual error check when the worksheet is complete.

In this lesson, we'll switch off Excel's background error checking and then manually scan a worksheet for errors.

1   Open *Operating Expenses-1 from* your sample files folder.

This workbook contains three errors. Excel has automatically detected them and indicates each by a small green triangle in the top left hand corner of each cell containing a suspected error.

	A	B	C	D
3	Month	Budget	Actual	Variance
4	Jan-09	42,000	45000	3,000
5	Feb-09	45,000	42000	-3,000
6	Mar-09	47,500	46000	-2,500
7	Apr-09	48,000	53000	5,000
8	May-09	47,000	47000	0
9	Jun-09	46,000	45000	-1,000
10	Total	275,500	186000	1,500

2   Switch off background error checking.

1.   Click: File→Options→Formulas.

2.   Clear the *Enable background error checking* check box:

Error Checking

☐ Enable background error checking

3.   Click the OK button.

Notice that the green triangles have now vanished, even though the error conditions remain.

3   Manually check the worksheet for errors.

1.   Click: Formulas→Formula Auditing→Error Checking.

2.   Cell D6 is selected (the first cell in the worksheet containing a suspected error) and the *Error Checking* dialog appears:

Error Checking

Error in cell D6

=C6-B6-1000

Inconsistent Formula

The formula in this cell differs from the formulas in this area of the spreadsheet.

Copy Formula from Above

Help on this error

Ignore Error

Edit in Formula Bar

Options...

Previous   Next

Operating Expenses-1

The dialog indicates that it has found an inconsistent formula. This means that the formula in cell D6 is not consistent with the other formulas in column D.

3. Click: Formulas→Formula Auditing→Show Formulas.

   The formulas behind the cells are now displayed:

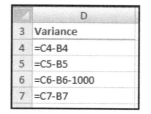

	D
3	Variance
4	=C4-B4
5	=C5-B5
6	=C6-B6-1000
7	=C7-B7

   The error is now apparent. For some reason an extra 1,000 has been deducted from the variance for March 2009.

4. Click: Formulas→Formula Auditing→Show Formulas.

   Values are once again shown in all cells.

5. Click the *Resume* button on the *Error Checking* dialog.

6. Click *Copy Formula from Above* to correct the error.

   The error is corrected and the active cell moves to cell C8, the next cell in the worksheet containing a suspected error.

   This time, the error is caused by a number being stored as text. This can happen when a numeric cell is formatted as text or when a value is typed into a cell preceded with an apostrophe like this:

   '47000

7. Click *Convert to Number*.

   The error is corrected and the active cell moves to cell C10, the next cell in the worksheet containing a suspected error.

   This time the error is another inconsistent formula. The formula in cell C10 is incorrectly adding the values in cells C4:C8 instead of C4:C9. Excel has noticed that this is inconsistent with the formulas in cells B10 and D10.

8. Click *Copy Formula from Left* to correct the error.

   Microsoft Office Excel

   The error check is complete for the entire sheet.

   OK

9. Click the OK button to end the error check.

4   Re-enable background error checking.

   1. Click: File→Options→Formulas.

   2. Check the *Enable background error checking* check box.

   3. Click the OK button.

      Notice that there are no longer any green triangles as we've corrected all of the errors.

5   Save your work as *Operating Expenses-2.*

Lesson 4-13: Audit a formula by tracing precedents

When you have a worksheet with cross-worksheet formulas and range names, there is a lot of scope for error. Ranges and formulas can often reference the wrong cells.

Excel's *trace precedents* tool provides an easy way to quickly audit cell references in order to confirm the integrity of your workbook.

1   Open *Profit Analysis-1 from* your sample files folder.

This workbook summarizes data from the *January, February* and *March* worksheets into a *First Quarter Summary*. The workbook also makes extensive use of range names.

	A	B	C	D	E	F
1	**First Quarter Summary**					
2						
3		Sales	Cost	Profit		
4	Jan	89,199	45,318	43,881		
5	Feb	99,197	42,510	56,687		
6	Mar	87,194	45,025	42,169		
7	Totals:	275,590	132,853	142,737		

⏮ ◀ ▶ ⏭   **First Quarter Summary**   January   February   March

2   Audit the formula in cell D7 of the *First Quarter Summary* worksheet using *Trace Precedents*.

1.   Click into cell D7.

Notice that it isn't possible to immediately see which cells are referenced by the *Profit* range name.

    fx =SUM(Profit)

2.   Click: Formulas→Formula Auditing→Trace Precedents.

The cells referenced by the *Profit* range name are now apparent.

	A	B	C	D
3		Sales	Cost	Profit
4	Jan	89,199	45,318	●43,881
5	Feb	99,197	42,510	56,687
6	Mar	87,194	45,025	42,169
7	Totals:	275,590	132,853	142,737

You might think that this isn't very impressive. You could have done the same thing by pressing the <F2> key, or by clicking the word *Profit* in the formula bar. But there's more to come!

3.   Click: Formulas→Formula Auditing→Trace Precedents again.

This time the next level of precedents is shown:

Profit Analysis-1

note

Use *trace error* to quickly find the first error in a chain

When a cell shows an error condition (such as #DIV/0!), it is often caused by an error in a precedent cell.

It is be possible to click:

Formulas→
Formula Auditing→
Trace Precedents

... several times in order to trace the cell causing the error.

However, Excel also provides a way of tracing all precedents in a single click when a cell shows an error condition, allowing you to save a few mouse clicks.

When the active cell contains an error condition, you can click:

Formula Auditing→
Error Checking→
Trace Error

To show all precedents, at all levels, with a single click.

	A	B	C	D
3		Sales	Cost	Profit
4	Jan	89,199	45,318	43,881
5	Feb	99,197	42,510	56,687
6	Mar	87,194	45,025	42,169
7	Totals:	275,590	132,853	142,737

You can see that the value in cell D4 is calculated from the values in cells B4 and C4. You can also see that the value in cell D7 is calculated from the range D4:D6.

But where are the values in cells B4:C6 coming from?

4. Click: Formulas→Formula Auditing→Trace Precedents again.

	A	B	C	D
2				
3		Sales	Cost	ofit
4	Jan	89,199	45,318	43,881
5	Feb	99,197	42,510	56,687
6	Mar	87,194	45,025	42,169
7	Totals:	275,590	132,853	142,737

The icons pointing to cells B4:C6 indicate that their values come from different worksheets in this (or even another) workbook.

5. Double-click the dotted line joining cell B4 and the icon.

The *GoTo* dialog appears showing the source of the value in cell B4.

6. Select the item shown in the *GoTo* window and then click the OK button.

Reference:

'[Profit Analysis-1.xlsx]January'!$D$10

Special...   OK   Cancel

You are taken to the cell in the *January* worksheet that provides the value shown in cell B4 on the *First Quarter Summary* worksheet.

7. Click: Formulas→Formula Auditing→Trace Precedents again.

Now you can see the precedents of cell D10 in the *January* worksheet (see sidebar).

8. Click: Formulas→Formula Auditing→Remove Arrows.

The precedent arrows are removed from the *January* worksheet.

9. Select the *First Quarter Summary* worksheet.

10. Click: Formulas→Formula Auditing→Remove Arrows.

The precedent arrows are removed from the *First Quarter Summary* worksheet.

	D	E
3	Sales	Cost
4	16,756	9,431
5	19,437	7,412
6	14,742	7,960
7	15,881	6,214
8	11,835	8,714
9	10,548	5,587
10	89,199	45,318

Lesson 4-14: Audit a formula by tracing dependents

1 Open *Profit Analysis-1 from* your sample files folder (if it isn't already open).

2 Select the *January* worksheet.

3 Audit the formula in cell D6 using *Trace Dependents*.

   1. Click cell D6 to make it the active cell.

   2. Click: Formulas→Formula Auditing→Trace Dependents.

      The direct dependents are shown for cell D6. These cells have formulas that directly reference cell D6.

	A	B	C	D	E	F
3	Team	First Name	Last Name	Sales	Cost	Profit
4	Blue	Johnny	Caine	16,756	9,431	7,325
5	Blue	George	Marley	19,437	7,412	12,025
6	Blue	Bill	Spears	14,742	7,960	6,782
7	Red	Gordon	Depp	15,881	6,214	9,667
8	Red	Tom	Marley	11,835	8,714	3,121
9	Red	Charles	Blair	10,548	5,587	4,961
10	Totals:			89,199	45,318	43,881
11						
12	Team			Average Sales	Average Cost	Average Profit
13	Blue			16,978	8,268	8,711
14	Red			12,755	6,838	5,916

You can see that:

- The *Profit* in cell F6 depends upon *Sales* in D6 (because Profit = Sales-Cost).

- The *Total Sales* in cell D10 depends upon the *Sales* in D6.

- The *Average Sales* for the *Blue* team also depends upon the value in D6 because Bill Spears is in the *Blue* team.

   3. Click: Formulas→Formula Auditing→Trace Dependents again.

	A	B	C	D	E	F
3	Team	First Name	Last Name	Sales	Cost	Profit
4	Blue	Johnny	Caine	16,756	9,431	7,325
5	Blue	George	Marley	19,437	7,412	12,025
6	Blue	Bill	Spears	14,742	7,960	6,782
7	Red	Gordon	Depp	15,881	6,214	9,667
8	Red	Tom	Marley	11,835	8,714	3,121
9	Red	Charles	Blair	10,548	5,587	4,961
10	Totals:			89,199	45,318	43,881
11						
12	Team			Average Sales	Average Cost	Average Profit
13	Blue			16,978	8,268	8,711
14	Red			12,755	6,838	5,916

Profit Analysis-1

The next level of dependents are shown. You can now see that:

- The *Total* in cell F10 depends upon the *Profit* value in cell F6.

- The Blue Team's *Average Profit* in cell F13 depends upon the *Average Sales* in cell D13.

There is also an icon pointing to cell D10 indicating that there is a dependent value in a different worksheet in this (or even another) workbook.

4. Double-click the dotted line joining cell D10 and the icon.

The *GoTo* dialog appears showing the source of the value in cell D10.

5. Select the item shown in the *GoTo* window and then click the OK button.

Reference:

'[Profit Analysis-1.xlsx]First Quarter Summary'!$B$4

Special...   OK   Cancel

You are taken to cell B4 in the *First Quarter Summary* worksheet as this cell depends upon the value in cell D10 on the *January* worksheet.

6. Click: Formulas→Formula Auditing→Trace Dependents again.

You can now see the cells whose formulas directly depend upon the value in cell B4.

	A	B	C	D
3		Sales	Cost	Profit
4	Jan	89,199	45,318	43,881
5	Feb	99,197	42,510	56,687
6	Mar	87,194	45,025	42,169
7	Totals:	275,590	132,853	142,737

7. Click: Formulas→Formula Auditing→Trace Dependents again.

The final level of dependents is shown:

	A	B	C	D
3		Sales	Cost	Profit
4	Jan	89,199	45,318	43,881
5	Feb	99,197	42,510	56,687
6	Mar	87,194	45,025	42,169
7	Totals:	275,590	132,853	142,737

8. Click: Formulas→Formula Auditing→Remove Arrows.

The precedent arrows are removed from the *First Quarter Summary* worksheet.

9. Select the *January* worksheet.

10. Click: Formulas→Formula Auditing→Remove Arrows.

The dependent arrows are removed from the *January* worksheet.

Lesson 4-15: Use the watch window to monitor cell values

The watch window is useful when developing workbooks that contain cross-worksheet formulas. You'll often want to monitor one or more result cells on a summary worksheet as you edit values in source worksheets.

1   Open *Profit Analysis-1 from* your sample files folder (if it isn't already open).

2   Select the *First Quarter Summary* worksheet.

	A	B	C	D
3		Sales	Cost	Profit
4	Jan	89,199	45,318	43,881
5	Feb	99,197	42,510	56,687
6	Mar	87,194	45,025	42,169
7	Totals:	275,590	132,853	142,737

3   Set up a watch window to monitor the values in cells B7, C7 and D7.

1.   Click cell B7 to make it the active cell.

2.   Click: Formulas→Formula Auditing→Watch Window.

The watch window appears.

3.   Click the *Add Watch…* button.

The *Add Watch* dialog appears:

> **Add Watch**   [?] [X]
>
> Select the cells that you would like to watch the value of:
>
> ='First Quarter Summary'!$B$7
>
>   [Add]   [Cancel]

4.   Click the Add button.

The watch cell details appear in the Watch window.

> **Watch Window**
> 🔁 Add Watch...   🔽 Delete Watch
>
> | Book | Sheet | Name | Cell | Value | Formula |
> |---|---|---|---|---|---|
> | Profit ... | First ... | | B7 | 275,590 | =SUM(Sales) |

5.   Click the *Add Watch...* button again.

6.   Click on cell C7.

7.   Click the *Add* button.

A second watch appears in the watch window.

8.   Add a watch for cell D7 in the same way.

Profit Analysis-1

The watch window now contains three watch conditions:

4   Dock the watch window to the top of the screen.

Drag the watch window to the top of the screen. It then snaps into place above the formula bar:

Book	Sheet	Name	Cell	Value	Formula
Profit...	First...		B7	275,590	=SUM(Sales)
Profit...	First...		C7	132,853	=SUM(Cost)
Profit...	First...		D7	142,737	=SUM(Profit)

J12

	A	B	C	D	E	F
3		Sales	Cost	Profit		
4	Jan	89,199	45,318	43,881		
5	Feb	99,197	42,510	56,687		
6	Mar	87,194	45,025	42,169		
7	Totals:	275,590	132,853	142,737		

5   Convert the watch window into a floating dialog box.

1.   Click the drop down menu at the top right corner of the Watch Window and then click *Move*.

Watch Window

Book	Sheet	Name	Cell	Value	F	Move
Profit...	First...		B7	275,590	=:	Size
Profit...	First...		C7	132,853	=SUM(Cost)	Close
Profit...	First...		D7	142,737	=SUM(Profit)	

L10

A	B	C	D	E	F

2.   Move the cursor into the worksheet grid.

The window is converted back into a floating dialog box.

(You can also do this simply by dragging the top window downward).

6   Change some values on the *February* worksheet while monitoring the values defined in the watch window.

1.   Click on the *February* worksheet tab.

2.   Change Johnny Caine's sales (in cell D4) to 20,000 and press the **<Enter>** key.

Note that the values in the watch window have changed to reflect the new value.

Book	Sheet	Name	Cell	Value
Profit...	First...		B7	276,841
Profit...	First...		C7	132,853
Profit...	First...		D7	143,988

3.   Close the watch window.

7   Save your work as *Profit Analysis-2*.

Lesson 4-16: Use Speak Cells to eliminate data entry errors

One of my favorite Excel features is the ability to read the workbook to me via the *Speak Cells* facility. When I need to input lots of numbers from a sheet of paper and want to check them, I get Excel to read them to me as I tick each off my list. This is much faster and nicer than continuously looking first at the screen, and then at the paper, for each entry.

This is one of those "secret" features that most Excel users will never discover because you won't find it anywhere on the Ribbon or standard Excel dialogs. In order to use this feature, you'll have to add some custom buttons to the Quick Access Toolbar or Ribbon (you'll learn how to create a custom Ribbon tab later in: *Lesson 8-20: Create a custom Ribbon tab*).

1   Open *Profit Analysis-2 from* your sample files folder (if it isn't already open).

2   Add custom buttons to the Quick Access Toolbar for all of the *speak cells* commands.

    1.   Click: File→Options→Quick Access Toolbar.

        The *Customize the Quick Access Toolbar* pane appears.

    2.   Select *Commands Not in the Ribbon* from the *Choose commands from* drop-down list:

    3.   Click the *Speak Cells* command in the list of commands window:

    4.   Click the *Add* button.

    5.   Click the *Add* button four more times to add all *Speak Cells* commands to the Quick Access toolbar.

    6.   Click the OK button.

3   Type **Bonus** into cell G3 on the *January* worksheet.

Profit Analysis-2

4   Apply the *Heading 3* cell style to cell G3.

5   Click in cell G4.

6   Click the *Speak Cells on Enter* button that you added to the Quick Access Toolbar.

You should hear the words "Cells will now be spoken on enter". If you don't hear this, your speakers are either muted or not working.

7   Add the following values to column G without looking at the Excel screen.

	E	F	G
3	Cost	Profit	Bonus
4	9,431	7,325	700
5	7,412	12,025	1200
6	7,960	6,782	600
7	6,214	9,667	900
8	8,714	3,121	300
9	5,587	4,961	400
10	45,318	43,881	

Notice that Excel speaks the number back to you every time you press the **<Enter>** key.

This means that you can be sure that you added the correct value without having to continually look from paper to screen.

8   Select cells G4:G9.

9   Click the *Speak Cells* button that you added to the Quick Access Toolbar.

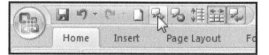

This time Excel speaks each value in the column in sequence. This is an alternative way to double-check that figures have been entered correctly.

10 Click the *Speak Cells on Enter* button that you added to the Quick Access Toolbar.

You should hear the words "Turned off speak on enter".

If you don't do this, Excel will continue to speak to you when you remove the toolbar buttons!

11 Remove the *Speak Cells* buttons from the Quick Access Toolbar.

Right-click upon each *Speak Cells* button in turn and then click *Remove from Quick Access Toolbar*.

12 Save your work as *Profit Analysis-3*.

note

Excel won't stop talking!

You may delete your *Quick Access Toolbar* buttons and then find that Excel continues to talk to you.

It's easy to run into this problem, as you would reasonably expect the *Stop Speaking Cells* button to switch off the voice.

However, Excel will continue speaking as long as the *Speak Cells on Enter* button is pressed.

Session 4: Exercise

1   Open *Excel Quiz-1* from your sample files folder.

2   Select cells A5:E9 on the *Choices* worksheet.

	A	B	C	D	E
4					
5	1	64,000	128,000	512,000	1,048,576
6	2	1985	1992	1995	1997
7	3	Excel 7	Excel 12	Excel 9	Excel 11
8	4	Lotus 1-2-3	SuperCalc	VisiCalc	Multiplan
9	5	256	512	16,585	22,256
10					

3   Create range names from the selected cells using the value in the left column to name each range.

4   Apply a list validation to cell C4 on the *Quiz* worksheet that will show a list of all valid answers to the first question.

	B	C	
3	Question	Answer	Corre
4	How many rows does Excel have?	▼	
5	When was the first Excel version released?	64,000	
6	What is another name for Excel 2007?	128,000 / 512,00 / 1,048,576	cel
7	What was the most popular worksheet before Excel?		tus

5   Copy and paste the validation from cell C4 to cells C5:C8.

6   Put an IF function into cell E4 that will show the text "CORRECT" if the answer in cell C4 equals the correct answer in cell D4, and a blank space if the answer is not correct.

	C	D	E
3	Answer	Correct Answer	Correct?
4	1048576	1,048,576	CORRECT

7   AutoFill cell E4 down to cells E5:E8.

8   Hide columns A and D.

9   Save your work as *Excel Quiz-2*.

	B	C	E
1	**Excel Quiz**		
2			
3	Question	Answer	Correct?
4	How many rows does Excel have?	1048576	CORRECT
5	When was the first Excel version released?	1985	CORRECT
6	What is another name for Excel 2007?	Excel 9 ▼	
7	What was the most popular worksheet before Excel?	Excel 7 / Excel 12	
8	How many columns does Excel support	Excel 9	
9		Excel 11	

Excel Quiz-1

If you need help slide the page to the left

Session 4: Exercise Answers

These are the four questions that students find the most difficult to answer:

Q 6	Q 5	Q 4	Q 3
1. The correct function is: **=IF(D4=C4, "CORRECT", "")** This was covered in: *Lesson 3-5: Use the IF logic function.*	1. Click in cell C4. 2. Click: Home→Clipboard→Copy. 3. Select the range C5:C8. 4. Click: Home→Clipboard→Paste→Paste Special. 5. Select *Validation* in the *Paste Special* dialog. Paste ○ All ○ Formulas ○ Values ○ Formats ○ Comments ● Validation 6. Click OK. This was covered in: *Lesson 4-8: Create two linked drop-down lists using range names.*	1. Click in cell C4 on the Quiz worksheet. 2. Click: Data→Data Tools→Data Validation. 3. Complete the Data Validation dialog like this: Allow: List Data: between Source: =INDIRECT(A4) The INDIRECT function allows you to use the number in column A to reference the range name containing the multiple-choice questions. This was covered in: *Lesson 4-8: Create two linked drop-down lists using range names.*	1. Click: Formulas→Defined Names→Create from Selection. 2. Make sure that only the *Left column* is checked in the *Create Names from Selection* dialog. Create names from ☐ Top row ☑ Left column ☐ Bottom row ☐ Right column 3. Click the OK button. This was covered in: *Lesson 4-8: Create two linked drop-down lists using range names.*

If you have difficulty with the other questions, here are the lessons that cover the relevant skills:

8   In order to hide a column, right-click the column header and select *Hide* from the shortcut menu.

This skill is covered in lesson 3-1 of the *Essential Skills* book in this series.

5

Session Five: Pivot Tables

> If the only tool you have is a hammer, you tend to see every problem as a nail.
>
> *Abraham Maslow (1908 - 1970)*

I'm constantly amazed at how many highly experienced Excel users are unable to understand Pivot tables.

"I manage to do everything I want to without them" they will tell me.

I've seen many cases where a user has spent hours creating a worksheet-based solution that could have been addressed in a few seconds using a pivot table.

This session will empower you with a complete mastery of this essential Excel tool.

Session Objectives

By the end of this session you will be able to:

- Create a one dimensional pivot table report from a table
- Create a grouped pivot table report
- Understand pivot table rows and columns
- Use an external data source
- Apply a simple filter and sort to a pivot table
- Use report filter fields
- Filter a pivot table visually using slicers
- Use slicers to create a date-driven interface
- Use report filter fields to automatically create multiple pages
- Format a pivot table using PivotTable styles
- Create a custom PivotTable style
- Understand pivot table report layouts
- Add/remove subtotals and apply formatting to pivot table fields
- Display multiple summations within a single pivot table
- Add a calculated field to a pivot table
- Add a calculated item to a pivot table
- Group by Text, Date and numeric value ranges
- Show row data by percentage of total rather than value
- Create a pivot chart from a pivot table
- Embed multiple pivot tables onto a worksheet
- Use slicers to filter multiple pivot tables

Lesson 5-1: Create a one dimensional pivot table report from a table

In this lesson, you'll jump straight into the deep end and create a simple one-dimensional pivot table. There's a huge amount to learn about pivot tables but it will be fun to do some useful work with one straight away.

Here's the sample file we'll use in this lesson:

	A	B	C	D	E	F	G	H
1	Order No	Order Date	Customer	Employee	Title	Genre	Qty	Total
2	136438	01-Oct-07	Silver Screen Video	Lee,Frank	Lawrence of Arabia	Biography	15	122.76
3	136438	01-Oct-07	Silver Screen Video	Lee,Frank	The Discreet Charm of the Bourgeoisie	Comedy	9	67.46
4	136438	01-Oct-07	Silver Screen Video	Lee,Frank	Berlin Alexanderplatz	Drama	25	250.60
5	136438	01-Oct-07	Silver Screen Video	Lee,Frank	Gone With The Wind	Drama	14	107.72
6	136439	02-Oct-07	Cinefocus DVD	Diamond,Elizabeth	Mouchette	Drama	5	31.77

This is the type of worksheet that pivot tables can work well with because the columns contain repeating data.

The sample file contains over 2,000 rows of transactional data listing sales during the 18 month period from October 2007 to March 2009 inclusive.

You can see from the data that the worksheet contains details of orders sold by a DVD wholesaler, along with the titles supplied on each order. Order *136438* was placed on *1st-Oct-07* and was ordered by *Silver Screen Video*. The order was sold by *Frank Lee* and there were four items on the order. Two of the films ordered were in the *Drama* genre and the other two were in the *Biography* and *Comedy* genres.

A business may wish to ask several questions about sales during this period such as:

- What were my sales by *Genre*?

- How many units did each *Employee* sell?

In this lesson, you'll use a pivot table to answer both questions in less than 10 seconds!

1 **Open *Transactions-1* from your sample files folder.**

This worksheet contains a large table named *Data* (see sidebar for more on using tables with Pivot Tables). The table looks like a regular range because it has had its *Filter* switched off and the *Table Style* set to *None*.

2 **Click anywhere inside the table.**

3 **Click Insert→Tables→Pivot Table.**

The first screen of the wizard appears.

Notice that, because you clicked inside the table, it has automatically detected the table's name of *Data*.

important

Pivot Tables, Ranges, Named Ranges and Tables

You can create a Pivot Table that is associated with a *Range*, a *Named Range* or a *Table*.

The fatal flaw of named ranges is that they only expand and contract when rows are *inserted* or *deleted* and NOT when data is added to the end of the range. You discovered a work-around to this problem in: *Lesson 4-6: Create dynamic formula-based range names using the OFFSET function.*

Fortunately, Excel 2010 has the fantastic new *Table* structure (introduced in Excel 2007).

Tables are wonderful to use as a data source for Pivot Tables because they are truly dynamic. You learned everything there is to know about tables in: *Session One: Tables, Ranges and Databases.*

Transactions-1

note

Drilling down into pivot table data

Whenever Excel shows a total, it is possible to "drill down" to see the transactions that were used to calculate the total.

When you double-click on a total, (such as the total sales for action movies in cell C5), a new worksheet opens showing the source transactions.

You'll have to manually delete this worksheet after viewing the transaction list.

note

Activating a pivot table

Pivot tables are a little like charts in that you cannot work upon their design unless they are activated.

To activate, you simply click anywhere inside the pivot table.

When the pivot table is activated, the *PivotTable Field List* appears along with the *PivotTable Tools* tab on the Ribbon.

	A	B
3	**Row Labels** ▾	**Sum of Qty**
4	Anderson,Jane	1109
5	Armstrong,Dan	1000
6	Ashe,Lucille	1116
7	Bell,Stephen	1409
8	Bradshaw,John	1196
9	Carrey,Julia	770
10	Davis,Charles	839
11	Diamond,Elizabeth	1153
12	Goodman,Paul	1163
13	Hawking,Alfred	1386
14	Hicks,Michael	921

4 Click the OK button.

An empty pivot table is shown on screen and the *PivotTable Field List* appears on the right of the screen.

Check the *Genre, Qty* and *Total* check boxes (in that order) on the *PivotTable Field List*.

Simply by clicking on three fields you have answered the first question:

- What were my sales by *Genre*?

5 Format the values shown in column C of the pivot table so that they show two decimal places with a comma separator.

1. Right-click on any value in column C.

2. Click *Number Format...* on the shortcut menu.

3. Click *Number* in the *Category* list.

4. Click the *Use 1000 Separator* check box.

Decimal places:	2
☑ Use 1000 Separator (,)	

5. Click the OK button.

	A	B	C
3		**Values**	
4	**Row Labels** ▾	**Sum of Qty**	**Sum of Total**
5	Action	4699	37,411.40
6	Adventure	1149	8,588.03
7	Animation	574	5,098.87
8	Biography	2229	17,174.78
9	Comedy	4747	37,614.16
10	Crime	2960	25,212.68
11	Drama	8439	67,097.47
12	Fantasy	1252	11,785.28
13	Sci Fi	989	7,289.18
14	Thriller	765	5,514.95
15	**Grand Total**	**27803**	**222,786.80**

6 Clear all check boxes and then select the *Employee* and *Qty* check boxes.

Once again, with very little effort, you have answered the second question:

- How many units did each *Employee* sell?

7 Name the pivot table: *Transactions*.

1. Click inside the Pivot Table.

2. Click PivotTable Tools→Options→PivotTable→ PivotTable Name.

3. Type **Transactions** into the *PivotTable Name* box.

8 Name the pivot table worksheet: *Pivot Table*.

9 Save your work as *Transactions-2*.

Lesson 5-2: Create a grouped pivot table report

1 Open *Transactions-2* from your sample files folder (if it isn't already open).

2 Select the *Pivot Table* worksheet (if it isn't already selected).

3 Click inside the pivot table to show the *PivotTable Field List*.

4 Click *Genre* in the PivotTable field list.

Each Employee's sales for each genre are now shown in the report.

	A	B
3	**Row Labels** ▾	**Sum of Qty**
4	⊟**Anderson,Jane**	**1109**
5	Action	199
6	Adventure	30
7	Biography	134
8	Comedy	233
9	Crime	79
10	Drama	345
11	Fantasy	21
12	Sci Fi	37
13	Thriller	31
14	⊟**Armstrong,Dan**	**1000**
15	Action	136
16	Adventure	26

5 Add *Title* information to the pivot table.

Click *Title* in the *PivotTable Field List*.

The report now breaks sales down by *Employee, Genre* and *Title*.

	A	B
3	Row Labels ▾	Sum of Qty
4	⊟Anderson,Jane	1109
5	⊟Action	199
6	A Touch of Zen	41
7	Drunken Master II	3
8	Get Carter	31
9	Once Upon a Time in the West	39
10	The Good, the Bad and the Ugly	42
11	The Lord of the Rings: The Fellowship of the Ring	13
12	The Lord of the Rings: The Return of the King (200	14
13	The Lord of the Rings: The Two Towers	8
14	Yojimbo	8
15	⊟Adventure	30
16	Aguirre, the Wrath of God	22
17	Interview With The Vampire	8
18	⊟Biography	134

6 Collapse the outline to show only sales by *Employee.*

1. Right-click cell A4.

   A shortcut menu appears.

note

You can also collapse an outline from the Ribbon

The fastest way to collapse and expand an outline is by using the right-click method described in the text.

It is also possible to do this in a less efficient way using the Ribbon:

1. Click cell A5.

A5 becomes the *Active Field.*

2. Click:

PivotTable Tools→Options→
Active Field→
Collapse Entire Field

Transactions-2

2.   Click: Expand/Collapse→Collapse Entire Field.

The Pivot Table collapses to the level of *Employee*.

	A	B
3	Row Labels ▼	Sum of Qty
4	⊞ Anderson,Jane	1109
5	⊞ Armstrong,Dan	1000
6	⊞ Ashe,Lucille	1116
7	⊞ Bell,Stephen	1409

7   Expand Dan Armstrong's sales to show full details.

Click the small + sign to the left of cell A5.

	A	B
5	⊞ Armstrong,Dan	1000
6	⊞ Ashe,Lucille	1116

Sales are expanded to show full details of Dan's sales.

	A	B
5	⊟ Armstrong,Dan	1000
6	⊟ Action	136
7	A Touch of Zen	24
8	Drunken Master II	22

8   Collapse the outline so that Dan's sales by *Genre* are shown without *Title* details.

1.   Right-click cell A6.

A shortcut menu appears.

2.   Click: Expand/Collapse→Collapse Entire Field.

The *Title* level of the Pivot Table collapses to show Dan's sales by *Genre* but not by *Title*.

	A	B
5	⊟ Armstrong,Dan	1000
6	⊞ Action	136
7	⊞ Adventure	26
8	⊞ Animation	22

9   Collapse the outline to only show sales by *Employee*.

Click the small minus sign to the left of cell A5.

The outline contracts to show only the *Employee* level.

	A	B
5	⊞ Armstrong,Dan	1000
6	⊞ Ashe,Lucille	1116
7	⊞ Bell,Stephen	1409

10   Save your work as *Transactions-3*.

Lesson 5-3: Understand pivot table rows and columns

1   Open *Transactions-3* from your sample files folder (if it isn't already open).

2   Select the *Pivot Table* worksheet (if it isn't already selected).

3   Click inside the pivot table to display the *Pivot Table Field List*.

At the lower right of the screen, you can see four panes:

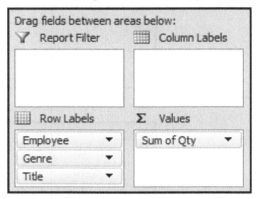

At the moment, we have three columns in the *Row Labels* list and one in the *Values* list. This creates a pivot table that shows sales first by *Employee,* then grouped by *Genre* and then grouped by *Title.*

	A	B
3	**Row Labels** ▼	**Sum of Qty**
4	⊟**Anderson,Jane**	1109
5	⊟Action	199
6	A Touch of Zen	41
7	Drunken Master II	3

4   Remove the *Genre* and *Title* rows from the Row Labels list.

1.   Click *Genre* and then click *Remove Field* from the shortcut menu.

2.   Click *Title* and then click *Remove Field* from the shortcut menu.

5   Add the *Genre* to the pivot table as a *Column Label*.

Instead of checking the *Genre* in the *PivotTable Field List,* you need to drag it from the *PivotTable Field List* to the *Column Labels* list below.

The pivot table now shows sales for each employee by genre with the genres listed along the top row as column labels:

	A	B	C	D	E
4	Row Labels ▼	Action	Adventure	Animation	Biography
5	Anderson,Jane	199	30		134
6	Armstrong,Dan	136	26	22	79
7	Ashe,Lucille	176	42	23	54

6   Add the *Title* field to the *Column Labels* list.

Drag the *Title* field from the *PivotTable Field List* to the *Column Labels* list.

Make sure that you place *Title* below *Genre*.

▼ Report Filter		Column Labels
		Genre ▼
		Title ▼
Row Labels		Σ Values
Employee ▼		Sum of Qty ▼

A small + sign is now shown next to each genre:

	A	B	C	D	E
4		⊞ Action	⊞ Adventure	⊞ Animation	⊞ Biography
5	Row Labels ▼				
6	Anderson,Jane	199	30		134
7	Armstrong,Dan	136	26	22	79
8	Ashe,Lucille	176	42	23	54

7   Expand and collapse the *Action* genre.

1. Click the small + sign to the left of *Action* in cell *B4*.

The field expands to show each title within the *Action* genre:

	A	B	C	D
4		⊟ Action		
5	Row Labels ▼	A Touch of Zen	Drunken Master II	Get Carter
6	Anderson,Jane	41	3	31

2. Click the small – sign that has now appeared to the left of *Action* in cell *B4*.

The outline collapses back to the genre level:

	A	B	C	D
4		⊞ Action	⊞ Adventure	⊞ Animation
5	Row Labels ▼			
6	Anderson,Jane	199	30	
7	Armstrong,Dan	136	26	22

8   Save your work as *Transactions-4*.

note

The difference between a relational database and Excel

A relational database (such as a Microsoft Access database) contains several tables joined together by relationships.

Conceptually, each table is similar to an Excel table but with more sophisticated validations.

In this respect, Excel is a little like a simple "one table database".

It is the relationships between the tables that make a true database "relational".

For example, the database used for this lesson has a *Director* table and a *Film* table. The relationship between them is defined as:-

One director may direct many films but a single film has one, and only one, director.

When this relationship is defined, Access will prevent a director from being deleted if there is an existing association with a film.

It is a huge mistake to store relational data in Excel, rather than in a true relational database.

Excel is the world's most powerful analytical tool, but it isn't a database!

note

You can also create a pivot table from an Access database like this:

1. Data→Get External Data→ From Access.

2. Select the Access database file and then click *Open*.

3. Select the table or query to use for the data source and click OK.

4. Select *PivotTable Report* in the *Import Data* dialog and then click OK.

Lesson 5-4: Use an external data source

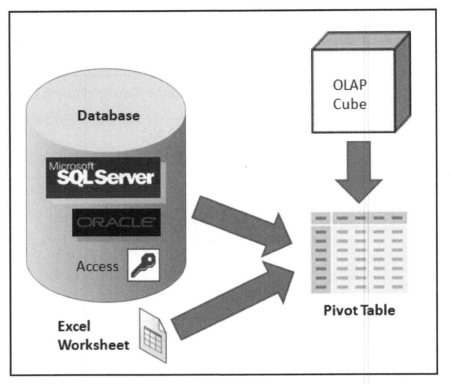

Excel is capable of importing data from a huge range of sources such as a CSV (comma separated variable) file. Once the data is imported into an Excel worksheet, it is then possible to create a pivot table from the worksheet.

It is also possible to use data directly (without first importing it) from an external data source. This is usually a database such as Microsoft Access or one of its big brothers; SQL Server or Oracle.

You can also use data directly from an OLAP cube. An Online Analytical Processing (OLAP) cube resides on an OLAP server and is a special sort of database that is optimized for reporting speed. OLAP technology would typically only be used when working with very large business databases.

In this lesson, we'll create a worksheet that analyses data from an Access database.

important

You may not be able to complete this lesson unless you have Microsoft Access 2010 installed on your machine. Access is included in the professional version of Office 2010 but, unfortunately, not the standard version.

If you don't have Access installed, you may still wish to read the lesson in order to understand how pivot tables can be used with an Access database.

1   Open a new blank workbook.

2   Save the new workbook as *Film Details-1.*

3   Click Insert→Tables→PivotTable.

The *Create PivotTable* dialog appears.

4   Create a pivot table using the *qryFilmDetails* query in the *Film Library* Access database as an external data source.

1. Click the *Use an external data source* option button.

2. Click the *Choose Connection…* button.

The *Existing Connections* dialog appears.

3. Click the *Browse for More…* button.

4. Navigate to your sample files folder and select the *Film Library* Access database file.

5. Click the *Open* button.

You are presented with a list of all tables and queries in the database.

6. Click the *qryFilmDetails* query and then click the OK button.

7. Click the OK button.

5   Use the pivot table to display all of the film titles, and each film's budget.

Check the *Film Budget (Millions $)* check box and the *Film Title* check box in the *PivotTable Field List*.

A list of films and budgets is displayed.

	A	B
1	**Row Labels** ▼	**Sum of Budget (Millions $)**
2	Blazing Saddles (1974)	26
3	Casablanca (1942)	4.75
4	Get Carter (1971)	3.75
5	Get Carter (2000)	200
6	Gone With The Wind (1939)	19.5
7	Interview With The Vampire (1994)	360
8	It's A Wonderful Life (1947)	18.9
9	**Grand Total**	**632.9**

6   Save your work (still with the name: *Film Details-1*).

---

important

A pivot table doesn't automatically update when the data source changes

Until you click:

PivotTable Tools→ Options→Data→Refresh

... a pivot table will not update to reflect changes to the source data (whether it is a worksheet or an external data source).

By default, Excel invisibly stores a local copy of data from an external data source. This means that you can still use the pivot table even if the source database is down.

If you are working with very large data sets you can switch off the local storage of data by unchecking:

PivotTable Tools→ Options→PivotTable→ Options→Data→ Save Source data with file.

Lesson 5-5: Apply a simple filter and sort to a pivot table

1 Open *Transactions-4* from your sample files folder (if it isn't already open).

2 Select the *Pivot Table* worksheet (if it isn't already selected).

3 Click inside the pivot table to display the *Pivot Table Field List.*

4 Remove the *Genre* and *Title* column Labels.

This was covered in: *Lesson 5-3: Understand pivot table rows and columns.*

5 Click the drop-down arrow next to *Row Labels* in cell A3.

Filter options appear.

These are very similar to the options that you learned to use in: *Lesson 1-2: Apply a simple filter to a range* and *Lesson 1-3: Apply a top 10 and custom filter to a range.*

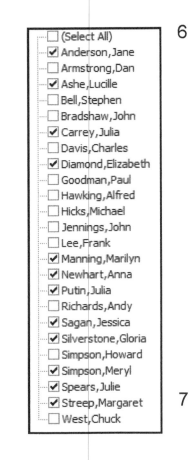

6 Filter the pivot table so that only female employees are shown.

1. Uncheck the check boxes next to each male employee (see sidebar).

	A	B
3	Row Labels 🔽	Sum of Qty
4	Anderson,Jane	1109
5	Ashe,Lucille	1116
6	Carrey,Julia	770
7	Diamond,Elizabeth	1153

2. Click the OK button.

Notice the filter icon in cell A3 showing that the pivot table has been filtered.

This is a very long winded way to filter out the male employees. In a real-world workbook you'd probably create a *Gender* column in the source data containing the values **M** or **F.** You could then filter by gender with a single check box.

7 Sort *Employee* names in Z-A order.

At the moment, the names are sorted in A-Z order.

1. Click cell A4.

When you click on any *Employee* name it makes *Employee* the active field.

2. Click: PivotTable Tools→Options→Sort & Filter→Z-A.

The Pivot Table is sorted in Z-A order.

Transactions-4

3	Row Labels	Sum of Qty
4	Streep,Margaret	1772
5	Spears,Julie	1314
6	Simpson,Meryl	822
7	Silverstone,Gloria	1040
8	Sagan,Jessica	1407
9	Putin,Julia	1054
10	Newhart,Anna	1081

note

Filters are not inherited from source data

If the data associated with a Pivot Table (whether a table, range or named range) has a filter applied to it (or contains subtotals) this will not be carried forward into the Pivot Table.

If you need the same filter in your Pivot Table, you must first create the Pivot Table and then apply the same filter.

Another way to achieve this is to copy the (filtered) data to a new worksheet and to create the Pivot Table from this subset of the actual data.

A useful technique for copying and pasting filtered data (visible cells) is described in: *Lesson 2-3: Automatically subtotal a range (sidebar).*

3	Row Labels	Sum of Qty
4	Newhart,Anna	1081
5	Diamond,Elizabeth	1153
6	Silverstone,Gloria	1040
7	Anderson,Jane	1109
8	Sagan,Jessica	1407
9	Carrey,Julia	770
10	Putin,Julia	1054
11	Spears,Julie	1314
12	Ashe,Lucille	1116
13	Streep,Margaret	1772
14	Manning,Marilyn	1161
15	Simpson,Meryl	822
16	Grand Total	13799

8 Sort *Employee* names by first name.

It isn't possible to automatically sort by first name. To do this, we would need *First Name* to be a different field to *Last Name*.

If there were a lot of names, we'd attend to this in the source data by splitting the *Employee Name* column into two. (You learned to do this in: *Lesson 2-1: Split fixed width data using Text to Columns* and in *Lesson 3-21: Extract text from delimited strings using the FIND and LEN functions).*

Because there are only twelve names, it will be quicker to manually sort the list.

1. Click in cell A4 to make it the active field.

2. Click: PivotTable Tools→Options→Sort & Filter→Sort.

   The *Sort* dialog appears.

3. Click the *Manual* option button.

4. Click OK.

5. Click and drag the border of each *Employee* name to move them to the desired position. Look for the four headed arrow cursor shape before clicking the mouse. (Sidebar shows sorted order).

4	Newhart,Anna
5	Diamond,Elizabeth
6	Silverstone,Gloria

9 Remove the filter.

1. Click the filter button at the top right of cell A3.

2. Check the *Select All* check box.

3. Click the OK button.

10 Save your work as *Transactions-5.*

Lesson 5-6: Use report filter fields

In pre-2007 versions of Excel, report filters were called *Page Fields*.

1 Open *Transactions-5* from your sample files folder (if it isn't already open).

2 Select the *Pivot Table* worksheet (if it isn't already selected).

3 Drag the *Genre* field from the *PivotTable Field List* to the *Report Filter* list.

	A	B		PivotTable Field List	
1	Genre	(All)		Choose fields to add to report:	
2				☑ Employee	
3	**Row Labels**	**Sum of Qty**		☐ Title	
4	West,Chuck	886		☑ Genre	
5	Newhart,Anna	1081		☑ Qty	
6	Diamond,Elizabeth	1153			
7	Silverstone,Gloria	1040		Drag fields between areas below:	
8	Anderson,Jane	1109		▽ Report Filter Column Labels	
9	Sagan,Jessica	1407		Genre	
10	Carrey,Julia	770		Row Labels Σ Values	
11	Putin,Julia	1054		Employee Sum of Qty	
12	Spears,Julie	1314			
13	Ashe,Lucille	1116		☐ Defer Layout Update Update	

Notice that a filter has appeared at the top left of the pivot table (in cells A1 and B1):

	A	B
1	Genre	(All) ▾

The filter currently shows all sales for all genres.

4 Use the report filter field to display sales for the *Comedy* genre.

1. Click the drop-down list arrow in cell B1.

2. Click *Comedy* in the drop-down list.

3. Click the OK button.

Notice that the *Sum of Qty* values now change to only show quantities sold in the *Comedy* genre.

5 Use a report filter field to show sales in the *Comedy* genre for June 2008.

1. Drag the *Order Date* field from the *PivotTable Field List* down to the *Report Filter List*.

▽ Report Filter	Column Labels
Genre ▾	
Order Date ▾	

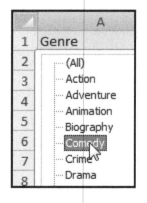

	A
1	Genre
2	⋯ (All)
3	⋯ Action
4	⋯ Adventure
	⋯ Animation
5	⋯ Biography
6	Comedy
7	⋯ Crime
8	⋯ Drama

Transactions-5

2.   Click the drop-down arrow in cell B2.

	A	B
1	Genre	Comedy
2	Order Date	(All)
3		

3.   Type **jun-08** into the *Search* box.

4.   (The search text is not case sensitive so exactly the same results would be displayed if you had typed JUN-08).

jun-08	×
01-Jun-08	
02-Jun-08	

The Search box is a brand new feature for Excel 2010 and filters the entries in the list to dates containing the text *jun-08*.

5.   Check the *Select Multiple Items* check box.

☑ Select Multiple Items

Every June 2008 date is now checked.

jun-08	×
☑ (Select All Search Results)	
☐ Add current selection to filter	
☑ 01-Jun-08	
☑ 02-Jun-08	

6.   Click the OK button.

7.   Only goods sold in the *Comedy* genre during *June 2008* are now displayed.

	A	B
1	Genre	Comedy
2	Order Date	(Multiple Items)
3		
4	**Row Labels**	Sum of Qty
5	West,Chuck	22
6	Silverstone,Gloria	22
7	Anderson,Jane	17
8	Sagan,Jessica	22
9	Putin,Julia	40
10	Spears,Julie	19
11	Ashe,Lucille	15
12	Streep,Margaret	8
13	Simpson,Meryl	9
14	Richards,Andy	24
15	Lee,Frank	6
16	Bradshaw,John	43
17	Bell,Stephen	37
18	**Grand Total**	**284**

Notice that the filter information in cell B2 *(Multiple Items)* gives no information to the user about the filter currently in place. In *Lesson 5-7: Filter a pivot table visually using slicers* you'll discover a much better way of showing the user which multiple item filters are currently active.

6   Save your work as *Transactions-6*.

Lesson 5-7: Filter a pivot table visually using slicers

Slicers are probably the most important new feature introduced in Excel 2010.

Unlike report filter fields, slicers show which filters are in place when a multiple-item filter is applied.

Slicers are also very useful for designing touch-screen user interfaces for tablet personal computers.

1   Open *2010 Transactions-1* from your sample files folder (if it isn't already open).

This workbook contains a single worksheet containing a table named *Data*. The table contains details of all sales during 2010.

2   Create a pivot table from the *Data* table.

1. Click anywhere in the data table.

2. Click: Insert→Tables→Pivot Table.

3. Click the OK button.

Choose fields to add to report:

- Order No
- Date
- Year
- Month
- Day
- Quarter
- Customer
- Employee
- Title
- ✓ **Genre**
- ✓ **Qty**
- ✓ **Total**

3   Display the *Total* and *Qty* values for each genre.

Click the check-boxes for *Genre, Qty* and *Total* in the *Pivot Table Field List*.

4   Change the number format for the values shown in column C to show two decimal places with a comma separator.

You learned how to do this in: *Lesson 5-1: Create a one dimensional pivot table report from a table*.

5   Change the number format for the values shown in column B to show no decimal places and a comma separator.

You learned how to do this in: *Lesson 5-1: Create a one dimensional pivot table report from a table*.

6   Change the text in cell A3 to *Genre*, in cell B3 to *Sales Qty* and in cell C3 to *Total Sales*.

Click in each cell and type the new text.

Your pivot table should now look like this:

	A	B	C
3	Genre	Sales Qty	Total Sales
4	Action	2,173	17,191.96
5	Adventure	464	3,508.95

7   Add slicers to filter by Genre and Customer.

In *Lesson 5-6: Use report filter fields*, you saw how this could be achieved using report filter fields. This time we'll implement the filter using a slicer.

1. Click anywhere in the pivot table to activate it.

2. Click: PivotTable Tools→Options→Insert Slicer.

2010 Transactions-1

The *Insert Slicers* dialog appears.

3. Check the *Genre* and *Customer* check boxes.

4. Click OK.

Two slicers appear on the worksheet.

8 **Move and Format the slicers so that they have an attractive appearance.**

1. Click on the *Genre* slicer to select it and then click and drag the border to move it next to the pivot table.

2. Click: Slicer Tools→Options→Buttons→Columns and type **5** into the text box.

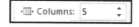

3. Re-size the slicer so that all genre names are visible.

4. Click: Slicer Tools→Options→Slicer Styles and select an attractive style.

5. Do the same for the *Customer* slicer, setting the *Columns* to 3.

Your worksheet should now look like this:

	A	B	C	D	E	F	G	H	I	J	K	L	M
3	**Genre**	▾ **Sales Qty**	**Total Sales**										
4	Action	2,173	17,191.96		Genre								🏷
5	Adventure	464	3,508.95										
6	Animation	242	2,151.44		Action		Adventure		Animation		Biography		Comedy
7	Biography	1,054	7,905.19		Crime		Drama		Fantasy		Sci Fi		Thriller
8	Comedy	2,793	22,485.98										
9	Crime	1,676	14,067.66										
10	Drama	5,308	41,990.25		Customer								🏷
11	Fantasy	501	4,819.98										
12	Sci Fi	380	2,801.34		Addison-Freelander Scr...		AV Supplies				Box Office Supplies		
13	Thriller	485	3,421.59		Cheapo Cheap DVD's Ltd		Cinefocus DVD				Classic Films		
14	**Grand Total**	**15,076**	**120,344.34**		Creative Films		Lights-Camera-Action Ltd				Magic Lantern Classic Fil...		
15					Silver Screen Video		Soft Focus Video Rental				Video Flicks International		
16													
17													

9 **Test the slicers.**

1. Click the *Action* button on the *Genre* slicer.

Notice that the pivot table filters to only show sales values for the *Action* genre.

Notice also that the *Action* button is highlighted on the *Genre* slicer and that three *Customer* buttons are dimmed. This is because there are no sales in the *Action* genre for those three customers.

2. Click the *Cinefocus DVD* button in the *Customer* slicer and then hold down the <Ctrl> key and click the *Classic Films* button.

Notice that only sales to the selected customers for the *Action* genre are now shown.

3. Clear the slicer filters by clicking the *Clear Filter* buttons in each slicer's top right corner.

10 **Save your work as** *2010 Transactions-2*.

note

Creating Years, Months, Days and Quarters from a date value

Year

The YEAR() function is covered in: *Lesson 3-8: Understand common date functions.*

Month as a string

The TEXT() function is covered in *Lesson 3-19: Use the TEXT function to format numerical values as strings.*

The custom format code "mmm" formats a date as a three character text value (such as Jan). The *Essential Skills* book in this series extensively covers the (rather cryptic) formatting codes available in Excel.

Day

The DAY() function is covered in: *Lesson 3-8: Understand common date functions.*

Quarter

1/ The Month is first returned as a number (1-12) using the MONTH() function (covered in: *Lesson 3-8: Understand common date functions*).

2/ The number of the month returned is then divided by three. For example May would return 5/3 = 2.666.

3/ The ROUNDUP function is used to round the number up to the nearest whole number. This returns the correct quarter (1-4).

The completed formula can be seen in the *Data* worksheet:

=ROUNDUP(
MONTH([@Date])/3,0)

Lesson 5-8: Use slicers to create a date-driven interface

A date-driven interface is one of the most impressive and useful implementations of Excel 2010's new slicer feature.

Before you can add a date-driven interface to a pivot table you will need to create fields in the underlying data table for *Year, Month, Day* and *Quarter*. This has already been done in the sample file for this session:

	B	C	D	E	F
1	Date	Year	Month	Day	Quarter
2	03-Jan-10	2010	Jan	3	1
3	02-Jan-10	2010	Jan	2	1

Before beginning this lesson you may find it useful to study the formulas used to create these fields from the *Date* field. If you do not understand how these formulas work, refer to the sidebar for more information.

1 Open *2010 Transactions-2 from* your sample files folder (if it isn't already open).

2 Add slicers to the pivot table for *Year, Quarter, Month* and *Day*.

You learned how to do this in: *Lesson 5-7: Filter a pivot table visually using slicers.*

3 Format the slicers so that they look the same as the screen grab at the bottom of the facing page.

You learned how to do this in: *Lesson 5-7: Filter a pivot table visually using slicers.*

Notice that a *Year* slicer has been included even though the underlying data only has a single year (2010).

When you use slicers to create a date-driven interface, it is good practice to always include a Year slicer because you can never be sure that more data will not be added to the underlying data table.

For example, if 2011 sales data were added to the table, selecting *Jan* would show sales for both Jan 2010 and Jan 2011 if the Year slicer was not included.

4 Use the slicers to show sales for the first two quarters of 2010 in the *Action, Animation and Comedy* genres.

1. Click the *1* button in the *Quarter* slicer and then hold down the <Ctrl> key and click the 2 button.

Quarter			
1	**2**	3	4

Notice that the months Jan-Jun are now selected in the *Month* slicer.

<u>OR</u>

2010 Transactions-2

Click the *Jan* button in the *Month* slicer and then hold down the **<Shift>** key and click the *Jun* button.

Month				𝕂
Jan	Feb	Mar	Apr	May
Jun	Jul	Aug	Sep	Oct
Nov	Dec			

Notice that the one and two buttons are now selected in the *Quarter* slicer

2. Click the *Action* button in the *Genre* slicer and then hold down the **<Ctrl>** key and click the *Animation* and *Comedy* buttons.

    Sales are now shown for the first two quarters of 2010 in the *Action, Comedy* and *Animation* genres.

	A	B	C	D	E	F	G	H	I	J	K	L	M
2													
3	**Genre** ⊤	**Sales Qty**	**Total Sales**		**Year** 𝕂		**Quarter** 𝕂						
4	Action	886	6,892.52		2010		1	2	3	4			
5	Animation	143	1,297.74										
6	Comedy	1,241	10,021.66										
7	**Grand Total**	**2,270**	**18,211.92**		**Month** 𝕂								

Month

Jan	Feb	Mar	Apr	May
Jun	Jul	Aug	Sep	Oct
Nov	Dec			

Day

1	2	3	4	5	6	7
8	9	10	11	12	13	14
15	16	17	18	19	20	21
22	23	24	25	26	27	28
29	30	31				

Genre

Action	Adventure	Animation	Biography	Comedy
Crime	Drama	Fantasy	Sci Fi	Thriller

Customer

Addison-Freelander Scr...	AV Supplies	Box Office Supplies
Cheapo Cheap DVD's Ltd	Cinefocus DVD	Classic Films
Creative Films	Lights-Camera-Action Ltd	Magic Lantern Classic Fil...
Silver Screen Video	Soft Focus Video Rental	Video Flicks International

5   Save your work as *2010 Transactions-3*.

Lesson 5-9: Use report filter fields to automatically create multiple pages

In this lesson, we cater for the following scenario:

You have been asked to print out a sales listing for each employee. This involves printing a total of 24 separate reports.

It is easy, but time consuming, to print each sheet manually. You would need to perform 24 filter and print operations. Surely there's a better way?

Of course there is. We can use a report filter to automate the whole task and print all 24 reports in one operation.

1 Open *Transactions-6* from your sample files folder (if it isn't already open).

2 Select the *Pivot Table* worksheet (if it isn't already selected).

3 Remove all filters.

There's a quick way to remove all filters from a pivot table.

1. Click inside the pivot table to activate it.

2. Click: PivotTable Tools→Options→Actions→Clear→ Clear Filters.

4 Change the fields displayed by the pivot table so that they match the following:

▽ Report Filter		▦ Column Labels	
Employee	▼	Σ Values	▼

▦ Row Labels		Σ Values	
Genre	▼	Sum of Qty	▼
		Sum of Total	▼

You learned to do this in: *Lesson 5-3: Understand pivot table rows and columns.* Note that the $\boxed{\Sigma\ \text{Values}}$ field automatically appears in the *Column Labels* list when you add more than one field to the *Values* list.

Your pivot table now looks like this:

	A	B	C
2	Employee	(All) ▼	
3			
4		**Values**	
5	Row Labels ▼	Sum of Qty	Sum of Total
6	Action	4699	37411.4
7	Adventure	1149	8588.03

5 Create separate worksheets detailing each employee's sales.

1. Click anywhere within the pivot table.

Transactions-6

2. Click: PivotTable Tools→Options→PivotTable→Options→
   Show Report Filter Pages…

The *Show Report Filter Pages* dialog appears.

Because there is only one report filter, there's only one choice.

If you had multiple report filters, you could choose which filter you wanted to use.

3. Click the OK button.

Something amazing happens!

24 worksheets are instantly created, one for each employee.

Here's Chuck West's sheet:

	A	B	C
1	Employee	West,Chuck ▼	
2			
3		**Values**	
4	**Row Labels** ▼	**Sum of Qty**	**Sum of Total**
5	Action	111	861.84
6	Adventure	5	44.77
7	Animation	76	677.02

You can see that it contains a copy of the original pivot table with a filter set for Chuck.

6 **Print preview all worksheets**.

1. Click on the first employee's tab (West, Chuck)

2. Hold down the **<Shift>** key.

3. Use the worksheet scroll bar buttons so that the last employee's tab (Armstrong, Dan) is visible.

4. Click on the last employee's tab (Armstrong, Dan).

   You have now selected all of the employee worksheets (you don't want to print the *Pivot Table* or *Data* worksheets).

5. Click: File→Print.

   Note that *Active Sheets* is selected by default.

   Note the preview pane. All employee sheets will be printed.

6. Click the *Home* tab to return to the worksheet.

7 **Save your work as** *Multiple Sheets-1.*

Lesson 5-10: Format a pivot table using PivotTable styles

In: *Lesson 1-9: Format a table using table styles and convert a table into a range,* you learned how to use a built-in style to format an Excel table. PivotTable styles are used in a similar way.

1 Open *Transactions-6* from your sample files folder.

2 Remove all existing fields from the pivot table.

A fast way to do this is to drag each field from the field selection panes to the field list above:

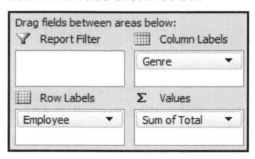

3 Select the fields shown below.

4 Filter to only show the genres: *Action, Adventure* and *Animation* for employees: *Chuck West, Julie Spears* and *Dan Armstrong.*

You learned how to do this in: *Lesson 5-5: Apply a simple filter and sort to a pivot table.*

	A	B	C	D	E
4	Sum of Total	Column Labels			
5	Row Labels	Action	Adventure	Animation	Grand Total
6	West,Chuck	861.84	44.77	677.02	1583.63
7	Spears,Julie	1032.11	284.58	109.37	1426.06
8	Armstrong,Dan	1199.7	195.56	218.1	1613.36
9	Grand Total	3093.65	524.91	1004.49	4623.05

Transactions-6

5   Apply the PivotTable style: *Dark 9.*

Click: PivotTable Tools→Design→PivotTable Styles→
Dark→Pivot Style Dark 9.

	A	B	C	D	E
4	Sum of Total	Column Labels			
5	Row Labels	Action	Adventure	Animation	Grand Total
6	West,Chuck	861.84	44.77	677.02	1583.63
7	Spears,Julie	1032.11	284.58	109.37	1426.06
8	Armstrong,Dan	1199.7	195.56	218.1	1613.36
9	Grand Total	3093.65	524.91	1004.49	4623.05

6   Enable *Banded Rows* and *Banded Columns.*

1. Check: PivotTable Tools→Design→PivotTable Style Options→
    Banded Rows.

2. Check: PivotTable Tools→Design→PivotTable Style Options→
    Banded Columns.

The pivot table changes to show colored lines separating each
row and column.

	A	B	C	D	E
4	Sum of Total	Column Labels			
5	Row Labels	Action	Adventure	Animation	Grand Total
6	West,Chuck	861.84	44.77	677.02	1583.63
7	Spears,Julie	1032.11	284.58	109.37	1426.06
8	Armstrong,Dan	1199.7	195.56	218.1	1613.36
9	Grand Total	3093.65	524.91	1004.49	4623.05

The other two options in the *PivotTable Style* options group are:
Row Headers and *Column Headers.*

In the *Dark 9* style, the column headers are shown in a
contrasting color. The *Column Headers* check box allows you to
switch this color off.

Some of the other designs also show row headers (cells A6:A8)
in a contrasting color. If you were using this type of design,
you could switch this colour off with the *Row Headers* check
box.

7   Save your work as *Transactions-7.*

Lesson 5-11: Create a custom PivotTable style

In: *Lesson 1-10: Create a custom table style,* you learned how to create a custom style for an Excel table. PivotTable custom styles are applied in a similar way.

1 Open *Transactions-7* from your sample files folder (if it isn't already open).

2 Remove the existing style.

    1. Click the pivot table to activate it.

    2. Click: PivotTable Tools→Design→PivotTable Styles→ Light→None.

    Notice that this style is different from the default style. The default pivot table style is *Light 16*.

3 Create a custom pivot table style called *Corporate* by duplicating the *Medium8* built in style.

    You'll usually find that modifying a duplicate of an existing style is easier than creating a style from scratch.

    1. Right-click on:

    PivotTable Tools→Design→PivotTable Styles→ Medium→Pivot Style Medium 8.

    2. Click *Duplicate…* from the shortcut menu.

    The *Modify Pivot Table Quick Style* dialog appears.

Transactions-7

Notice that some of the Table Elements are shown in bold face. These are the elements that have had formatting applied to them:

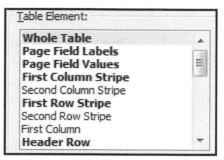

3.   Type the name **Corporate** into the *Name* text box.

4.   Click the OK button to dismiss the dialog.

4   Apply the new *Corporate* style to the pivot table.

Click: PivotTable Tools→Design→PivotTable Styles→ Custom→Corporate.

5   Modify the *Corporate* style so that it shows the *Grand Total* column in boldface.

1.   Right-click on:

PivotTable Tools→Design→PivotTable Styles→ Custom→Corporate.

2.   Click *Modify…* from the shortcut menu.

3.   Select *Grand Total Column* from the *Table Element* list.

4.   Click the *Format* button.

5.   Select the *Font* tab.

6.   Select the *Font style:* Bold.

7.   Click the OK button.

8.   Click the OK button again.

The Grand Total column is now shown in bold face.

	A	B	C	D	E
4	Sum of Total	Column Labels ▼			
5	Row Labels ▼	Action	Adventure	Animation	Grand Total
6	West,Chuck	861.84	44.77	677.02	**1583.63**
7	Spears,Julie	1032.11	284.58	109.37	**1426.06**
8	Armstrong,Dan	1199.7	195.56	218.1	**1613.36**
9	**Grand Total**	3093.65	524.91	1004.49	**4623.05**

6   Save your work as *Transactions-8*.

Lesson 5-12: Understand pivot table report layouts

1 Open *Transactions-8* from your sample files folder (if it isn't already open).

2 Remove all existing fields from the pivot table by dragging them up into the *PivotTable Field List*.

It's important to realize that when you drag a field back to the PivotTable Field List, you do not clear any filter conditions associated with the field. You can still see the filter icon next to each filtered field (see sidebar).

3 Select the fields shown below.

You learned how to do this in: *Lesson 5-3: Understand pivot table rows and columns*.

4 Expand the *Employee* field to also display *Genres*.

You learned how to do this in: *Lesson 5-2: Create a grouped pivot table report*.

The pivot table is shown in *compact form layout*. This is the default layout.

	A	B
4	Row Labels	Sum of Total
5	⊟West,Chuck	1583.63
6	Action	861.84
7	Adventure	44.77
8	Animation	677.02
9	⊟Spears,Julie	1426.06
10	Action	1032.11

This layout is useful when you need the report to take up the minimum amount of space on screen or paper.

Subsidiary fields are only slightly indented from their parent field.

Transactions-8

5 Change the report layout to *Outline Form.*

Click:

PivotTable Tools→Design→Layout→
Report Layout→Show in Outline Form

	A	B	C
4	Employee 🔽	Genre 🔽	Sum of Total
5	⊟West,Chuck		1583.63
6		Action	861.84
7		Adventure	44.77
8		Animation	677.02
9	⊟Spears,Julie		1426.06
10		Action	1032.11

Outline Form is the classic pivot table layout that was the default in pre-2007 versions of Excel.

It takes up more space but is more readable as each field has its own column label.

6 Change the report layout to *Tabular Form.*

Click:

PivotTable Tools→Design→Layout→
Report Layout→Show in Tabular Form

	A	B	C
4	Employee 🔽	Genre 🔽	Sum of Total
5	⊟West,Chuck	Action	861.84
6		Adventure	44.77
7		Animation	677.02
8	West,Chuck Total		1583.63
9	⊟Spears,Julie	Action	1032.11
10		Adventure	284.58
11		Animation	109.37
12	Spears,Julie Total		1426.06
13	⊟Armstrong,Dan	Action	1199.7
14		Adventure	195.56
15		Animation	218.1
16	Armstrong,Dan Total		1613.36
17	Grand Total		4623.05

This layout is very easy to read because it is similar to a regular Excel table with totals shown at the bottom of each column.

7 Save your work as *Transactions-9.*

Lesson 5-13: Add/remove subtotals and apply formatting to pivot table fields

1 Open *Transactions-9 from* your sample files folder (if it isn't already open).

2 Apply a Filter to show only the *Biography* and *Thriller* genres.

You learned to do this in: *Lesson 5-5: Apply a simple filter and sort to a pivot table.*

3 Add the *Title* field to the pivot table as a third-level row label.

Drag the *Title* field from the *PivotTable Field List* to the *Row Labels* list.

▼ Report Filter	▦ Column Labels

▦ Row Labels	Σ Values
Employee ▼	Sum of Total ▼
Genre ▼	
Title ▼	

4 Expand all of the *Genre* fields to show all *Titles*.

You learned to do this in: *Lesson 5-2: Create a grouped pivot table report.*

Because the pivot table layout is set to *Tabular Form,* subtotals are displayed by all subsidiary groups. Both *Employee* and *Genre* are showing subtotals.

	A	B	C	D
4	**Employee** ▼	**Genre** ▼	**Title** ▼	**Sum of Total**
5	⊟**West,Chuck**	⊟**Biography**	Goodfellas	99.27
6			Lawrence of Arabia	87.68
7			Raging Bull	236.49
8			Schindler's List	333.37
9		**Biography Total**		756.81
10		⊟**Thriller**	Chinatown	35.67
11			Psycho	196.41
12		**Thriller Total**		232.08
13	**West,Chuck Total**			988.89
14	⊟**Spears,Julie**	⊟**Biography**	Bonnie and Clyde	58.2

5 Format the *Genre subtotal* fields using the *Total* cell style.

1. Hover the mouse cursor over the left edge of the *Biography Total* label in cell B9.

2. Make sure you see the black arrow cursor shape and then click to select.

Transactions-9

	A	B	
9		→Biography Total	
10		⊟ Thriller	Chin

Notice that when you select the field all *Genre subtotal* cells are selected.

3. Click: Home→Styles→Cell Styles→Total.

4. The *Total* style is applied to all *Genre subtotal* fields.

	A	B	C	D
4	Employee	Genre	Title	Sum of Total
5	⊟ West,Chuck	⊟ Biography	Goodfellas	99.27
6			Lawrence of Arabia	87.68
7			Raging Bull	236.49
8			Schindler's List	333.37
9		Biography Total		756.81
10		⊟ Thriller	Chinatown	35.67
11			Psycho	196.41
12		Thriller Total		232.08
13	West,Chuck Total			988.89
14	⊟ Spears,Julie	⊟ Biography	Bonnie and Clyde	58.2

6   Remove *Genre* subtotals.

1. Right-click any of the Genres in column B.

2. Click Subtotal "Genre" on the shortcut menu.

⿻	Copy
☝	Format Cells...
⿻	Refresh
	Sort ▶
	Filter ▶
√	Subtotal "Genre"
	Expand/Collapse ▶

The *Genre* subtotal fields are removed.

7   Remove the *Grand Total.*

1. Click: PivotTable Tools→Design→Layout→Grand Totals.

2. Select *Off for Rows and Columns.*

8   Save your work as *Transactions-10.*

Lesson 5-14: Display multiple summations within a single pivot table

It is possible to show the same *Value* field many times in the same pivot table.

This is useful when you need to display different summations (such as Average, Sum and Total) on a single pivot table.

1   Open *Transactions-10 from* your sample files folder (if it isn't already open).

2   Remove the *Genre* and *Title* fields from the *Row Labels* list.

3   Add two more *Total* fields to the *Values* list.

> | ⧩ Report Filter | ⧎ Column Labels |
> |---|---|
> | | Σ Values ▼ |
> | ⧎ Row Labels | Σ Values |
> | Employee ▼ | Sum of Total ▼ |
> | | Sum of Total2 ▼ |
> | | Sum of Total3 ▼ |

4   Change the new totals to show *Average* sales and *Maximum* sales for each employee.

     1.   Right-click anywhere in column C within the pivot table.

     2.   Click *Value Field Settings…* on the shortcut menu.

     3.   Select *Average* in the *Summarize value field by* list.

> **Value Field Settings**   ？ ✕
>
> Source Name: Total
>
> Custom Name: Average of Total2
>
> Summarize by   Show values as
>
> **Summarize value field by**
>
> Choose the type of calculation that you want to use to summarize the data from selected field
>
> Sum
> Count
> Average
> Max
> Min
> Product
>
> Number Format   OK   Cancel

     4.   Click the OK button.

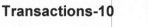

Transactions-10

5. Use the same technique to make the *Sum of Total3* field display the maximum (*Max*) value.

	A	B	C	D
4		Values		
5	Employee	Sum of Total	Average of Total2	Max of Total3
6	West,Chuck	6847.74	96.44704225	239.05
7	Spears,Julie	10683.14	99.84242991	243.85
8	Armstrong,Dan	7880.51	96.10378049	248.73

5 Format the *Average of Total2* field so that it displays two decimal places.

1. Right-click on any value in column C within the pivot table.

2. Click *Number Format…* on the shortcut menu.

3. Select the *Number* category with two decimal places.

```
Number

Category:
General          Sample
Number
Currency
Accounting       Decimal places:  2
Date
```

4. Click the OK button.

	A	B	C	D
4		Values		
5	Employee	Sum of Total	Average of Total2	Max of Total3
6	West,Chuck	6847.74	96.45	239.05
7	Spears,Julie	10683.14	99.84	243.85
8	Armstrong,Dan	7880.51	96.10	248.73

6 Add a *Grand Total*.

Click: PivotTable Tools→Design→Layout→ Grand Totals→On for Rows and Columns.

	A	B	C	D
4		Values		
5	Employee	Sum of Total	Average of Total2	Max of Total3
6	West,Chuck	6847.74	96.45	239.05
7	Spears,Julie	10683.14	99.84	243.85
8	Armstrong,Dan	7880.51	96.10	248.73
9	**Grand Total**	**25411.39**	**97.74**	**248.73**

7 Save your work as *Transactions-11*.

note

Switching grand totals on and off with the right-click method

In this lesson, you used the Ribbon to enable or disable the *Grand Total*.

It is also possible to do this faster using the following right-click method:

1. Right click anywhere within the pivot table.

2. Click *PivotTable Options...* from the shortcut menu.

3. Click the *Totals & Filters* tab.

4. Click one, or both of the *Grand Totals* check boxes to enable/disable.

```
Grand Totals
  ☑ Show grand totals for rows
  ☑ Show grand totals for columns
```

Lesson 5-15: Add a calculated field to a pivot table

1   Open *Transactions-11* from your sample files folder (if it isn't already open).

2   Remove the *Average of Total2* and *Max of Total3 Fields*.

You learned how to do this in: *Lesson 5-3: Understand pivot table rows and columns*.

	A	B
4	Employee	Sum of Total
5	West,Chuck	6847.74
6	Spears,Julie	10683.14
7	Armstrong,Dan	7880.51
8	Grand Total	25411.39

3   Format the *Sum of Total* field to show a comma thousand separator.

1.   Right-click any of the values in column B within the pivot table.

2.   Click *Number Format…* on the shortcut menu.

3.   Click the *Number* category.

4.   Check the *Use 1000 Separator (,)* check box.

5.   Click OK.

4   Add a calculated field called *Bonus* that will calculate 3% of total sales.

1.   Click: PivotTable Tools→Options→Calculations→ Fields, Items & Sets→Calculated Field…

2.   Type **Bonus** in the *Name* text box.

Insert Calculated Field	
Name:	Bonus

3.   Click in the *Formula* text box and remove the zero, leaving only an = sign.

Formula:	=

4.   Select *Total* in the *Fields* list and then click the *Insert Field* button.

5.   The word **Total** is added to the Formula.

Formula:	= Total

6.   Type *3% to complete the formula.

Formula:	= Total*3%

7. Click the OK button.

A new field called *Bonus* has now appeared in the *PivotTable Field List* and a *Sum of Bonus* field has appeared in column C.

	A	B	C
4		Values	
5	Employee	Sum of Total	Sum of Bonus
6	West,Chuck	6,847.74	205.43
7	Spears,Julie	10,683.14	320.49
8	Armstrong,Dan	7,880.51	236.42
9	**Grand Total**	**25,411.39**	**762.34**

5 Change the names at the top of columns B and C to *Sales* and *Bonus Due*.

1. Click cell B5.

2. Type the new name **Sales**.

3. Press the **<Enter>** key.

4. Use the same technique to change the name in cell C5 to *Bonus Due.*

6 Remove the *Field Header* (this is currently shown in row 4).

Click: PivotTable Tools→Options→Show→Field Headers.

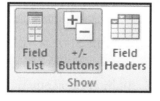

The three items in the Show group are toggle buttons allowing you to add and remove different pivot table artefacts.

The pivot table is now well formatted.

	A	B	C
3			
4		Sales	Bonus Due
5	West,Chuck	6,847.74	205.43
6	Spears,Julie	10,683.14	320.49
7	Armstrong,Dan	7,880.51	236.42
8	**Grand Total**	**25,411.39**	**762.34**

The *Values* label has disappeared but so has the *Employee* label. If you wanted to keep the *Employee* label you would have had to hide row 4 instead (see sidebar).

7 Save your work as *Transactions-12*.

---

tip

Hiding pivot table rows

In this lesson, we switched off the field headers in order to suppress the *Values* label in cell B4.

This had the side-effect of also removing the word *Employee* from cell A5.

	A	B
3		
4		Sales
5	West,Chuck	6,847.74

If you wanted to keep the *Employee* label but suppress the *Value* label you would need to hide row 4.

To hide the row, right-click the row header (the number 4 on the left of the row) and then click *Hide* from the shortcut menu.

	A	B
3		
5	Employee	Sales
6	West,Chuck	6,847.74
7	Spears,Julie	10,683.14
8	Armstrong,Dan	7,880.51
9	**Grand Total**	**25,411.39**

Lesson 5-16: Add a calculated item to a pivot table

One *field* will usually consist of several *items*. For example, the *Genre* field consists of items such as *Drama, Comedy, Action, Biography* etc.

If you wanted to show a sales target of **Sales + 10%**, you'd simply create a calculated field (as described in: *Lesson 5-15: Add a calculated field to a pivot table*).

Sometimes, you will want to perform a calculation upon a selected number of items within a field. In this lesson's example, you are interested in total sales for the *Drama, Comedy* and *Action* genres, as they are your top sellers.

Calculated items provide a solution to this problem. In this lesson, we'll add a calculated item to find the total sales in these genres.

1   Open *Transactions-12* from your sample files folder (if it isn't already open).

2   Clear all filters from the pivot table.

Click: PivotTable Tools→Options→Actions→Clear→Clear Filters.

3   Remove all of the existing fields from the pivot table and replace them with the following:

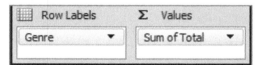

4   Format the *Sum of Total* to show two decimal places with a thousand comma separator.

1.   Right-click on any of the values in column B within the pivot table.

2.   Click *Number Format…* on the shortcut menu.

3.   Click the *Number* category.

4.   Check the *Use 1000 Separator (,)* check box.

5.   Click OK.

Your pivot table now looks like the one shown in the sidebar.

5   Add a calculated item to show total sales for the genres: *Drama, Comedy and Action.*

1.   Click any pivot table cell in column A.

2.   Click: PivotTable Tools→Calculations→Fields, Items & Sets→ Calculated Item…

The *Insert Calculated Item* dialog appears.

This is very similar to the *Insert Calculated Field* dialog. The dialog is confusing because it shows many fields and items that would not be valid for the *Genre* field. They are not grayed out as you would expect.

	A	B
4		**Sum of Total**
5	Action	37,411.40
6	Adventure	8,588.03
7	Animation	5,098.87
8	Biography	17,174.78
9	Comedy	37,614.16
10	Crime	25,212.68
11	Drama	67,097.47
12	Fantasy	11,785.28
13	Sci Fi	7,289.18
14	Thriller	5,514.95
15	**Grand Total**	222,786.80

Transactions-12

3. Name the calculated item: **Drama, Comedy & Action.**

Name: Drama, Comedy & Action

4. Select the *Genre* field and the *Drama* item and then click the *Insert Item* button.

   The formula changes to include the *Drama* item.

Formula: =Drama

5. Type a + operator into the formula.

Formula: =Drama+

6. Add the *Comedy* and *Action* items in the same way so that your formula is the same as the following:

Formula: =Drama+Comedy+Action

7. Click the OK button.

   A total for *Drama, Comedy & Action* appears at the bottom of the pivot table.

	A	B
14	Thriller	5,514.95
15	Drama, Comedy & Action	142,123.03
16	**Grand Total**	**364,909.83**

Notice that this addition has corrupted the *Grand Total* as *Drama, Comedy and Action* are included in the *Grand Total* twice.

6   Filter the individual *Drama*, *Comedy* and *Action* fields so that they are no longer shown or included in the *Grand Total*.

Because the *Field Headers* are currently switched off, you cannot apply a filter.

1. Click: PivotTable Tools→Options→Show→Field Headers.

2. The *Genre* field header appears in cell A4.

	A	B
4	Genre ▼	Sum of Total
5	Action	37,411.40

3. Click the drop-down arrow to the right of cell A4.

4. Remove the individual *Drama*, *Comedy* and *Action* items by un-checking their check boxes.

☐ (Select All)
☐ Action
☑ Adventure
☑ Animation
☑ Biography
☐ Comedy
☑ Crime
☐ Drama
☑ Fantasy
☑ Sci Fi
☑ Thriller
☑ Drama, Comedy & Action

5. The *Grand Total* is now correct.

	A	B
11	Thriller	5,514.95
12	Drama, Comedy & Action	142,123.03
13	**Grand Total**	**222,786.80**

7   Save your work as *Transactions-13*.

Lesson 5-17: Group by text

In *Lesson 5-16: Add a calculated item to a pivot table,* we used a calculated item to show a group total for the *Action, Comedy* & *Drama* genres.

Another solution to this problem would be to create a *group* for these three genres. The pivot table could then show group totals.

We'll push things a little further, in this lesson, by placing each of the genres into three groups:

- Action, Comedy & Drama
- Crime, Biography & Fantasy
- Adventure, Sci Fi, Thriller & Animation

1   Open *Transactions-13* from your sample files folder (if it isn't already open).

2   Remove all of the existing fields and filters from the pivot table (including the calculated item added in the last lesson).

You'll often want to remove all fields and filters from your pivot table to start again. To do this, click:

PivotTable Tools→Options→Actions→Clear→Clear All

3   Add the following fields to the pivot table.

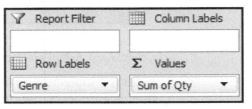

4   Format the *Sum of Qty* field so that it shows 0 decimal places and a comma separator for thousands.

1.   Right-click anywhere in column B within the pivot table.

2.   Click *Number Format…* on the shortcut menu.

3.   Click the *Number* category.

4.   Select the *Number* category and set 0 decimal places with a thousand separator.

> Decimal places: 0
> ☑ Use 1000 Separator (,)

5.   Click the OK button.

5   Add a group for the *Action, Comedy* and *Drama* genres.

1.   Click on the *Drama* field in column A (cell A11).

2.   Hold down the **<Ctrl>** key and then click on the *Comedy* (A9) and *Action* (A5) fields in column A.

Cells A11, A9 and A5 are now selected.

3.   Right-click on any of the selected fields and click *Group* in the shortcut menu.

Transactions-13

The fields are grouped:

	A	B	C
4	Genre2 ▼	Genre ▼	Sum of Qty
5	⊟ Group1	Action	4,699
6		Comedy	4,747

6 Change the *Genre2* label to *Category* and the *Group1* label to *Action, Comedy & Drama*.

The default names are not very descriptive. Single-click (be careful not to double-click) on each field (cells A4 and A5) and then type in the new labels.

	A	B	C
4	Category ▼	Genre ▼	Sum of Qty
5	⊟ Action, Comedy & Drama	Action	4699
6		Comedy	4747

7 Create the *Crime, Biography & Fantasy* group and the *Adventure, Sci Fi, Thriller & Animation* group.

Do this in exactly the same way. (This time you will select the *Genres* in column B).

8 AutoSize column A and collapse all categories.

This was covered in: *Lesson 5-2: Create a grouped pivot table report.*

Your pivot table should now look like this:

	A	B	C
4	Category ▼	Genre ▼	Sum of Qty
5	⊞ Action, Comedy & Drama		17,885
6	⊞ Adventure, Sci-Fi, Thriller & Animation		3,477
7	⊞ Crime, Biography & Fantasy		6,441
8	Grand Total		27,803

9 Add subtotals for each group.

1. Right-click anywhere in column A within the pivot table.

2. Click *Field Settings* from the shortcut menu.

   The *Field Settings* dialog appears.

3. Click the *Automatic* option button in the *Subtotals* section.

4. Click OK.

5. Expand the category groups.

   Subtotals are shown for each defined group.

	A	B	C
4	Category ▼	Genre ▼	Sum of Qty
5	⊟ Action, Comedy & Drama	Action	4,699
6		Comedy	4,747
7		Drama	8,439
8	Action, Comedy & Drama Total		17,885
9	⊟ Crime, Biography & Fantasy	Adventure	1,149

Subtotals

◉ Automatic
○ None
○ Custom

10 Save your work as *Transactions-14.*

Lesson 5-18: Group by date

Out of all of the skills covered in my classroom *Expert Skills* course, this is surely the star of the show.

Excel's ability to summarize transactional data by monthly totals is extremely difficult to achieve without a pivot table.

In previous versions of Excel, this feature was so well hidden that most Excel users didn't even know it was there. Things are a little better with the new Ribbon interface.

1   Open *Transactions-14* from your sample files folder (if it isn't already open).

2   Remove all of the existing fields from the pivot table.

You'll often want to remove all fields and filters from your pivot table to start again. To do this, click:

PivotTable Tools→Options→Actions→Clear→Clear All

3   Add the following fields to the pivot table.

▽ Report Filter	▦ Column Labels
	Order Date ▼
▦ Row Labels	Σ Values
Employee ▼	Sum of Total ▼

Sales are now shown for every employee and for every date.

	A	B	C	D
4	Sum of Total	Order Date ▼		
5	Employee ▼	01-Oct-07	02-Oct-07	03-Oct-07
6	West,Chuck			
7	Newhart,Anna			308.11
8	Diamond,Elizabeth		363.65	

Sales are summarized by day but it is more likely that you will want to show sales by week, month, quarter or year.

4   Show monthly sales for each employee.

   1.   Right-click on any of the dates in row 5.

   2.   Click *Group* on the shortcut menu.

        The *Grouping* dialog appears.

   3.   Select *Months* and *Years*.

        When you group by months, be very careful that you also group by years. If you don't, you'll get October 2007, 2008 and 2009 grouped into a single total!

Seconds
Minutes
Hours
Days
Months
Quarters
Years

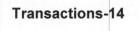

Transactions-14

4.   Click the OK button.

The pivot table is now grouped by year and by month.

	A	B	C	D	E
4	Sales				
5		⊟ 2007			⊟ 2008
6		Oct	Nov	Dec	Jan
7	West,Chuck	433.24	86.12	706.73	77.16
8	Newhart,Anna	308.11	121.95	351.70	515.33
9	Diamond,Elizabeth	363.65	123.67	736.27	827.05

5   Collapse the pivot table to show sales by year.

1.   Right-click cell B5 to display the shortcut menu for the *Years* field.

2.   Click: Expand/Collapse→Collapse Entire Field.

Sales are now shown by year.

	A	B	C	D	E
4	Sales				
5		⊞ 2007	⊞ 2008	⊞ 2009	Grand Total
6					
7	West,Chuck	1,226.09	3,745.62	1,876.03	**6,847.74**
8	Newhart,Anna	781.76	7,994.02	161.88	**8,937.66**
9	Diamond,Elizabeth	1,223.59	5,561.00	2,180.70	**8,965.29**

6   Expand the pivot table to show sales by month and year.

1.   Right-click cell B5 to display the shortcut menu for the *Years* field.

2.   Click: Expand/Collapse→Expand Entire Field.

Sales are now shown by month and year.

7   Apply a filter to show sales for Jan, Feb and Mar 2009.

1.   Select cells Q5:S6.

Make sure that you include the year (Q5) otherwise you'll see sales for Jan/Feb/Mar 2008 and 2009.

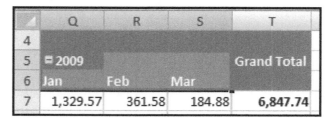

2.   Right-click the selected cells.

3.   Click: Filter→Keep Only Selected Items on the shortcut menu.

4.   Scroll the screen left so that you can see column A.

8   Save your work as *Transactions-15*.

Lesson 5-19: Group by numeric value ranges

1 Open *Employee Age Profile-1* from your sample files folder.

2 Convert the range A3:C27 into a table named **Data**.

In Excel 2010, it is best practice to base pivot tables upon tables (we would have used a named range in pre 2007 Excel versions).

1. Click anywhere in the range A3:C27.

2. Click: Insert→Tables→Table.

3. Click OK.

4. Type the name **Data** into:

   Table Tools→Design→Properties→Table Name

3 Create a pivot table from the Data table.

1. Click anywhere inside the table.

2. Click: Insert→Tables→PivotTable.

3. Click OK.

4 Add the following fields to the pivot table:

▼ Report Filter	⊞ Column Labels
⊞ Row Labels	Σ Values
Age ▼	
Name ▼	

(The order is important. *Age* must come before *Name*).

The pivot table now groups employees by age.

	A
23	⊟ **40**
24	Frank Lee
25	⊟ **44**
26	Charles Davis
27	Lucille Ashe

Where two or more employees are of the same age, they are grouped together.

The challenge for this lesson will be to group employees into different age bands.

5 Group the pivot table into the age bands: *Under 25, 25-34, 35-45* and *Over 45*.

1. Right-click any of the ages in column A (for example: cell A6).

2. Click *Group* from the shortcut menu.

Employee Age Profile-1

The *Grouping* dialog is displayed.

3. Type the following values into the dialog:

Grouping	?	✕
Auto		
☐ Starting at:	25	
☐ Ending at:	45	
By:	10	
	OK	Cancel

This tells Excel to group into the ages:

-   Less than 25
-   Between 25 and 45 in bands of 10 years
-   Over 45

4. Click the OK button.

Ages are now grouped as defined:

	A
3	**Row Labels** ▾
4	⊟ **<25**
5	Alfred Hawking
6	Elizabeth Diamond
7	Jane Anderson
8	Julie Spears
9	Meryl Simpson
10	⊟ **25-34**
11	Howard Simpson

When data is grouped in this way it is sometimes referred to as a frequency distribution.

6 Change the *Row Labels* label in cell A3 to *Age Group*.

1. Click once on cell A3.

2. Type **Age Group** into the cell.

	A
3	**Age Group**|
4	⊟ **<25**
5	Alfred Hawking

3. Press the **<Enter>** key.

7 Save your work as *Employee Age Profile-2*.

	A
3	**Age Group**
4	⊟ **<25**
5	Alfred Hawking
6	Elizabeth Diamond
7	Jane Anderson
8	Julie Spears
9	Meryl Simpson
10	⊟ **25-34**
11	Howard Simpson
12	Jessica Sagan
13	Julia Putin
14	Stephen Bell
15	⊟ **35-45**
16	Charles Davis
17	Dan Armstrong
18	Frank Lee
19	Julia Carrey
20	Lucille Ashe
21	Margaret Streep
22	Paul Goodman
23	⊟ **>45**
24	Andy Richards
25	Anna Newhart
26	Chuck West
27	Gloria Silverstone
28	John Bradshaw
29	John Jennings
30	Marilyn Manning
31	Michael Hicks
32	**Grand Total**

Lesson 5-20: Show row data by percentage of total rather than value

In this lesson, we will discover which genres each employee is best at selling. This will enable the company to allocate sales leads for each genre to the most competent salesperson in that genre.

This time we're not interested in total sales but the percentage sales by genre for each employee.

As a bonus, we'll see the percentage market share of each genre.

1 Open *Transactions-15* from your sample files folder (if it isn't already open).

2 Remove all of the existing fields and filters from the pivot table.

You'll often want to remove all fields and filters from your pivot table to start again. To do this, click:

PivotTable Tools→Options→Actions→Clear→Clear All

3 Add the following fields to the pivot table.

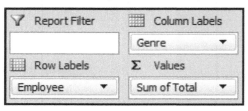

4 Format the *Sum of Total* field to show two decimal places and thousand separators.

This was covered in: *Lesson 5-17: Group by text.*

Sales are now shown for every employee and for every genre.

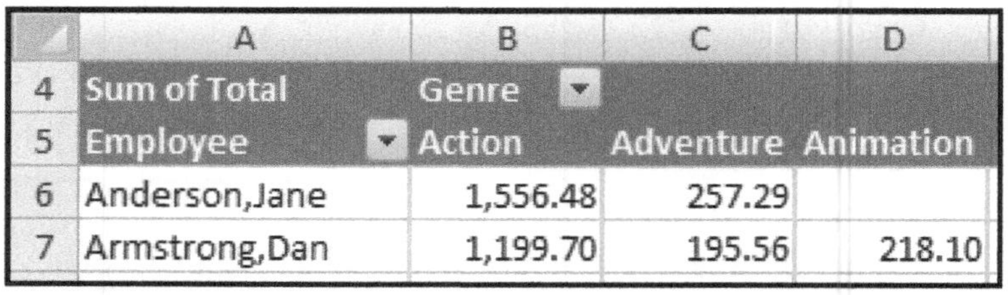

	A	B	C	D
4	Sum of Total	Genre ▼		
5	Employee ▼	Action	Adventure	Animation
6	Anderson,Jane	1,556.48	257.29	
7	Armstrong,Dan	1,199.70	195.56	218.10

5 Show sales values as a percentage of each row total.

1. Right-click on any of the numerical values in the pivot table.

2. Click *Value Field settings* in the shortcut menu.

The *Value Field Settings* dialog is displayed.

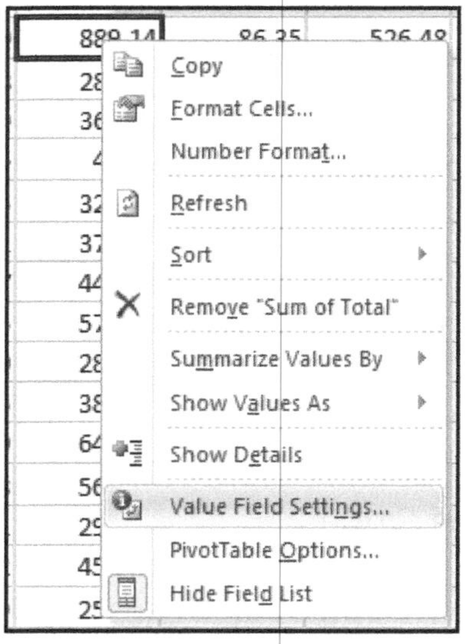

Context menu (left margin):

- Copy
- Format Cells...
- Number Format...
- Refresh
- Sort ▶
- X Remove "Sum of Total"
- Summarize Values By ▶
- Show Values As ▶
- Show Details
- Value Field Settings...
- PivotTable Options...
- Hide Field List

Transactions-15

3. Click the *Show values as* tab.

4. Select *% of Row Total* in the *Show values as* drop down list.

5. Click the OK button.

    Values are now shown as a percentage of each employee's sales:

5	Employee	Action	Adventure	Animation	Biography	Comedy	Crime	Drama	Fantasy	Sci Fi
14	Goodman,Paul	14.57%	3.94%	0.98%	7.17%	15.31%	7.75%	40.02%	4.26%	1.55%
15	Hawking,Alfred	25.86%	4.03%	2.38%	4.57%	16.36%	9.44%	29.77%	2.66%	4.71%
16	Hicks,Michael	12.18%	8.07%	0.00%	9.71%	16.53%	14.92%	31.40%	5.83%	0.00%
17	Jennings,John	16.77%	2.55%	1.76%	4.93%	14.76%	16.04%	31.26%	6.15%	3.35%
18	Lee,Frank	14.50%	2.83%	0.00%	9.12%	19.30%	9.45%	31.79%	9.46%	1.98%
19	Manning,Marilyn	13.37%	7.09%	1.02%	12.65%	15.28%	12.47%	30.31%	3.18%	4.64%
20	Newhart,Anna	16.43%	6.29%	2.81%	3.76%	16.41%	11.90%	23.36%	6.70%	8.56%
21	Putin,Julia	11.78%	3.39%	0.00%	3.48%	25.05%	9.91%	38.17%	4.34%	2.19%
22	Richards,Andy	11.76%	5.50%	0.90%	9.88%	19.06%	17.14%	22.99%	5.47%	3.67%
23	Sagan,Jessica	24.79%	2.32%	7.58%	3.31%	23.17%	4.24%	28.64%	1.90%	3.77%
24	Silverstone,Gloria	21.40%	3.56%	1.02%	9.23%	8.15%	7.86%	23.46%	11.18%	2.98%
25	Simpson,Howard	19.86%	4.61%	1.96%	4.16%	10.04%	10.65%	32.38%	8.44%	4.25%
26	Simpson,Meryl	15.52%	4.01%	3.50%	6.30%	13.78%	6.88%	37.61%	3.41%	5.72%
27	Spears,Julie	9.66%	2.66%	1.02%	11.43%	17.98%	17.54%	32.40%	5.23%	0.00%

You can see at a glance that *Alfred Hawking* does very well with sales in the *Action* genre, and that *Paul Goodman* is our star performer in the *Drama* genre.

We should keep *Michael Hicks* and *Julie Spears* away from *Science Fiction* sales!

6   Save your work as *Transactions-16*.

Lesson 5-21: Create a pivot chart from a pivot table

Excel is one of the world's most powerful charting tools. Every aspect of charting is covered in the *Essential Skills* book in this series, where a whole session (21 lessons) covers everything there is to know about Excel charts.

This *Expert Skills* book assumes that you already understand normal Excel charts.

When you create a pivot chart from a pivot table, it is important to realize that the chart always matches the data shown in the pivot table. You make changes to the source data of the chart by modifying the pivot table underpinning it.

1 Open *Transactions-16* from your sample files folder (if it isn't already open).

2 Change the *Sum of Total* field so that it displays cash values rather than a percentage of the total.

    1. Right-click on any of the percentage values in the pivot table.

    2. Click *Value Field settings* in the shortcut menu.

        The *Value Field Settings* dialog is displayed.

    3. Click the *Show values as* tab.

    4. Select *No Calculation* from the drop-down list.

    5. Click the OK button.

3 Filter the pivot table so that sales are only shown for the three employees: *Jane Anderson, Dan Armstrong* and *Lucille Ashe.*

    This was covered in: *Lesson 5-5: Apply a simple filter and sort to a pivot table.*

4 Filter the pivot table so that sales are only shown for the three categories: *Action, Comedy* and *Crime.*

	A	B	C	D	E
4	Sum of Total	Genre			
5	Employee	Action	Comedy	Crime	Grand Total
6	Anderson,Jane	1556.48	1848.54	644.05	4049.07
7	Armstrong,Dan	1199.7	1368.84	903.71	3472.25
8	Ashe,Lucille	1375.72	1476.78	1135.23	3987.73
9	Grand Total	4131.9	4694.16	2682.99	11509.05

5 Create a *Clustered Column* pivot chart from the pivot table.

    1. Click anywhere in the pivot table to activate it.

    2. Click: PivotTable Tools→Options→Tools→PivotChart.

    The *Insert Chart* dialog appears.

Transactions-16

3. Click the *Clustered Column* chart type.

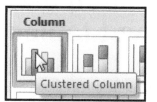

4. Click the OK button.

A clustered column chart is shown embedded in the worksheet.

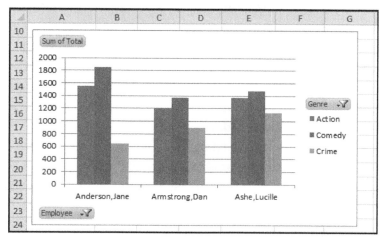

While this is sometimes what you want, most of the time you'll want to place your chart into a worksheet of its own (see sidebar).

6 Move the chart to its own worksheet.

1. Click on the chart to activate it.

2. Click: PivotChart Tools→Design→Location→Move Chart.

3. The *Move Chart* dialog appears.

4. Complete the dialog as follows:

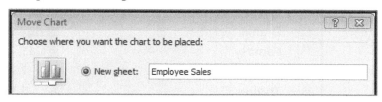

5. Click the OK button.

The chart now resides in its own chart sheet.

7 Save your work as *Transactions-17*.

Lesson 5-22: Embed multiple pivot tables onto a worksheet

In this lesson, we'll create the following Sales Summary worksheet containing three embedded pivot tables:

	A	B	C	D	E	F
1		**Sales Summary**				
3		**Customer** ▾	**Sales**		**Employee** ▾	**Sales**
4		Addison-Freelander Screen Agency	17,135.23		Anderson,Jane	8,833.40
5		AV Supplies	15,199.30		Armstrong,Dan	7,880.51
6		Box Office Supplies	22,923.09		Ashe,Lucille	8,755.66
7		Cheapo Cheap DVD's Ltd	20,145.10		Bell,Stephen	11,649.76
8		Cinefocus DVD	22,277.45		Bradshaw,John	9,329.37
9		Classic Films	17,549.80		Carrey,Julia	6,091.91
10		Creative Films	14,637.39		Davis,Charles	6,800.56
11		Lights-Camera-Action Ltd	18,106.20		Diamond,Elizabeth	8,965.29
12		Magic Lantern Classic Film Rental	20,055.78		Goodman,Paul	9,578.01
13		Silver Screen Video	20,757.07		Hawking,Alfred	10,946.28
14		Soft Focus Video Rental	17,870.60		Hicks,Michael	7,091.10
15		Video Flicks International	16,129.79		Jennings,John	11,190.73
16		**Grand Total**	222,786.80		Lee,Frank	13,488.16
17					Manning,Marilyn	9,064.16
18		**Genre** ▾	**Sales**		Newhart,Anna	8,937.66
19		Action	37,411.40		Putin,Julia	8,590.69
20		Adventure	8,588.03		Richards,Andy	8,302.17
21		Animation	5,098.87		Sagan,Jessica	11,004.66
22		Biography	17,174.78		Silverstone,Gloria	8,349.05
23		Comedy	37,614.16		Simpson,Howard	9,370.30
24		Crime	25,212.68		Simpson,Meryl	6,522.80
25		Drama	67,097.47		Spears,Julie	10,683.14
26		Fantasy	11,785.28		Streep,Margaret	14,513.69
27		Sci Fi	7,289.18		West,Chuck	6,847.74
28		Thriller	5,514.95		**Grand Total**	222,786.80
29		**Grand Total**	222,786.80			

When several key performance indicators are combined to produce an overview of a business process (in thus case Sales) the worksheet is sometimes called a *Dashboard* or *Executive Information System*.

This lesson will also confirm your understanding of many of the skills learned in this session.

1   Open *Transactions-17* from your sample files folder (if it isn't already open).

2   Add a new worksheet and name it: *Summary*.

3   Type **Sales Summary** into cell B1.

Transactions-17

4   Apply the *Title* style to cell B1.

Click: Home→Styles→Cell Styles→Titles and Headings→Title.

5   Embed a pivot table starting at cell B3 to show sales by *Customer*.

1. Click in cell B3.

2. Click: Insert→Tables→PivotTable.

3. Type **Data** into the *Table/Range* box.

4. Click OK.

5. Select the *Customer* and *Total* fields from the *PivotTable Field List*.

6   Embed a pivot table starting at cell B18 to show sales by *Genre*.

7   Embed a pivot table starting at cell E3 to show sales by *Employee*.

8   Format all values to show two decimal places and thousand separators.

This was first covered in: *Lesson 5-15: Add a calculated field to a pivot table*.

9   Change the *Row Labels* text in cells B3, B18 and E3 to read *Customer*, *Genre* and *Employee*.

This was first covered in: *Lesson 5-15: Add a calculated field to a pivot table*.

10   Change the *Sum of Total* labels in cells C3, C18 and F3 to read *Sales*.

11   Add a *3 Traffic Lights (Unrimmed)* conditional format to cells C4:C15.

Conditional formatting is covered in depth in the *Essential Skills* book in this series.

1. Select cells C4:C15.

2. Click: Home→Styles→Conditional Formatting→ Icon Sets→3 Traffic Lights (Unrimmed).

12   Add a *Light Blue Data Bar* conditional format to cells C19:C28.

13   Add a *5 Ratings (Icon Set)* conditional format to cells F4:F27.

14   Re-size column widths to enhance visual appearance.

15   Save your work as *Transactions-18*.

Lesson 5-23: Use slicers to filter multiple pivot tables

Earlier in this session you learned how to use slicers to provide an elegant user interface when filtering pivot tables.

Slicers become even more powerful when used to filter multiple pivot tables (such as the one created in: *Lesson 5-22: Embed multiple pivot tables onto a worksheet*).

In this lesson we'll refine this workbook to create an overview of sales using slicers to enable the user to filter all of the pivot tables at the same time.

1   Open *Transactions-18 from* your sample files folder (if it isn't already open).

2   Name the pivot tables *Customer Employee* and *Genre*.

When working with multiple pivot tables it is useful to give each an intuitive name.

1.   Click on the *Customer* pivot table to activate it.

2.   Click: PivotTable Tools→Options→Pivot Table→ Pivot Table Name.

3.   Type **Customer** in the *Pivot Table name* box and press the <Enter> key.

4.   Repeat the process to name the *Employee* and *Genre* pivot tables.

3   Add three slicers that will filter the *Customer* pivot table by *Employee, Customer* and *Genre*.

You learned how to do this in: *Lesson 5-7: Filter a pivot table visually using slicers.*

4   Size and format the slicers so that they provide a compact and attractive user interface.

You learned how to do this in: *Lesson 5-7: Filter a pivot table visually using slicers.*

When you have finished, your user interface should be similar to the screen grab on the facing page.

5   Test your slicers.

Notice that the slicers only affect the *Customer* pivot table. No matter what filter condition you set in the slicers, the values in the *Genre* and *Employee* pivot tables remain unaffected.

6   Connect the slicers to all three pivot tables.

1.   Click the *Genre* pivot table to activate it.

2.   Click: Slicer Tools→Options→Slicer→PivotTable Connections.

The *PivotTable Connections* dialog appears.

3.   Check the *Employee* and *Genre* check boxes to connect this slicer to all three pivot tables on the *Summary* worksheet.

PivotTable Name:

Customer

Options ▾
PivotTable

Transactions-18

note

How can I stop Excel changing pivot table column widths?

This is caused by a glitch in Excel's *Autofit* feature.

The easy solution is to switch off Autofit and size the column widths manually.

To switch off Autofit:

1/ Right-click on each pivot table in turn.

2/ Select *PivotTable Options→Layout & Format* from the shortcut menu.

3/ Clear the *Autofit column widths on update* check box.

4/ Manually resize each column width so that they are wide enough to display their contents correctly.

4. Click OK.

5. Repeat this process for the *Customer* and *Employee* slicers.

7 Test your slicers.

Notice that the slicers now work the way you want them to. All three pivot tables are filtered in accordance with the slicer filters you select.

You may find that the columns are not wide enough to display their values when a filter is applied. See sidebar for a solution to this problem.

8 Save your work as *Transactions-19*.

Session 5: Exercise

1   Open *Film Sales-1* from your sample files folder.

2   Convert the range to a table named *Data*.

3   Create a pivot table from the *Data* table.

4   Add *Row Labels* and *Values* so that your pivot table looks like this:

	A	B	C
3	Row Labels ▼	Sum of Qty	Sum of Total
4	Fedex	6929	55793.38
5	Royal Mail	6606	52965.68
6	TNT	7366	58884.38
7	UPS	6902	55143.36
8	Grand Total	27803	222786.8

5   Re-format the values in the pivot table and change the text in the header, so that your pivot table looks like this:

	A	B	C
3	Carrier ▼	Units	Cost
4	Fedex	6,929	55,793.38
5	Royal Mail	6,606	52,965.68
6	TNT	7,366	58,884.38
7	UPS	6,902	55,143.36
8	Grand Total	27,803	222,786.80

6   Add a calculated field to calculate the average cost per unit for each carrier formatted to two decimal places.

	A	B	C	D
3	Carrier ▼	Units	Cost	Cost per Unit
4	Fedex	6,929	55,793.38	8.05
5	Royal Mail	6,606	52,965.68	8.02
6	TNT	7,366	58,884.38	7.99
7	UPS	6,902	55,143.36	7.99
8	Grand Total	27,803	222,786.80	8.01

7   Embed a second pivot table starting in cell A10 of the same worksheet that will display sales by studio in an attractive format.

	A	B
11	Studio ▼	Sales
12	20th Century Fox	12,819.76
13	BBC TV	2,891.99
14	Columbia Pictures	11,007.66

8   Save your work as *Film Sales-2*.

If you need help slide the page to the left

Film Sales-1

Session 5: Exercise Answers

These are the four questions that students find the most difficult to answer:

Q 7	Q 6	Q 4	Q 2
1. Click in cell A10.	1. Click: PivotTable Tools→Options→ Calculations→Fields, Items & Sets→ Calculated Field...	Drag the following fields from the *PivotTable Field List* to the *Row Labels* and *Values* lists:	1. Click anywhere inside the range.
2. Click: Insert→Tables→ PivotTable.			2. Click:
3. Type **Data** into the *Table/Range* box.	2. Complete the Calculated field dialog as follows:		Insert→Tables→ Table
4. Click the OK button.		Row Labels / Carrier	3. Click:
5. Drag the following fields from the *PivotTable Field List* to the *Row Labels* and *Values* lists:	Name: Cost/Units / Formula: = Total/ Qty	Σ Values / Sum of Qty / Sum of Total	Table Tools→ Design→Properties→ Table Name
Row Labels / Studio	3. Click the OK button.	This was covered in: *Lesson 5-3: Understand pivot table rows and columns.*	4. Type **Data** into the *Table Name* box.
Σ Values / Sum of Total	4. Right-click one of the values in column D.		5. Press the <Enter> key.
6. Format the values to show two decimal places and a thousands comma separator (as detailed in the question 6 answer).	5. Click *Number Format...* on the shortcut menu.		This was covered in: *Lesson 1-8: Convert a range into a table and add a total row.*
7. Click in cell A10 and type: **Studio**.	6. Select the *Number* category and set two decimal places.		
8. Click in cell B10 and type: **Sales**.	7. Click OK.		
9. Press the <Enter> key.	8. Click cell D3 once and type **Cost per Unit.**		
This was covered in: *Lesson 5-3: Understand pivot table rows and columns.*	9. Type **Carrier, Units** and **Cost** into cells A3, B3 and C3.		
	This was covered in: *Lesson 5-15: Add a calculated field to a pivot table.*		

If you have difficulty with the other questions, here are the lessons that cover the relevant skills:

3   Refer to: *Lesson 5-1: Create a one dimensional pivot table report from a table.*

5   Refer to: *Lesson 5-15: Add a calculated field to a pivot table.*

6

Session Six: What If Analysis and Security

> The superior man, when resting in safety, does not forget that danger may come. When in a state of security, he does not forget the possibility of ruin. When all is orderly, he does not forget that disorder may come. Thus his person is not endangered, and his States and all their clans are preserved.
>
> *Confucius (551 BC - 479 BC)*

The concept of "What If" is very simple. A business may wish to know what will happen in a given set of circumstances (called a scenario). For example, a simple scenario might be: "What if I reduced my profit margins by 5% and my sales increased by 20%?" Excel provides several tools that are geared to more complex scenarios. In this session you'll learn how to use these tools effectively.

Sometimes you'll want to keep the contents of a workbook secure. This session will show you how to prevent unauthorized users from opening or changing your workbooks. You'll also learn how to restrict the cells a user is able to edit within a workbook. We'll also discover how to hide rows and columns and then create multiple custom views of the worksheet – each view hiding and showing different information.

Session Objectives

By the end of this session you will be able to:

- Create a single-input data table
- Create a two-input data table
- Define Scenarios
- Create a scenario summary report
- Use Goal Seek
- Use Solver
- Hide and unhide worksheets, columns and rows
- Create custom views
- Prevent unauthorized users from opening or modifying workbooks
- Control the changes users can make to workbooks
- Restrict the cells users are allowed to change
- Allow different levels of access to a worksheet with multiple passwords
- Create a digital certificate
- Add an invisible digital signature to a workbook
- Add a visible digital signature to a workbook

Lesson 6-1: Create a single-input data table

Don't be fooled by the name. A *data table* has nothing to do with a regular Excel table. Data tables are another of those wonderful Excel features that are a complete mystery to virtually all Excel users.

In this lesson we'll use a data table to list the monthly repayments for a loan at different interest rates.

1   Open *Mortgage-1 from* your sample files folder.

> This is a simple worksheet that calculates four result values from four input values. When performing what-if analysis, it is a good idea to separate the input values from the result values on your worksheet.
>
> The worksheet uses the PMT function that was covered in: *Lesson 3-3: Use the formula palette and the PMT function.*

	A	B
3	Input Cells	
4	Loan Amount	250,000
5	Deposit (%)	10%
6	Term (Years)	25
7	Interest Rate (APR%)	6.6%
8		
9	Result Cells	
10	Loan Financed	225,000
11	Monthly Repayment	1,533.31
12	Total amount to be repaid	459,992
13	Total interest to be repaid	234,992

> During the last 20 years, mortgage interest rates have never dropped below 2.5% or increased to more than 15.5%.
>
> Based upon the assumption that future rates will stay in this range, we will create a data sheet to show how potential changes in interest rates will affect monthly payments.

2   Create a single input data table to display all result cells for interest rates between 2.5% and 15.5% in half percent increments.

1.   Type **Interest** % into cell D3.

2.   Type **Monthly Payment** into cell E3.

3.   Type **Total Payments** into cell F3.

4.   Type **Total Interest** into cell G3.

5.   AutoSize columns D, E, F and G so that all of the headers are readable.

6.   Type **2.5**% into cell B7.

> When you create a data table, you should always put the lowest input value into the relevant input cell. You'll see why in a moment.

note

Single-input data tables can have the input cells along rows or columns

It is also possible to place the result cells along the left of the data table and the input cells along the top.

In this case, you would specify a *Row input cell* rather than a *Column input cell* in the *Data Table* dialog.

Mortagage-1

note

Data tables are read only

You cannot change or delete a cell in a data table.

If you try to do this, Excel will produce an error message.

If you need to remove a cell in a data table, you must delete the entire table.

7. Put formulas in cells D4:G4 that refer to the relevant input and result cells. The correct formulas are shown below:

	D	E	F	G
3	Interest %	Monthly Payment	Total Payments	Total Interest
4	=B7	=B11	=B12	=B13

8. Type **=D4+0.005** into cell D5.

9. AutoFill cell D5 down to cell D30 (15.5%).

10. Select cells D3:G3.

11. Click: Home→Styles→Cell Styles→Heading 3.

    Your worksheet should now look like this:

	D	E	F	G
	Interest %	Monthly Payment	Total Payments	Total Interest
	2.5%			
	3.0%			

12. Convert cells D5:D30 from formulas to values.

    Excel 2010 data tables have a problem with certain formulas in the left-hand column. For this reason you need to *Copy* the values in cells D4:D30 and then *Paste Special* them back to the same location as *Values*.

    A work-around for this limitation is discussed in: *Lesson 8-8: Add a single input data table to a form*.

    You are now ready to create your data table.

13. Select cells D4:G30.

14. Click: Data→Data Tools→What-If Analysis→Data Table...

    The *Data Table* dialog appears.

15. Set the *Column input cell* to cell B7.

    Because the interest rates are shown in column D, Excel must change the value in cell B7 to the value in column D in order to calculate values for columns E, F and G.

16. Click the OK button.

    The data table is populated to show all result cells for all interest rates.

17. Select cells E4:G30.

18. Click: Home→Styles→Cell Styles→Comma[0].

	D	E	F	G
3	Interest %	Monthly Payment	Total Payments	Total Interest
4	2.50%	1,009	302,816	77,816
5	3.00%	1,067	320,093	95,093
6	3.50%	1,126	337,921	112,921
7	4.00%	1,188	356,290	131,290

You are now able to change any of the *Input Cells* to explore the effect of different *Loan Amount, Interest Rate, Deposit* or *Term* values.

3   Save your work as *Mortgage-2*.

Lesson 6-2: Create a two-input data table

A two-input data table is similar to a one-input data table.

However, in a two-input data table, input cells are arranged along both the top and the left-hand side of the table.

In this lesson we'll use a two-input data table to show monthly repayments for different loan amounts and different interest rates.

1   Open *Mortgage-2 from* your sample files folder (if it isn't already open).

2   Create a new worksheet and name it: *Variable Interest and Capital*.

| ⏮ ◀ ▶ ⏭ | Variable Interest | **Variable Interest and Capital** | ↻ |

3   Copy cells A1:B13 from the *Variable Interest* worksheet and paste them into the same cells in the *Variable Interest and Capital* worksheet.

4   AutoSize columns A and B so that they are wide enough to display all values.

5   Create rows for your data table in cells E3:L3 showing capital amounts from 125,000 to 300,000 in increments of 25,000.

    1.   Type **125,000** into cell E3.

    2.   Type **150,000** into cell F3.

    3.   Select cells E3:F3 and AutoFill to cell L3.

6   Create column labels for your data table in cells D4:D30 showing interest rates from 2.5% to 15.5% in increments of 0.5%.

    1.   Type **2.5%** into cell D4.

    2.   Type **3%** into cell D5.

    3.   Select cells D4:D5 and AutoFill to cell D30.

7   Format cells D4:D30 to show one decimal place.

    1.   Select cells D4:D30.

    2.   Click: Home→Number→Decrease Decimal.

8   Put a formula in cell D3 that will reference the *Monthly Repayment* result cell.

	D	E	F
3	=B11	125000	150000

9   Apply the *Note* cell style to cells D3:D30 and cells D3:L3.

    1.   Select cells D3:D30 and cells E3:L3.

Mortagage-2

2. Click: Home→Cell Styles→Note.

Your worksheet should now look like this:

	C	D	E	F	G
2					
3		1,009.39	125,000	150,000	175,000
4		2.5%			
5		3.0%			
6		3.5%			
7		4.0%			

You are now ready to create your two-input data table.

10 Create a two-input data table to show monthly payments for each capital amount and interest rate.

1. Select cells D3:L30.

2. Click: Data→Data Tools→What-If Analysis→Data Table...

   The *Data Table* dialog appears.

   The *row input cell* is the *Loan Amount* in cell B4.

   The *column input cell* is the *Interest Rate* in cell B7.

   Note that you could take the view that the amount financed in cell B10 is the operative row input cell. I'm using cell B4 as it represents how much capital you would have available if your lender demands a 10% deposit.

3. Enter these values into the dialog and then click OK.

Data Table	? ⊠
Row input cell:	$B$4
Column input cell:	$B$7
OK	Cancel

4. Select cells E4:L30.

5. Click: Home→Number→Comma Style.

   This will format the numbers with a thousand comma separator and two decimal places.

   The two-input data table is complete.

	C	D	E	F	G	H
2						
3		1,009.39	125,000	150,000	175,000	200,000
4		2.5%	504.69	605.63	706.57	807.51
5		3.0%	533.49	640.19	746.88	853.58
6		3.5%	563.20	675.84	788.48	901.12
7		4.0%	593.82	712.58	831.34	950.11

The value in cell D3 looks a little untidy. If you'd like it to become invisible see the sidebar tip.

11 Save your work as *Mortgage-3*.

---

tip

Hiding values with the three semicolon custom format

You will often want to hide numbers or text in specific cells.

A common way of doing this is to format the cell as white text upon a white background.

A better solution is to create a custom format consisting of three semicolons. This is better because the cell contents will remain hidden no matter which background and foreground colors are set for the cell.

Here's how you would hide the value in cell D3:

1. Right-click cell D3.

2. Click *Format Cells...* on the shortcut menu.

3. Click the *Custom* category.

4. Type three semicolons into the *Type* box.

	D	E
3		125,000
4	2.5%	504.69
5	3.0%	533.49

5. Click OK.

The value in cell D3 has now become invisible:

	D	E
3		125,000
4	2.5%	504.69
5	3.0%	533.49

Lesson 6-3: Define scenarios

When you create a set of input values, it is referred to as a scenario.

For example, here's a scenario:

Forecasted sales for next month are: 1,500 Grommets, 4,300 Sprockets, 3,100 Widgets and 2,800 Flugel Valves.

You enter the scenario's values into the input cells:

	A	B
3	Input Cells	Units
4	Grommets	1,500
5	Sprockets	4,300
6	Widgets	3,100
7	Flugel valves	2,800

... and the result cells display the result:

	A	B
15	Result Cells	
16	Sales	842,280.00
17	Cost	643,230.00
18	Profit	199,050.00
19	Gross Profit Pct	23.6%

Sometimes, you will have several different scenarios that you want to compare side-by-side. For example, you may ask your salesmen for *"worst case, expected case* and *best case"* scenarios.

	A	B	C	D
21	Scenarios			
22	Product	Worst Case	Expected Case	Best Case
23	Grommets	750	1,500	2200
24	Sprockets	4100	4,300	4350
25	Widgets	2000	3,100	3750
26	Flugel valves	2400	2,800	2950

Excel's *Scenario Manager* is designed to allow you to easily compare these scenarios side-by-side.

1   Open *Profit Forecast-1 from* your sample files folder.

Notice that this worksheet has been grouped to show four sets of values:

- Input Cells (referred to as *changing cells* in Excel scenarios).
- Constants (cells that do not change their values).
- Result Cells (cells that change when input cells change).
- Scenarios (values for best, worst and expected case).

2   Create single-cell range names for the input and result cells.

This was covered in depth in: *Lesson 4-1: Automatically create single-cell range names.*

As you'll see later, in:*Lesson 6-4: Create a scenario summary report,* the *Scenario Manager* expects you to define range names for input

---

note

The scenario manager can only handle 32 changing cells

If you try to define more than 32 changing cells, Excel will display an error message.

Profit Forecast-1

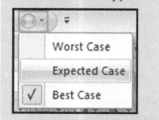
and result cells in order to correctly display scenario summary reports.

1. Select cells A4:B7.

2. Click: Formulas→Defined Names→Create from Selection.

3. Click the OK button.

4. Repeat for cells A16:B19.

3 **Define the scenarios listed in cells A22:D26.**

1. Click: Data→Data Tools→What-If Analysis→Scenario Manager...

   The *Scenario Manager* dialog appears.

2. Click the *Add* button to add a new scenario.

3. Type **Worst Case** into the *Scenario name* box.

4. Click in the *Changing cells* box and select cells B4:B7 with the mouse.

Scenario name:
Worst Case

Changing cells:
$B$4:$B$7

   The Scenario Manager uses the term *Changing cells* to refer to *Input Cells*.

5. Click the OK button.

6. Enter the following values for the *Worst Case* scenario:

Scenario Values		
Enter values for each of the changing cells.		
1:	Grommets	750
2:	Sprockets	4100
3:	Widgets	2000
4:	Flugel_valves	2400

   Add   OK   Cancel

7. Click the *Add* button and then use the same technique to add the *Expected Case* and *Best Case* scenarios.

8. Click the OK button.

4 **Use the Scenario Manager to view result cells for each scenario.**

1. Select one of the cases in the *Scenarios* list.

2. Click the *Show* button to display the scenario on the worksheet.

3. Select a different case and click the *Show* button.

4. Click the *Close* button to close the Scenario Manager.

5 **Save your work as *Profit Forecast-2*.**

Lesson 6-4: Create a scenario summary report

When scenarios have been defined, it is possible to display a neatly formatted report or pivot table, listing each scenario side-by-side.

1 Open *Profit Forecast-2 from* your sample files folder (if it isn't already open).

2 Open the Scenario Manager.

Click: Data→Data Tools→What-If Analysis→Scenario Manager...

The *Scenario Manager* dialog is displayed:

3 Create a *Scenario Summary* Report.

1. Click the *Summary...* button.

   The *Scenario Summary* dialog is displayed.

   This dialog asks which result cells should be displayed on the report.

2. Delete the current contents of the *Result cells* box.

3. Select cells B16:B19 with the mouse:

   Note that it is possible to show the report as either a *Scenario Summary* or as a *Scenario PivotTable* report.

4. Click the OK button.

Profit Forecast-2

The Scenario Summary report is displayed on its own worksheet.

	Current Values:	Worst Case	Expected Case	Best Case
Scenario Summary				
		Created by Mike Smart on 29/09/2009	Created by Mike Smart on 29/09/2009	Created by Mike Smart on 29/09/2009
Changing Cells:				
Grommets	750	750	1,500	2,200
Sprockets	4,100	4,100	4,300	4,350
Widgets	2,000	2,000	3,100	3,750
Flugel_valves	2,400	2,400	2,800	2,950
Result Cells:				
Sales	661,725.00	661,725.00	842,280.00	950,415.00
Cost	519,680.00	519,680.00	643,230.00	715,235.00
Profit	142,045.00	142,045.00	199,050.00	235,180.00
Gross_Profit_Pct	21.5%	21.5%	23.6%	24.7%

Notes: Current Values column represents values of changing cells at time Scenario Summary Report was created. Changing cells for each scenario are highlighted in gray.

Notice that the report is shown as an outline and that it is possible to collapse and expand the outline by clicking the plus and minus buttons or on the number buttons at the top left corner.

You can now see how important it was to define named ranges for the input and result cells. Without these the report would show cell references rather than descriptive names such as *Flugel_valves*.

4   Create a *Scenario PivotTable report*.

1. Select the *Profit Forecast* worksheet.

2. Click: Data→Data Tools→What-If Analysis→ Scenario Manager…

3. Click the *Summary* button.

4. Click the *Scenario PivotTable report* option button.

5. Click the OK button.

The *Scenario PivotTable* is displayed:

	A	B	C	D	E
1	$B$4:$B$7 by	(All)			
2					
3		**Result Cells**			
4	**Row Labels**	**Sales**	**Cost**	**Profit**	**Gross_Profit_Pct**
5	Best Case	950415	715235	235180	0.247449798
6	Expected Case	842280	643230	199050	0.236322838
7	Worst Case	661725	519680	142045	0.214658657

This time Excel hasn't done such a good job. You'd need to spend a little time re-formatting this report!

5   Save your work as *Profit Forecast-3*.

Lesson 6-5: Use Goal Seek

It is very easy to view result values by changing input values. You simply type the new values into the input cells.

	A	B
1	**Mortgage**	
2		
3	Input Cells	
4	Loan Amount	300,000
5	Deposit (%)	20%
6	Term (Years)	20
7	Interest Rate (APR%)	6.6%
8		
9	Result Cells	
10	Loan Financed	240,000
11	Monthly Repayment	1,803.53
12	Total amount to be repaid	432,847.92
13	Total interest to be repaid	192,848

In the above worksheet, I wanted to know the monthly repayment for a 300,000 loan with a 20% deposit over 20 years at 6.6%. I simply typed the values into the input cells and viewed the results in the result cells.

Consider the case where you want to know the maximum *Loan Amount* if you can only afford a monthly payment of 1,000. This is more difficult because the result cells contain formulas rather than values.

By using Goal Seek, Excel will change one (and only one) input cell so that the desired value is shown in one result cell.

There's a much more complex tool called Solver (you'll learn about this later in: *Lesson 6-6: Use Solver*), that is a more advanced goal seek tool, able to automatically set multiple input cells.

For now, we'll examine the simple and extremely useful goal seek tool.

1 Open *Mortgage-3 from* your sample files folder.

2 Create a new worksheet called: *Goal Seek*.

3 Copy cells A1:B13 on the *Variable Interest and Capital* worksheet to the same cells on the *Goal Seek* worksheet.

4 Autosize columns A and B so that all text and values are visible.

5 Use *Goal Seek* to find the maximum *Loan Amount* available if you can afford only 1,000 per month.

    1. Click in cell B11 (the *Monthly Repayment* cell).

Mortgage-3

2. Click: Data→Data Tools→What-If Analysis→Goal Seek…

    The *Goal Seek* dialog appears:

    We want to set the *Monthly Repayment* (B11) to the value 1,000 by changing the *Loan Amount* (B4).

3. Complete the dialog as follows:

4. Click OK.

    Goal Seek advises that it has found a solution:

5. Click OK.

    The solution to the problem is shown on the worksheet:

	A	B
3	Input Cells	
4	Loan Amount	247,675
5	Deposit (%)	10%
6	Term (Years)	25
7	Interest Rate (APR%)	2.5%
8		
9	Result Cells	
10	Loan Financed	222,907
11	Monthly Repayment	1,000.00
12	Total amount to be repaid	300,000
13	Total interest to be repaid	77,093

    The maximum *Loan Amount* I could raise will be 247,675 if I can only afford 1,000 per month. I could, of course, have also used goal seek to change any of the other input cells. The key limitation of Goal Seek is that it can only change one input cell.

6   Save your work as *Mortgage-4.*

Lesson 6-6: Use Solver

What is Solver?

Conceptually, Solver is similar to Goal Seek. While Goal Seek can only change one input cell to set a value in one result cell, Solver can change any number of input cells. This makes the tool more complex.

You can also define a set of rules (called constraints) that Solver needs to observe when finding a solution.

1   Open *Bicycle Manufacturing Schedule-1 from* your **sample files folder.**

This worksheet models a bicycle manufacturing company. The company manufactures four different types of bicycle but has a limited number of parts available.

- Cells B4:E4 are the input cells (or changing cells) for the worksheet. They define how many bicycles of each model will be manufactured.

- The parts needed to manufacture each type of bicycle are shown in cells B7:E11. For example, a *Street Bike* needs 2 wheels, 1 steel chassis and 1 set of derailleur gears.

- Column I shows how many parts are available.

- Cells B14:F14 show the profit for each bicycle type along with the total profit for all bicycle types.

	A	B	C	D	E	F	G	H	I
3		Mountain Bike	Street Bike	Racing Bike	Commuter Bike		Input (Changing) Cells		
4	Qty To Manufacture	20	20	20	20				
5								Constraints	
6	Parts List				Constraints		Parts needed	Operator	Parts Available
7	Wheels	2	2	2	2		160	<=	180
8	Alloy Chassis	1		1			40	<=	40
9	Steel Chassis		1		1		40	<=	60
10	Hub Gears	1			1		40	<=	50
11	Derailleur Gears		1	1			40	<=	40
12									
13	Profit Analysis			Profit Per Unit		Total Profit	Result (Target) Cell		
14		$ 45	$ 60	$ 55	$ 50	$ 4,200			

Our challenge is to maximize profit by manufacturing the optimum number of each type of bicycle.

2   Install the Solver add-in (if it is not already installed).

1.   Click: File→Options→Add-ins→ Solver Add-In.

2.   Click the GO button.

Bicycle Manufacturing Schedule-1

3. Check the *Solver Add*-in check box and click the OK button.

   Solver now appears on the Ribbon's *Data* tab in a new *Analysis* group (see sidebar).

3 **Open Solver.**

   Click: Data→Analysis→Solver.

   Solver appears.

4 **Let Solver know which are the *Changing* (Input) cells and which is the *Objective* (Result) cell.**

   Complete the dialog as follows:

   We are telling Solver to maximize profit by changing the *Input Cells* (or *Changing Cells*) B4:E4.

5 **Define the constraints for the problem.**

   1. Click the *Add* button next to the *Subject to the Constraints* list box.

   2. Complete the dialog as follows:

      This tells Solver that it cannot manufacture a negative number of bicycles.

   3. Click Add.

   4. Set up a second constraint as follows:

      This tells Solver that it cannot use more parts than are available.

   5. Click OK.

6 **Solve the problem.**

   1. Click the *Solve* button.

   2. Click the OK button.

      Solver has solved the problem.

	A	B	C	D	E
3		Mountain Bike	Street Bike	Racing Bike	Commuter Bike
4	Qty To Manufacture	25	35	5	25

   This mix of bicycles maximizes profits to $4,750.

7 **Save your work as *Bicycle Manufacturing Schedule-2*.**

Lesson 6-7: Hide and unhide worksheets, columns and rows

note

Hiding and unhiding a worksheet using the Ribbon

The right-click method is much faster than using the Ribbon but here's how it can be done:

To hide a worksheet:

Click: Home→Cells→
Format→
Hide & Unhide→
Hide Sheet.

To Unhide a worksheet:

1. Click: Home→Cells→
Format→
Hide & Unhide→
Unhide Sheet.

2. Select the sheet you want to hide/unhide from the dialog and click the OK button.

important

Don't rely on hidden worksheets for security

There is no password associated with hiding and unhiding a worksheet, row or column. A knowledgeable user can easily unhide any hidden item.

If you need to hide items more securely, it is possible to protect the structure before distributing a workbook.

When this is done, it isn't possible to unhide and view the hidden items unless you know the password.

Protecting the structure of a workbook will be covered in: *Lesson 6-10: Control the changes users can make to workbooks.*

1   Open *Human Resources-1* from your sample files folder.

2   Hide the *Headcount & Salaries* worksheet.

The *Payroll* worksheet depends upon the *Headcount & Salaries* worksheet in order to calculate each employee's hourly rate.

Because this data is sensitive, you may decide to hide the entire *Headcount & Salaries* worksheet.

1.   Select the *Headcount & Salaries* worksheet.

2.   Right-click the worksheet tab.

3.   Click *Hide* on the shortcut menu.

The worksheet disappears.

3   Unhide the *Headcount & Salaries* worksheet.

1.   Right-click any worksheet tab (at the moment the only visible worksheet tab is *Payroll*).

2.   Click *Unhide* on the shortcut menu.

The *Unhide* dialog is displayed listing all currently hidden worksheets.

3.   Click the OK button.

The *Headcount & Salaries* worksheet reappears.

You can see that this is not a good way to hide confidential information, as any knowledgeable user can simply unhide the worksheet (see sidebar).

4   Hide rows 3:6, rows 19:23 and row 9 on the *Payroll* worksheet.

Perhaps you would like to print out the *Payroll* worksheet for the floor manager so that each employee's hours can be reviewed.

This might be a problem if the salaries had to be kept confidential.

For this reason, you are going to hide the confidential rows on the *Payroll* worksheet before printing.

1.   Select the *Payroll* worksheet.

2.   Select rows 3 to 6.

3.   Right-click anywhere in the selected cells area.

4.   Click *Hide* on the shortcut menu.

Human Resources-1

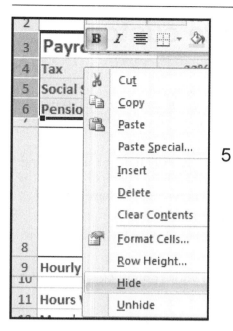

The rows disappear.

5. Do the same to hide rows 19:23.

6. Do the same to hide row 9.

   The payroll no longer shows any financial values. It would now be possible to print the worksheet without showing the hidden rows.

5 **Hide columns E:O on the *Payroll* worksheet.**

This is very similar to hiding rows.

1. Select columns E:O.

2. Right-click anywhere in the selected cells area.

3. Click *Hide* on the shortcut menu.

   The columns disappear.

	A	B	C	D	P
1	Payroll				
2					
8		Johnny Caine	George Marley	Betty Anan	
11	Hours Worked				
12	Monday	9	10	10	
13	Tuesday	8	9	8	
14	Wednesday	10	9	8	
15	Thursday	6	8	6	
16	Friday	10	7	10	
17	Total	43	43	42	
18					

6 **Unhide columns E:O on the *Payroll* worksheet.**

1. Select columns D:P (the columns that are on either side of the hidden columns).

2. Right-click anywhere in the selected cells area.

3. Click *Unhide* on the shortcut menu.

   The columns re-appear.

7 **Unhide all hidden rows on the *Payroll* worksheet.**

1. Click the *Select All* button (at the top left corner of the worksheet) to select every cell.

2. Right-click any of the row headers (the numbered buttons on the left of the worksheet).

3. Click *Unhide* on the shortcut menu.

4. All hidden rows re-appear.

There is no need to save this worksheet as it has not been changed in any way.

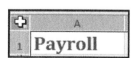

tip

A faster way to hide a single row or column

A hidden column is simply a column whose width has been set to zero.

You can quickly hide a row or column by dragging its border to make it so narrow that it is no longer visible.

Lesson 6-8: Create custom views

In: *Lesson 6-7: Hide and unhide worksheets, columns and rows,* we discussed how useful it can be to hide columns and rows when printing a worksheet.

Sometimes you may find that you are continuously hiding and unhiding the same rows and columns in order to print selected parts of a worksheet. When you notice that this is happening, you have an ideal candidate for a custom view.

Custom views allow you to save and recall worksheet layouts that have hidden columns and rows.

1   Open *Human Resources-1* from your sample files folder (if it isn't already open).

2   Select the *Payroll* worksheet.

3   Save the current view as *HR*.

   1.   Click: View→Workbook Views→Custom Views.

      The *Custom Views* dialog appears:

   2.   Click the *Add...* button.

      The *Add View* dialog appears.

   3.   Type **HR** into the *Name* box.

      Notice that custom views don't only save hidden rows and columns. Custom views also save *Print settings,* including any *Page Layout* settings, along with any filters that are currently applied to the worksheet. This includes the zoom factor, window sizes and positions, the currently active cell and the current worksheet view (*Normal, Page Layout* or *Page Break Preview*).

4. Click the OK button.

Nothing seems to have happened but you have, in fact, stored a view with all rows and columns visible.

4 Hide rows 3:6, rows 19:23 and row 9 on the *Payroll* worksheet.

This was covered in: *Lesson 6-7: Hide and unhide worksheets, columns and rows.*

5 Save the current view as *Hours Worked*.

6 Hide columns B,C,F,G,H,I,J,K,L and N.

7 Save the current view as *Hours Worked (Female)*.

8 Show the *Hours Worked* view.

1. Click: View→Workbook Views→Custom Views.

The *Custom Views* dialog is displayed and shows the three saved views:

2. Click the *Hours Worked* view in the *Views* list.

3. Click the *Show* button.

The worksheet changes to show the *Hours Worked* view.

9 Show the *Hours Worked (Female)* view.

10 Show the *HR* view.

11 Save your work as *Human Resources-2*.

important

Secure passwords

Hacking tools (freely available on the Internet) commonly use five methods to discover passwords:

1. Dictionary attack

In a matter of seconds the tool tries every word in the dictionary. For this reason your password should never be a real word such as *London*.

2. Dictionary + numbers

The tool makes several passes through the dictionary, appending a sequential number to the front or back of the password. For this reason, your password should never be a real word with leading or trailing numbers, such as *London99* or *99London*.

3. Reverse words

The tool tries every word in the dictionary spelled backwards.

4. Words with the letter O replaced with a zero

5. *Brute force* attack

The tool tries every possible combination of the letters of the alphabet. It currently takes up to 13 minutes for a dual-core Pentium to crack a seven letter single-case password such as: *xcoekfh*.

For ultimate security against brute force attacks, include upper and lower case letters, numbers, and symbols in your passwords. The best approach is to create a password from a phrase such as: "I like to ride my Honda motorcycle at 100 MPH". This gives the extremely secure password: *IltrmHm@100MPH*

This password would take up to 5 million years to crack with a dual-core Pentium, and would even take up to 53,000 years with the fastest supercomputer on the planet!

Human Resources-2

Lesson 6-9: Prevent unauthorized users from opening or modifying workbooks

There are two levels of password protection available when you save a workbook. You can:-

* Prevent users from opening the workbook.

* Prevent users from changing a workbook once they have opened it.

In this lesson we'll implement both types of protection.

1 Open *Human Resources-2* from your sample files folder (if it isn't already open).

2 Protect the workbook with a password that will prevent other users from opening it.

1. Click: File→Save As.

The *Save As* dialog is displayed.

2. Click: Tools→General Options at the bottom-right of the dialog.

(If you are using the Windows XP operating system your screen may differ slightly from the screen grab).

3. Type a password in the *Password to open* box.

See the *secure passwords* sidebar for important information about choosing an appropriate password.

See the facing page sidebar for a discussion of the *Always Create Backup* and *Read-only recommended* check box options.

4. Click OK.

Excel reminds you not to forget the password and prompts for it again to protect against accidental typing errors.

5. Type the password again.

note

Excel passwords do not provide 100% security

Even if you choose a secure password that is nine or more characters long (such as *IltrmHm@100MPH*), there are tools freely available on the Internet that can crack most of the Excel 2010 worksheet protection passwords in minutes.

Currently, only the *password to open* is not easily cracked.

The password to open is encrypted using AES 128 (Advanced Encryption Standard with a 128-bit key).

This encryption standard is approved by the US government to encrypt classified documents up to SECRET level. This suggests that it is extremely secure.

note

General Options check boxes

The *Always Create Backup* check box provides you with an escape route if you need to return to the previous version of the workbook.

A copy of the old workbook is saved every time you save, so that you always have two copies of each workbook. One copy is a *Microsoft Excel Backup* file with the file extension .xlk.

If you check the *Read-only recommended* check box, the user is presented with a dialog when opening a protected workbook.

The dialog suggests that the book be opened read-only.

If the user ignores this suggestion, a read/write copy will be opened. As you discovered in this lesson, this copy cannot be used to overwrite the protected file but can be used to create a new file with a different name.

6. Click OK.

7. Click *Save.*

8. Click *Yes* to overwrite the existing file.

3 Close the *Human Resources-2* workbook and then try to re-open it.

Without the password you are unable to open the workbook.

4 Enter the password and open the workbook.

5 Remove the password from the workbook.

1. Click: File→Save As.

2. Click: Tools→General Options at the bottom-right of the dialog.

3. Remove the password from the *Passsword to open* box.

4. Click OK.

5. Click *Save.*

6. Click *Yes* to overwrite the existing file.

6 Protect the workbook with a password that will prevent other users from changing it.

Follow the same procedure as you did when adding a *Password to open* but, this time specify a *Password to modify.*

7 Save and Close the workbook.

8 Open *Human Resources-2* read only.

1. Click: File→Open→Human Resources-2.

2. The Password dialog appears.

3. Click the *Read Only* button without entering a password.

   This doesn't have the effect you would expect. You've opened the workbook without a password and are able to change it.

9 Attempt to save the workbook.

Surprisingly, Excel will only disallow you from saving the workbook with the same name as the password-protected workbook. It is quite happy for you to make a copy and even prompts you to do so when you attempt to save the file.

10 Save the workbook as *Human Resources-3.*

This workbook no longer has password protection.

Lesson 6-10: Control the changes users can make to workbooks

Sometimes you are quite happy for any user to open your workbook, but you need to prevent them from inserting, deleting, renaming, moving, hiding or unhiding any of the worksheets or worksheet elements. This is called protecting the *Structure* of a workbook.

Some worksheets are intended to be viewed in a worksheet window that has been set to a specific size. In this case, you need to prevent your users from moving or re-sizing the worksheet windows. This is called protecting the *Windows* of a workbook.

In this lesson, we'll discover how to protect a workbook's structure, windows, or both.

1   Open *Human Resources-3* from your sample files folder (if it isn't already open).

2   Display the *Hours Worked (Female)* custom view.

   This was covered in: *Lesson 6-8: Create custom views.*

3   Restore down the worksheet window so that it floats within the application window.

   Click the *Restore Window* button in the top right corner of the Payroll worksheet.

4   Hide the *Headcount & Salaries* worksheet.

   This was covered in: *Lesson 6-7: Hide and unhide worksheets, columns and rows.*

5   Re-size the Payroll worksheet window so that it is a perfect fit for cells A1:O17.

6   Protect the structure and windows of the workbook.

    1.   Click: Review→Changes→Protect Workbook.

       The *Protect Structure and Windows* dialog is displayed:

    2.   Check both of the check boxes and add a password.

    3.   Click OK.

    4.   Enter the password again when prompted and click OK.

       Because you checked the *Windows* check box you are unable to re-size or move the worksheet window.

       Because you checked the *Structure* check box you are also unable to insert, delete, rename, move, hide or unhide any of the worksheets in this workbook.

7   Remove password protection from the structure and windows.

    1.   Click: Review→Changes→Protect Workbook.

       You are prompted for the password to remove protection:

    2.   Enter the password and click the OK button.

       Protection is removed.

8   Unhide the *Headcount & Salaries* worksheet.

9   Display the *HR* custom view.

    There's no need to save the workbook as it has not changed.

Lesson 6-11: Restrict the cells users are allowed to change

1   Open *Human Resources-3* from your sample files folder (if it isn't already open).

2   Display the *Hours Worked* custom view.

This was covered in: *Lesson 6-8: Create custom views*.

3   Hide the *Headcount and Salaries* worksheet.

This was covered in: *Lesson 6-7: Hide and unhide worksheets, columns and rows*.

4   Re-size columns B:O so that they are just wide enough to display their contents:

	Johnny Caine	George Marley	Betty Anan	Paris Winfrey	Ozzy Dickens	Johnny Roberts	Charles Monroe	Ronnie Bush	Michal Jolie	JK Spears	Ozzy Rowling	Oprah Hilton	Bill Biggs	Angelina Osbourne
Payroll														
Hours Worked														
Monday	9	10	10	10	7	7	7	7	7	7	7	10	8	6
Tuesday	8	9	8	6	10	10	10	7	6	10	7	8	7	9
Wednesday	10	9	8	7	9	8	6	8	7	8	8	6	6	8
Thursday	6	8	6	10	9	7	6	6	7	8	8	6	6	9
Friday	10	7	10	7	9	10	9	8	8	10	8	9	10	6
Total	43	43	42	40	44	42	38	36	35	43	38	39	37	38

The challenge this time will be to prevent the user from changing any value other than those in the yellow shaded cells (cells B12:O16).

We will solve this problem by *unlocking* these cells and then *protecting* the worksheet. This will only allow the user to enter values into the *unlocked* cells.

5   Unlock cells B12:O16.

All cells on a worksheet are (by default) *locked*. You are able to type values into them because the worksheet is not yet *protected*.

In order to prevent the user from changing any cell except cells B12:O16 we need to do two things:

- Unlock the cells that you want the user to be able to change.

- Protect the worksheet.

Here's how to unlock the cells:

1.   Select cells B12:O16.

tip

Use cell locking to make forms more user-friendly

Excel is often used to create forms (such as booking forms). The form is sent to the user by e-mail and the user completes and returns it.

This type of form becomes much easier to use if you do the following:

1. Unlock the cells that the user should type data into.

2. Protect the worksheet making sure that only the *Select unlocked cells* option is checked.

When this is done, the user can use the **<Tab>** key to navigate through all of the cells in the form that need to be completed.

Human Resources-3

note

You can keep your formulas secret with the *Hidden* attribute

If you set the *Hidden* attribute on the *Format Cells Protection* tab, users cannot see any of your formulas.

Even if a cell is unlocked, the formula does not display on the formula bar when the cell is selected.

This could be used if the formula used to calculate a value was a "trade secret".

This will only take effect when the worksheet is protected.

tip

Leave all cells locked to distribute a read-only workbook

If you protect a workbook without unlocking any cells, you have effectively created a read-only workbook.

To prevent the user from copying and pasting the contents, you should also un-check the *Select locked cells* check box. Note that the user will still be able to click:

Insert→Illustrations→Screenshot

... from any another Office application to copy an image of the worksheet. (Screenshots are a new Office 2010 feature).

2. Right click anywhere in the selected area.

3. Click *Format Cells...* from the shortcut menu.

4. Click the *Protection* tab.

5. Uncheck the *Locked* check box.

See sidebar for more about the *Hidden* attribute.

6. Click the OK button.

6 Protect the *Payroll* worksheet so that the user is unable to change or select any of the locked cells.

When you protect a worksheet, it is no longer possible to change the contents of a *locked* cell.

1. Click: Review→Changes→Protect Sheet.

   The *Protect Sheet* dialog appears

   The default settings allow the user to select (but not change) the contents of locked cells. This normally makes sense as you want the user to be able to copy and paste any part of the worksheet.

   In this case, however, it creates a huge security problem as the user can easily copy the entire worksheet, paste it into a new worksheet, and then unhide the hidden rows.

   For this reason, we want to prevent the user from selecting locked cells.

2. Uncheck the *Select locked cells* check box.

   Notice that by default, the user is prevented from doing many more things to the worksheet (such as formatting cells). You can selectively allow these actions by checking the appropriate check box.

3. Enter a password.

4. Click the OK button.

7 Test the protected worksheet.

You are unable to change (or even select) any of the locked cells but you can select and change any of the unlocked cells.

8 Unprotect the worksheet.

1. Click: Review→Changes→Unprotect Sheet.

2. If you set a password, enter it, and then click OK.

9 Lock cells B12:O16.

Do this in the same way that you unlocked the cells, but this time, check the *Locked* check box (instead of un-checking it).

10 Save your work as *Human Resources-4*.

note

You can allow access based upon the Windows log-in password or user group

You can also use your existing windows passwords and user groups to allow access to specific ranges of cells.

To use Windows permissions click :

Review→Changes→ Allow Users to Edit Ranges→ New...→Permissions...

Lesson 6-12: Allow different levels of access to a worksheet with multiple passwords

Sometimes you will want different users to be able to change different ranges in your worksheet. In this lesson, we'll set the following levels of access to the *Hours Worked* worksheet.

	A	B	C	D	E
3	**Payroll Rules**				
4	Tax	32%			
5	Social Security	8%			
6	Pension	5%			
7					
8		Johnny Caine	George Marley	Betty Anan	Paris Winfrey
9	Hourly Rate	18.20	12.57	12.66	11.32
10					
11	Hours Worked				
12	Monday	9	10	10	10
13	Tuesday	8	9	8	6
14	Wednesday	10	9	8	7
15	Thursday	6	8	6	10
16	Friday	10	7	10	7
17	Total	43	43	42	40

Group	Permission	Password
Human Resources	Access to cells B4:B6, B9:O9 and B12:O16. This allows the HR department to change *Tax, Social Security, Pension* and *Hourly Rate* values.	cat
Floor Manager	Access to cells B12:O16 only. Floor managers can only change the hours worked.	dog
Administrator	All rights (this is the unprotect password).	cow

I have deliberately used very insecure passwords in order to save you the effort of typing long (and more secure) ones. If security was important, you would use secure passwords (see sidebar in: *Lesson 6-9: Prevent unauthorized users from opening or modifying workbooks* for details of how to construct a secure password).

1   Open *Hours Worked-1* from your sample files folder.

Hours Worked-1

2   Set up the *Human Resources* password and permissions.

1. Select cells B4:B6.

2. Hold down the **<Ctrl>** key and select cells B9:O9 and cells B12:O16.

3. Click: Review→Changes→Allow Users to Edit Ranges.

   The *Allow Users to Edit Ranges* dialog appears.

4. Click the *New...* button

5. Type **Human Resources** as the *Title*.

6. Type **cat** as the *Range password*.

7. Click OK.

8. Type the password again when prompted and click OK.

3 Set up the *Floor Manager* password and permissions.

1. Click the *New...* button.

2. Type **Floor Manager** as the *Title*.

3. Click in the *Refers to cells* box and delete the current contents.

4. Select cells B12:O16.

5. Type **dog** as the *Range password*.

6. Click OK.

7. Type the password again when prompted and click OK.

8. Click OK to close the dialog.

4 Protect the worksheet.

1. Click: Review→Changes→Protect Sheet.

2. Type the administrator password: **cow** into the *Password to unprotect sheet* box.

3. Click OK, re-enter the password when prompted and click OK.

5 Test the worksheet.

1. Try to change any of the numbers in cells B12:O16.

   A dialog appears asking for a password.

2. Type **dog** for the password.

   You are now able to freely change any value in cells B12:O16 for as long as the workbook stays open.

3. Try to change any of the values in cells B4:B6 or cells B9:O9.

   In each case, a dialog appears asking for a password.

4. Type **cat** for the password.

   You are now able to freely change any value in cells B4:B6, B9:O9 or B12:O16 for as long as the workbook stays open.

6 Save your work as *Hours Worked-2*.

Lesson 6-13: Create a digital certificate

Why digital certificates are needed.

If you receive a workbook via e-mail, you cannot be sure where it has really come from. It is remarkably easy to send an e-mail that appears to have been sent by a different person.

You may also worry that the workbook may have been altered by somebody since the author sent it to you.

The solution to both of these problems is to digitally sign your workbooks.

If a workbook is digitally signed, it confirms the identity of the author. Excel will also warn the recipient if it has been changed since the author signed it.

Digital certificates are of great use when you need to distribute workbooks that contain macros within an organization. (You'll learn all about macros in: *Session Eight: Forms and Macros*). Macros can contain destructive macro viruses and you wouldn't ever want to open a workbook containing macros without being absolutely sure of its origin.

Self-certification and third-party certification.

There are two ways to create a digital certificate in Excel 2010:

1. Create your own digital certificate. This isn't very secure, as it is easy to forge a self-certified digital certificate. When another user opens a workbook with a self-certified signature it will display the message:

    > ![Signatures icon] **Signatures**   This document contains invalid signatures.   [View Signatures...]

    This isn't likely to inspire a great deal of confidence in the recipient. In fact, I'd go so far as to say that a self-certified digital certificate has no value as it doesn't really increase security at all.

2. Buy a certificate from a trusted third party such as VersiSign. Third-party certificates provide a high level of security as they are certified to be genuine by an outside agency. When the user opens a workbook, Excel will confirm that the certificate is genuine by contacting the third-party's server. Most third-party subscriptions cost between US$100 and US$500 per year.

In this lesson, you'll create your own digital certificate. Although this doesn't really improve security, it will give you all of the skills you need to effectively use digital certificates should you eventually purchase a third party subscription.

1   Create a self-certified digital certificate.

   Because this is a Windows feature, you need to begin by clicking the *Windows start button* at the bottom left of your screen.

1. Click: Windows Start→All Programs→ Microsoft Office→Microsoft Office Tools→ Digital Certificate for VBA Projects.

    If you do not see this option on your computer, you may have to install it (see sidebar for instructions).

    The *Create Digital Certificate* dialog appears:

    The dialog refers to macros because workbooks containing macros present the most serious security threat. You'll learn more about macros in: *Session Eight: Forms and Macros*.

    Notice that there is a hyperlink on this dialog that will direct you to several commercial certificate authorities should you wish to purchase a third-party certificate.

2. Type a name for your certificate into the *Your certificate's name* box.

3. Click the OK button.

    A dialog appears showing that the certificate has been created.

Lesson 6-14: Add an invisible digital signature to a workbook

As discussed in: *Lesson 6-13: Create a digital certificate,* a self-certified digital certificate has no value as it doesn't increase security at all. As you'll see in this lesson, Microsoft go out of their way to warn the user of this.

Should your organization purchase a "real" digital certificate this lesson will give you all of the skills you need to effectively attach them to workbooks.

1   Open *Salary Increase-1* from your sample files folder (if it isn't already open).

This worksheet details salary increases for the coming year:

You want your HR department to be confident that this workbook was really created by you and that nobody has changed any of the salary increases since it was sent out.

This can be achieved by adding a digital certificate.

2   Add an invisible digital signature.

1.   Click: File→Info→Protect Workbook→Add a digital signature.

If this is the first time you have added a signature, you will see a dialog informing you about how digital certificates are used.

2.   Click the OK button.

The *Sign* dialog appears.

3.   Type a *reason for signing* into the box:

4.   Click the *Sign* button.

Salary Increase-1

If this is the first time you have added a digital signature, the *Signature Confirmation* dialog appears.

5. You are warned that a self-certified certificate cannot be verified. Click *Yes* to confirm that you really do want to use the self-certified certificate.

    The document is now digitally signed.

    Notice that Excel warns you that a self-certified signature cannot be relied upon as it cannot be verified:

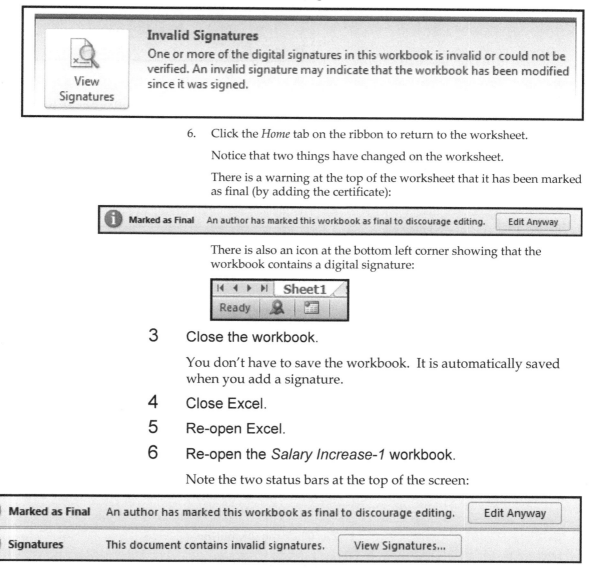

Invalid Signatures
One or more of the digital signatures in this workbook is invalid or could not be verified. An invalid signature may indicate that the workbook has been modified since it was signed.

View Signatures

6. Click the *Home* tab on the ribbon to return to the worksheet.

    Notice that two things have changed on the worksheet.

    There is a warning at the top of the worksheet that it has been marked as final (by adding the certificate):

ⓘ **Marked as Final**   An author has marked this workbook as final to discourage editing. | Edit Anyway |

There is also an icon at the bottom left corner showing that the workbook contains a digital signature:

|◀ ◀ ▶ ▶| Sheet1
Ready   🜲   🔲

3   Close the workbook.

You don't have to save the workbook. It is automatically saved when you add a signature.

4   Close Excel.

5   Re-open Excel.

6   Re-open the *Salary Increase-1* workbook.

Note the two status bars at the top of the screen:

ⓘ **Marked as Final**   An author has marked this workbook as final to discourage editing. | Edit Anyway |

ⓘ **Signatures**   This document contains invalid signatures. | View Signatures... |

You can see that a self-certified digital signature is presented to the user as *invalid* by Microsoft. This is Microsoft's way of saying "the signature is not verified by a third-party agency and cannot be relied upon"!

Note also that the top status bar indicates that the workbook has been opened as read-only.

Salary Increase-1.xlsx [Read-Only] - Microsoft Excel

Lesson 6-15: Add a visible digital signature to a workbook

1   Open *Salary Increase-1* from your sample files folder (if it isn't already open).

2   Remove the invisible digital signature.

    1. Click the signature icon at the bottom-left of the screen.

       The *Signatures* pane appears.

    2. Click the certificate issuer name in the signature pane

       A drop-down arrow appears to the right of the certificate issuer.

    3. Click the drop-down arrow and then click *Remove Signature* from the menu.

    4. The *Remove Signature* dialog appears.

    5. Click Yes

       The *Signature Removed* dialog appears.

> Signature Removed
>
> (i) The signature has been removed and the document has been saved.
>
> ☐ Don't show this message again
>
> OK

    6. Check the *Don't show this message again* check box to prevent this dialog from displaying in future.

    7. Click the OK button.

3   Add a visible signature.

    1. Click: Insert→Text→Signature Line→ Microsoft Office Signature Line.

    2. If a help dialog appears, click OK.

       The *Signature Setup* dialog appears.

    3. Enter a *Name, Title* and *E-mail Address* into the relevant boxes:

Salary Increase-1

Signature Setup

Suggested signer (for example, John Doe):

Joe Kerr

Suggested signer's title (for example, Manager):

HR Director

Suggested signer's e-mail address:

joekerr@miriad.com

Instructions to the signer:

Before signing this document, verify that the content you are signing is correct.

☐ Allow the signer to add comments in the Sign dialog

☑ Show sign date in signature line

OK   Cancel

4. Click the OK button.

A graphic appears on the worksheet with a blank space for the signature. This graphic may be freely dragged to any location on the screen.

	A	B	C	D	E
22	Bill Biggs	19,345	12%	21,666	
23	Angelina Osbourne	38,158	8%	41,211	
24					
25					
26					
27		X			
28					
29		Joe Kerr			
30		HR Director			

5. Double-click the signature graphic.

6. If a help dialog appears, click OK.

The *Sign* dialog allows you to either select a signature image (created from a scan of your handwritten signature) or to type a name into the box.

7. Type a name into the box.

8. Click the *Sign* button.

A signature confirmation dialog appears warning that your self-certified digital signature cannot be verified.

9. Click the *Yes* button.

Microsoft flags the signature as invalid because it is self-certified, easily forged, and thus not of any real use as a security measure.

	B	C	D	E
24	🗎 Invalid signature			
25				
26				
27	X Joe Kerr			
28				
29	Joe Kerr			
30	HR Director			

4   Close the *Salary Increase-1* workbook.

Session 6: Exercise

1 Open *Selling Price Calculator-1* from your sample files folder.

	A	B
3	**Input Cells**	
4	Cost	$ 4.50
5	Retail Price	$ 17.95
6	Wholesale Discount	60%
7	Annual Units	2,000.00
8		
9	**Result Cells**	
10	Sales (at wholesale price)	$14,360.00
11	Total Cost	$ 9,000.00
12	Gross Profit	$ 5,360.00
13	Gross Profit Percent	37%

2 Create an attractively formatted single input data table in cells D3:F18 to display the *Gross Profit* and *Gross Profit Percent* that would result from a *Retail Price* of $17.95 to $24.95 in increments of $0.50.

	D	E	F
3	Retail Price	Gross Profit	Gross Profit Percent
4	$ 17.95	$ 5,360.00	37%
5	$ 18.45	$ 5,760.00	39%
6	$ 18.95	$ 6,560.00	42%

3 Hide columns D:F.

4 Use *Goal Seek* to calculate the *Retail Price* that would be needed to produce exactly 50% *Gross Profit*.

5 Create named ranges for cells B4:B7 and cells B10:B13 using the names in cells A4:A4 and A10:A13.

6 Use the scenario manager to create three scenarios:

Worst Case: 2,000 Annual Units
Expected Case: 3,500 Annual Units
Best Case: 5,000 Annual Units

7 Create a *Scenario Summary* report to show *Sales, Total Cost, Gross Profit* and *Gross Profit Percent* for each scenario.

Scenario Summary					
		Current Values:	Worst Case	Expected Case	Best Case
Changing Cells:					
	Annual_Units	5,000.00	2,000.00	3,500.00	5,000.00
Result Cells:					
	Sales__at_wholesale_price	$ 44,997.45	$ 17,998.98	$ 31,498.22	$ 44,997.45
	Total_Cost	$ 22,500.00	$ 9,000.00	$ 15,750.00	$ 22,500.00
	Gross_Profit	$ 22,497.45	$ 8,998.98	$ 15,748.22	$ 22,497.45
	Gross_Profit_Percent	50%	50%	50%	50%

8 Protect the worksheet so that only cells B4:B7 (the cells shaded yellow) can be changed.

9 Save your work as *Selling Price Calculator-2*.

Selling Price Calculator-1

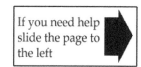

If you need help slide the page to the left

Session 6: Exercise Answers

These are the four questions that students find the most difficult to answer:

Q 6	Q 5	Q 4	Q 2
1. Click: Data→ Data Tools→ What-If Analysis→ Scenario Manager…	1. Select cells A4:B7.	1. Click: Data→ Data Tools→ What-If Analysis→ Goal Seek…	1. Type **Retail Price, Gross Profit** and **Gross Profit Percent** into cells D3, E3 and F3.
2. Click the *Add…* button.	2. Click: Formulas→ Create from Selection.	2. Complete the dialog as follows:	2. AutoSize columns D:F so that all text is visible.
3. Type **Worst Case** into the *Scenario name* box.	3. Click OK.	*Set cell:* $B$13 / *To value:* 50% / *By changing cell:* $B$5	3. Enter the formula: =**B5** into cell D4, =**B12** into cell E4 and =**B13** into cell F4.
Scenario name: Worst Case	4. Repeat for cells A10:B13.	3. Click OK and OK again.	4. Enter the formula: =**D4+0.50** into cell D5.
4. Click in the *Changing cells* box and then click on cell B7.	This was covered in: *Lesson 4-1: Automatically create single-cell range names.*	This was covered in: *Lesson 6-5: Use Goal Seek.*	5. Autofill cell D5 to cells D6:D18.
Changing cells: $B$7			6. Select cells D4:F18.
5. Click the OK button.			7. Click: Data→ Data Tools→ What-If Analysis→ Data Table…
6. Type **2000** into the value box.			8. Set the *Column input cell* to: B5 and click OK.
$B$7 2000			9. Use the *Format Painter* to attractively format each column.
7. Click the OK button.			This was covered in: *Lesson 6-1: Create a single-input data table.*
8. Click the *Add…* button.			
9. Complete the same steps for the *Expected Case* and *Best Case* scenarios.			
This was covered in: *Lesson 6-3: Define scenarios.*			

If you have difficulty with the other questions, here are the lessons that cover the relevant skills:

3   Refer to: *Lesson 6-7: Hide and unhide worksheets, columns and rows.*

7   Refer to: *Lesson 6-4: Create a scenario summary report.*

8   Refer to: *Lesson 6-11: Restrict the cells users are allowed to change.*

7

Session Seven: Working with the Internet, Other Applications and Workgroups

> Teamwork is the ability to work together toward a common vision. The ability to direct individual accomplishments toward organizational objectives. It is the fuel that allows common people to attain uncommon results.
>
> *Andrew Carnegie (1835-1919)*
> *Industrialist, businessman and entrepreneur*

The Internet is one of the defining inventions of our age. Excel has many features that enable you to interact with web sites. In this session you'll learn how to publish data to the Internet. You'll also use web queries to import data from web pages.

Excel objects can be embedded into Word documents. This session shows you how, and you can use the same skills to embed Excel objects into other Office applications such as PowerPoint and Outlook.

Team projects may require several members of a workgroup to open and update a workbook at the same time. In this session you'll learn how to use all of Excel's powerful shared workbook features.

Session Objectives

By the end of this session you will be able to:

- Publish a worksheet as a single web page
- Publish multiple worksheets as a web site
- Hyperlink to worksheets and ranges
- Hyperlink to other workbooks and the Internet
- Hyperlink to an e-mail address and enhance the browsing experience
- Execute a web query
- Embed an Excel worksheet object into a Word document
- Embed an Excel chart object into a Word document
- Link an Excel worksheet to a Word document
- Understand the three different ways to share a document
- Share a workbook using the lock method
- Share a workbook using the merge method
- Share a workbook on a network
- Accept and reject changes to shared workbooks

important

Single file web pages

Traditional web pages store their information in more than one file.

The main file contains all of the text that will be shown on the web page along with formatting information.

The other files contain pictures and other supporting files. You'll see these files in a folder called *Sales Competition-1_files* in the directory you saved the web page file to.

It has long been realized that this is a clumsy arrangement and a new file format was developed as an alternative way to store an entire web page in a single file

Because this is clearly an easier and better way to work, Microsoft added the ability to create *Single File Web Page* files from Word, Excel, PowerPoint and other applications.

You can view a *Single File Web Page* file in Internet Explorer. Unfortunately, (as I write this in 2011), most other browsers (including Firefox, Safari and Google Chrome) don't support single file web pages.

If you are absolutely certain that everybody that views your web page will be using Internet Explorer, you may find a use for single file web pages. In all other cases, you should stay with the traditional *Web Page* format.

In *Lesson 7-2: Publish multiple worksheets as a web site*, you will publish a multi-page workbook. When you publish multiple worksheets you are only able to save in the *single file web page* format.

Sales Competition-1

Lesson 7-1: Publish a worksheet as a single web page

You wouldn't really think about Excel as a web page design tool, but just like Word and PowerPoint, it can create excellent web pages and even an entire web site (using worksheet tabs for navigation).

Nobody would pretend that Excel is a professional web page design tool. Web design professionals tend to use Microsoft Expression Web or Adobe Dreamweaver. Both are powerful web design tools but demand intimate knowledge of HTML and CSS to get the most out of them.

When you need to author a simple web page quickly (or a set of pages using worksheet tabs to navigate between pages), Excel will deliver. All you need are your existing Excel skills. You don't need to know anything about HTML or CSS!

1   Open *Sales Competition-1* from your sample files folder.

Make sure that you open the Excel file and not the web page file. The Excel file has an Excel icon:

Sales Competition-1

This is an attractively formatted workbook containing two worksheets. It provides up-to-date sales figures to encourage rivalry between the five sales teams.

The workbook has two worksheets, one showing the sales figures and the other detailing the wonderful prize for the winning team.

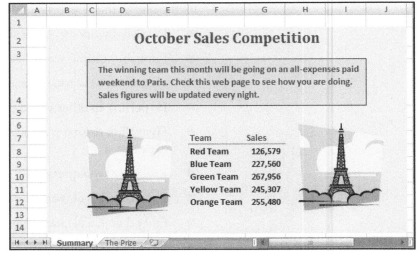

2   Save the *Summary* worksheet as a web page.

It is a good idea to save this to the folder above your sample files folder so that you don't over-write the sample file of the same name.

1.   Click: File→Save As.

2.   Select *Web Page* from the *Save as Type* drop-down list.

note

How does my page get onto the Internet for the world to see?

In this lesson we publish a web page to a set of files on your hard drive. These files can then be opened with a web browser.

The simplest way to share your work with a wider audience is to save the files onto a shared server drive. Anybody in the organisation can then type the file location into their web browser. For example:

F:/web/competition.htm

The example would open a web page called competition.htm stored in the /web directory on the F: shared drive.

To create a "real" web site that can be accessed by typing an http:// address into a browser window, you need to save the files to a special location that is used by a web server.

The web server makes the files available across either an Intranet (a closed-circuit Internet that only people in your organisation can see) or to the Worldwide Web.

While a free web server comes with Windows (called IIS), it is quite challenging to configure and most organizations would leave this to their own IT professionals.

Most web servers are not run in-house but rented from outside suppliers. For a few dollars a month, they will set you up with a domain name (like www.mikesmart.com) and provide disk space to store your HTML files. You then simply copy your HTML files to their server and the world can see your work.

Single File Web Page
Web Page
Excel Template

Notice that there is also a *Single File Web Page* option. See the facing page sidebar for the advantages and disadvantages of choosing this instead.

A new dialog now appears at the bottom of the *Save As* dialog. This contains several options for the web page.

3. Change the *Save* selection from *Entire Workbook* to *Selection: Sheet*.

Save: ○ Entire Workbook
◉ Selection: Sheet
Publish...

This will create a web page showing the contents of the single *Summary* worksheet.

4. Click the *Publish...* button.

The *Publish as Web Page* dialog appears.

5. Make sure that the *Open published web page in browser* check box is checked.

☑ Open published web page in browser

This will allow you to view the web page immediately.

6. Click the *Publish* button.

A web page appears in Internet Explorer (or your default web browser if different). The page looks very professional – it looks no different to a page that one of those professional designers might have created in Dreamweaver or Expression Web!

3   Close the web browser.

4   Save your work as *Sales Competition-2*.

note

Advanced web page options

When you save a web page, the default options are usually the ones that you want.

If you understand a little more about the technicalities of web page design, you may find the web options dialog interesting.

To view the web options dialog:

1. In the *Save As* dialog, click the *Tools* button.

2. Select *Web Options...* from the drop-down menu.

You can view help about all of the options by clicking the help button:

Lesson 7-2: Publish multiple worksheets as a web site

In the last lesson we published a single worksheet as a web page.

Very few web sites consist of only one web page. You'll often need several pages.

In *Lesson 7-3: Hyperlink to worksheets and ranges* we'll learn how to use traditional hyperlinks to jump between workbooks and worksheets. A really fast way to create a multiple page web site is to use the worksheet tabs, instead of hyperlinks, to navigate around the site.

In this lesson we'll use this method to create a two-page web site.

1   Open *Sales Competition-2* from your sample files folder (if it isn't already open).

2   Save the workbook as a two-tab web page.

   It is a good idea to save this to the folder above your sample files folder so that you don't over-write the sample file of the same name.

   1.   Click: File→Save As.

   2.   Select *Web Page* from the *Save as type* drop-down list.

   A new dialog now appears at the bottom of the *Save As* dialog listing several options for the web page.

   3.   Change the *Save* option to *Entire Workbook*.

   This will create a web page with a tab for each worksheet.

   4.   Click the *Publish...* button.

   The *Publish as Web Page* dialog appears.

   5.   In the *Item to publish* drop-down list, select *Entire Workbook*.

   When you choose the *Entire workbook* option, Excel quietly does two things without telling you. It changes the file type to an single-file web page (see facing page sidebar), and changes the *File name* to *Page*. If you'd prefer a more meaningful name you can change it in the *File name* box.

   6.   Make sure that the *Open published web page in browser* check box is checked.

Sales Competition-2

This will allow you to view the web site immediately.

7. Click the *Publish* button.

If you are using Internet Explorer you may hear a beep and then see a warning at the top or bottom of the browser window (depending upon your version of Internet Explorer):

Internet Explorer 8:

Internet Explorer 9:

Because this is a simple web page, the warning will not stop the pages displaying correctly. See the sidebar if you want to know more about Internet Explorer security warnings.

The web site is displayed:

You are able to freely move between web pages by clicking the tabs at the bottom of the dialog.

3   Close the web browser.

4   Save your work as *Sales Competition-3*.

Lesson 7-3: Hyperlink to worksheets and ranges

Because just about everybody uses a web browser, the "point and click" method of doing things comes naturally to most users.

It is possible to give users the same browser-like experience by adding hyperlinks to your workbooks in order to mimic web browser navigation. This isn't just a presentational gimmick. Hyperlink browsing is the most efficient way to quickly navigate to specific parts of long multi-page documents.

note

Adding screen tips to hyperlinks

When you hover the mouse cursor over a hyperlink, a screen tip is displayed showing additional information about the hyperlink's destination.

The default screen tip is rather verbose. It is better to define your own custom screen tips.

To add a screen tip:

1. Select the cell containing the hyperlink you want to add a screen tip to.

2. Click:

Insert→Links→Hyperlink

3. Click the *Screen Tip* button.

4. Add the screen tip text to the box and then click OK and OK again.

Set Hyperlink ScreenTip

ScreenTip text:

Short description of Monaco's history

When you hover the mouse cursor over the hyperlink, the tip is displayed.

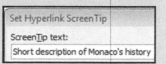

	A	B
5	Background	
6	Geogr	Short description of
7	People	

Monaco-1

1 Open *Monaco-1* from your sample files folder.

This worksheet has a lot of information about Monaco (the second smallest independent state in the world at only 2 sq km).

2 Create a worksheet hyperlink from cell A5 in the *Main Menu* worksheet to the *Background* worksheet.

1. Select cell A5 on the *Main Menu* worksheet.

2. Click: Insert→Links→Hyperlink.

The *Insert Hyperlink* dialog appears.

3. Select *Place in this Document* from the left-hand navigation bar.

4. Select *Background* from the *Or select a place in this document* tree view.

Insert Hyperlink

Link to:	Text to display: Background
Existing File or Web Page	Type the cell reference: A1 Or select a place in this document:
Place in This Document	Cell Reference 'Main Menu' Background Geography People Defined Names
Create New Document	

5. Click OK.

The text in cell A5 has been changed into a hyperlink:

	A
3	**Main Sections**
5	Background
6	Geography
7	People

It is also possible to define a screen tip for the hyperlink (see sidebar).

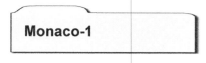

	A	B	C	D
5	Background			
6	Geogr	Short description of Monaco's history		
7	People			

3   Create worksheet hyperlinks from cells A7 and A8 to the *Geography* and *People* worksheets.

Do this in the same way you created the *Background* hyperlink.

	A
3	**Main Sections**
5	Background
6	Geography
7	People
8	Imports

4   Create a range name called *Climate* for cells A32:A33 on the *Geography* worksheet.

1. Select cells A32:A33 on the *Geography* worksheet.

2. Click: Formulas→Defined Names→Create From Selection.

3. Click OK.

5   Create range names called *Population* and *Life expectancy at birth* for cells A3:A5 and A50:A54 on the *People* worksheet.

Note that the range name: *Life_expectancy_at_birth* will be created with underscores as range names cannot have a space.

6   Make cells A12:A14 on the *Main Menu* worksheet into hyperlinks pointing to the range names that you created.

1. Select cell A12 on the *Main Menu* worksheet.

2. Click: Insert→Links→Hyperlink.

The *Insert Hyperlink* dialog appears.

3. Select *Place in this Document* from the left-hand navigation bar.

4. Select *Climate* from the *Or select a place in this document* tree view (*Defined Names* section).

5. Click the OK button.

6. Do the same for *Population* and *Life Expectancy*.

	A
10	**Of Specific Interest**
12	Climate
13	Population
14	Life Expectancy

7   Test your hyperlinks.

When you click upon any of the six defined hyperlinks, you are taken to the relevant defined worksheet or range.

8   Save your work as *Monaco-2*.

Lesson 7-4: Hyperlink to other workbooks and the Internet

1. Open *Monaco-2* from your sample files folder (if it isn't already open).

2. Create a hyperlink from cell A8 in the *Main Menu* worksheet to the *Monaco Economy-1* workbook.

    1. Select cell A8.

    2. Click Insert→Links→Hyperlink.

    3. Click *Existing File or Web Page* in the left-hand navigation bar.

    4. Select *Current Folder* and then the *Monaco Economy-1* file in the center window.

Look in:	Session 7
Current Folder	International Customers-2
	Monaco Economy-1
	Monaco-1

    5. Click OK.

    6. Click the *Imports* hyperlink in cell A8.

    7. The *Monaco Economy-1* workbook opens. Note that the hyperlink took you to cell A1 but the *Imports* data is actually in cells A74:A77

74	Imports:
75	$916.1 million (2005)
76	country comparison to the world: 171
	note: full customs integration with Fran
77	participates in EU market system throug
78	

3. Expand the hyperlink to include cells A74:A77.

    Once Excel has done the hard work of constructing a hyperlink to a different workbook it is easy to expand it to point to a range if required.

    1. Click: View→Window→Switch Windows→Monaco-2

        You are returned to the *Monaco-2* workbook.

    2. If not already selected, move the cursor to cell A8 using the keyboard arrow keys (if you simply click the cell you will fire the hyperlink).

    3. Click: Insert→Links→Hyperlink.

        The hyperlink address is visible in the *Address* box.

Address:	Monaco%20Economy-1.xlsx

    Notice that a hyperlink must have a %20 code in place of any spaces.

tip

Selecting a hyperlink cell with the mouse

In this lesson, you used the keyboard arrow keys to select a cell containing a hyperlink.

There's also a way to do this using the mouse.

If you click and hold the mouse button down for a second or two, you can select a hyperlinked cell without activating the hyperlink.

Monaco-2

note

You can also hyperlink to non Excel files such as Word documents

When you set the *Link to hyperlink* type to *Existing File or Web Page,* you are able to link to any file on your computer.

Most files know which application opens them, so if you link to a Word document, the document will open in Word when you click the hyperlink.

This opens up a huge range of possibilities. You could create a hyperlink on a worksheet that will:

- Play an MP3 sound file.
- View an MPEG video.
- Open a Word document.

... and do anything else that any application installed on your computer is capable of.

4. Edit the hyperlink to reference the range A74:A77 on the *Economy* worksheet by changing the *Address* to the following:

Address:	Monaco%20Economy-1.xlsx#Economy!A74:A77

5. Click the OK button.

4 Test the hyperlink.

When you click the *Imports* hyperlink, you are taken to the *Economy* worksheet in the *Monaco Economy-1* workbook with cells A74:A77 selected.

	A
73	
74	Imports:
75	$916.1 million (2005)
76	country comparison to the world: 171
77	note: full customs integration with France, which collects and rebates Monegasque trade duties; also participates in EU market system through customs union with France

5 Return to the *Monaco-2* workbook.

Click: View→Window→Switch Windows→Monaco-2.

6 Make cell A17 on the *Main Menu* worksheet into a *Web Page* hyperlink pointing to the *Monaco Tourist Office* website at *www.visitmonaco.com*.

1. Select cell A17 on the *Main Menu* worksheet.

2. Click: Insert→Links→Hyperlink.

3. Click *Existing File or Web Page* in the *Link to* navigation bar.

4. Type **www.visitmonaco.com** into the *Address* box.

Address:	http://www.visitmonaco.com

5. Click the OK button.

Cell A17 is converted into a hyperlink pointing to the *Monaco Tourist Office* website.

	A
16	**Useful Web resources**
17	Monaco Government Tourist Office

7 Save your work as *Monaco-3*.

Lesson 7-5: Hyperlink to an e-mail address and enhance the browsing experience

By now you've probably noticed a big problem when creating Excel hyperlinks. The links take you to the desired destination without problems, but how do you get back to the main menu? Excel has sold us a one-way ticket!

In a regular web browser you have a *Back Button, Forward Button* and *Name Box:*

This lesson will show you how to add the same controls to Excel.

You may want to also allow your users to quickly send you e-mail feedback. The easiest way to do this is to add a clickable e-mail link to the worksheet.

1   Open *Monaco-3* from your sample files folder (if it isn't already open).

2   Add a *Back* button to the *Quick Access Toolbar.*

This is another of those really useful Excel features that can only be accessed by customizing the *Quick Access Toolbar* or the *Ribbon.* (You'll learn how to create a custom Ribbon tab later in: *Lesson 8-20: Create a custom Ribbon tab*).

1. Click the drop-down arrow on the right of the *Quick Access Toolbar.*

2. Click *More Commands...* from the drop-down menu.

The *Customize the Quick Access Toolbar* dialog appears.

3. Click *Commands Not in the Ribbon* from the *Choose commands from* drop-down list.

![Choose commands from dropdown showing Popular Commands, Commands Not in the Ribbon, All Commands]

A list appears showing all of the commands that are not normally available in Excel.

4. Select the *Back* command from the commands list.

![Back command button]

5. Click the *Add>>* button to add the *Back* command to the *Quick Access Toolbar.*

Monaco-3

6. Click the OK button.

A back button is now displayed on the *Quick Access Toolbar*.

3 Add a *Forward* button to the *Quick Access Toolbar*.

Forward

4 Add a *Document Location* box to the *Quick Access Toolbar*.

Document Location

5 Test the new navigation controls.

Your Quick Access Toolbar now has familiar browser-like controls.

Click on an Excel hyperlink and then use the *Back* button to return to the *Main Menu* worksheet.

6 Add an e-mail hyperlink to cell A20 on the *Main Menu* worksheet.

1. Type your e-mail address into cell A20 on the *Main Menu* worksheet.

2. Press the **<Enter>** key.

When you press the **<Enter>** key the e-mail address changes into a hyperlink.

	A
19	**Any questions e-mail me...**
20	notta.realname@notreal.com

7 Edit the hyperlink to show a subject link for any generated e-mails.

1. If not already selected, move the cursor to cell A20 using the keyboard arrow keys (if you simply click the cell you will fire the hyperlink).

2. Click: Insert→Links→Hyperlink.

3. Type **Feedback from Monaco Excel workbook** into the *Subject* box.

Subject:

Feedback from Monaco Excel workbook

4. Click the OK button.

8 Test the hyperlink.

When you click the hyperlink, you are taken to your default e-mail application with the destination e-mail address and subject lines already completed.

9 Save your work as *Monaco-4*.

Lesson 7-6: Execute a web query

There are many sites on the Internet containing useful data that is constantly changing. Obvious examples are currency exchange rates and stock prices.

This type of information is usually held in a web page construct called a *table*. Excel allows you to create a web query that refers to a specific table on a specific web page. The web query goes to the web page, takes the current value of the table's contents, and uses it to populate a range of cells on a worksheet.

When a web query has been created, it is possible to update the information in your worksheet at any time. You can even set a timed automatic update so that the information is always current.

1   Open a new blank worksheet.

2   Create a web query to bring back currency exchange rates from the Internet.

    I'm going to use Oanda.com for this lesson. Because this book will have a very long life, and because the Internet is ever-changing, there's a possibility that the site will have changed (or even ceased to exist) between my writing this lesson and your completing it. In this case, you will have to simply use another currency exchange site with a table.

    1.   Select cell A1

    2.   Click: Data→Get External Data→From Web.

       A mini web-browser appears.

    3.   Type www.oanda.com into the *Address* box and press the **<Enter>** key.

    The Oanda web site appears in the browser window.

    Notice that there are small yellow arrows pointing to every table on the web page.

	USD	GBP	EUR	JPY
Real-time exchange rates				
USD	1.0000	1.5646	1.3599	0.01303
GBP	0.6392	1.0000	0.8693	0.00833
EUR	0.7353	1.1504	1.0000	0.00958
JPY	76.738	120.059	104.359	1.0000

note

Setting web query properties

There are many ways in which you can customize the way that your web query operates.

1. Right-click anywhere in the range returned by the web query.

2. Click *Data Range Properties...* from the shortcut menu.

The *External Data Range Properties* dialog appears offering many web query options.

The first option is *Query definition.*

> **Query definition**
> ☑ Save query definition
> ☐ Save password

This allows you to break the link with the web query, converting the web query range into a regular Excel range.

You can also refresh the range automatically at a defined interval using the *Refresh Control* settings.

> **Refresh control**
> ☑ Enable background refresh
> ☑ Refresh every 1 ⬍ minutes

The example above would automatically update the currency exchange rates every minute.

You may find that when the data refreshes the column widths are changed. To prevent this happening clear *the Adjust column width* check box.

> **Data formatting and layout**
> ☑ Include field names
> ☐ Include row numbers
> ☑ Adjust column width

4. Click the yellow arrow to the left of the exchange rate table.

The yellow arrow changes to a green tick and the table is highlighted.

5. Click the *Import* button at the bottom right of the dialog.

The *Import Data* dialog appears.

6. Click the OK button.

After a few seconds, the data from the currency table appears in the worksheet.

If necessary re-size the columns so that they are just wide enough to contain the data.

⬙	A	B	C	D	E
1		USD	GBP	EUR	JPY
2	USD	1	1.5646	1.3599	0.01303
3	GBP	0.6392	1	0.8693	0.00833
4	EUR	0.7353	1.1504	1	0.00958
5	JPY	76.738	120.059	104.359	1

3 Refresh the web query data.

Because the range A1:E5 originates in a web query, you are able to requery the web site whenever you want to bring the data up to date.

1. Right-click anywhere in the range.

2. Click *Refresh* from the short cut menu.

After a short pause, the data refreshes to show current exchange rates.

You may find that the column widths adjust when you refresh. (See sidebar for a solution to this problem).

You can even automate this process to refresh your data as often as once every minute (see sidebar for more details).

4 Save your work as *Exchange Rates-1.*

Lesson 7-7: Embed an Excel worksheet object into a Word document

Microsoft Office is an object-orientated application. Simply put, this means that everything you work with in Office is an object.

An Excel cell, an Excel range of cells, an Excel table, an Excel chart, a Word document and a PowerPoint slide are all objects.

The wonderful thing about this object-orientated architecture is that you can freely embed objects inside other objects. For example, you can embed an Excel range into a Word document, or an Excel chart into a PowerPoint presentation.

In this lesson we'll embed an Excel worksheet into a Word document.

1   Open Microsoft Word.

2   Use Word to open *The World's Best Selling Cars-1* (Word document) from your sample files folder.

This file contains the beginning of a Word document:

> **The World's Best Selling Cars**
> Some cars sell well, others hardly sell at all. Once every few years a car comes along that is demonstrably better than its competition. The car may beat the competition on price, performance, reliability, style, or a combination of these factors.
>
> Here is a list of the world's most successful cars to date:

3   Embed an Excel worksheet at the end of the word document.

1.   Click just to the right of the sentence *"Here is a list of the world's most successful cars to date:"*

2.   Press the **<Enter>** key to move to the next line.

3.   Click: Insert→Text→Object→Object…

The *Object* dialog appears.

4.   Select *Microsoft Excel Worksheet* from the *Object type* list.

> Object type:
> Microsoft Excel Chart
> Microsoft Excel Macro-Enabled Worksheet
> Microsoft Excel Worksheet

5.   Click the OK button.

An empty Excel worksheet is embedded into the Word document.

> Here is a list of the world's most successful cars to date:
>
> | | A | B | C | D | E |
> |---|---|---|---|---|---|
> | 1 | | | | | |
> | 2 | | | | | |

6.   Notice that something has happened to the Ribbon. The Word Ribbon has been replaced by the Excel Ribbon!

The World's Best Selling Cars-1

4   Enter the following data into the worksheet:

	A	B	C
1	Make	Model	Sales (Million)
2	Ford	Model T	16.5
3	Volkswagen	Beetle	21.5
4	Volkswagen	Golf	24
5	Ford	F Series	25
6	Toyota	Corolla	35

(When you have entered the data AutoSize each column so that each is wide enough to display the contents).

5   Return to Word.

Click anywhere on the Word document text (outside the Excel object).

Notice that the appearance of the worksheet has changed and that the Excel Ribbon has changed back to the Word Ribbon.

6   *Print Preview* the document.

Click: File→Print.

Notice that the worksheet looks just as it would in Excel. The worksheet is too big, however, as there are many empty cells.

7   Return to Excel.

1.   Click the *Home* tab on the ribbon.

2.   Double click anywhere in the Excel object.

Notice that the Excel Ribbon has returned.

8   Size the worksheet window so that it is the same size as the data entered.

1.   Hover over the sizing handle on the bottom right corner of the worksheet until you see the double-headed arrow.

2.   Click and drag upwards and to the left to re-size the worksheet object so that it is the same size as its contents.

9   Return to Word.

Click anywhere on the Word document text (outside the Excel object).

> Here is a list of the world's most successful cars to date:
>
> | Make | Model | Sales (Million) |
> |------|-------|-----------------|
> | Ford | Model T | 16.5 |
> | Volkswagen | Beetle | 21.5 |
> | Volkswagen | Golf | 24 |
> | Ford | F Series | 25 |
> | Toyota | Corolla | 35 |

10 Save your work as *The World's Best Selling Cars-2*.

Lesson 7-8: Embed an Excel chart object into a Word document

1   Open Microsoft Word.

2   Use Word to open *The World's Best Selling Cars-2* (Word document) from your sample files folder (if it isn't already open).

3   Convert the range to a table.

> **Create Table**
>
> Where is the data for your table?
>
> `=$A$1:$C$6`
>
> ☑ My table has headers
>
> OK   Cancel

      1.   Double-click the Excel object to return to Excel.

         The Excel Ribbon replaces the Word Ribbon.

      2.   Click inside the range.

      3.   Click: Insert→Tables→Table.

      4.   Click OK to accept the automatically detected range.

         The range is converted to a table.

4   Remove the AutoFilter from the table.

      The AutoFilter buttons don't look good in a Word document.

      Click: Data→Sort & Filter→Filter.

      The filter buttons vanish.

5   Sort the table from bestselling to least selling.

      1.   Click anywhere in column C.

      2.   Click Data→Sort & Filter→Sort Largest to Smallest.

6   Format the values in column C so that they display one decimal place.

      1.   Select the values in column C.

      2.   Click Home→Number→Increase decimal.

7   Add the text **... and here is the same data as a chart** to the end of the document.

      1.   Click anywhere on the document text to return to Word.

      2.   Click slightly to the right of the table.

      3.   Press the **<Enter>** key to move to the next line.

      4.   Type the text: **... and here is the same data as a chart.**

      5.   Press the **<Enter>** key to move to the next line.

Make	Model	Sales (Million)
Toyota	Corolla	35.0
Ford	F Series	25.0
Volkswagen	Golf	24.0
Volkswagen	Beetle	21.5
Ford	Model T	16.5

... and here is the same data as a chart.

The World's Best Selling Cars-2

note

Use the same technique to embed objects into (and from) PowerPoint and other applications

The mechanism that allows you to embed and link documents is called OLE (Object Linking and Embedding).

Any application that supports OLE is happy to work with any other OLE compatible application.

Applications supporting OLE include (of course) the entire Office suite along with many Adobe and other third-party applications.

You'll find OLE fantastically useful to add Excel ranges and charts to Word documents and PowerPoint presentations, but there's no need to stop there!

8 Copy the Excel object to the end of the document.

1. Click the Excel object once to select it (be careful to only click once, if you double-click you will go back into Excel).

2. Copy.

3. Click on the line after the text: **... and here is the same data as a chart.**

4. Paste.

An identical Excel object now appears in both places.

9 Convert the duplicated Excel object into a chart.

1. Double-click the lower Excel object to go back into Excel.

2. Select cells A1:C6.

3. Click: Insert→Charts→Pie→2-D Pie→Pie.

The worksheet now contains a pie chart.

4. Right-click just inside the top-left corner of the pie chart.

5. Click *Move Chart...* on the shortcut menu.

6. Click the *New Sheet* option button.

> ⦿ New sheet: Chart1

7. Click OK.

A tiny pie chart is shown in the Excel object.

10 Re-size the Excel chart object so that the legend shows each make and model.

This was covered in: *Lesson 7-7: Embed an Excel worksheet object into a Word document.*

11 Return to Word.

Click anywhere on the document text.

Here is a list of the world's most successful cars to date:

Make	Model	Sales(Million)
Toyota	Corolla	35.0
Ford	F Series	25.0
Volkswagen	Golf	24.0
Volkswagen	Beetle	21.5
Ford	Model T	16.5

... and here is the same data as a chart.

Sales(Million)

- Toyota Corolla
- Ford F Series
- Volkswagen Golf
- Volkswagen Beetle
- Ford Model T

12 Save your work as *The World's Best Selling Cars-3.*

Lesson 7-9: Link an Excel worksheet to a Word document

1 Open Microsoft Word.

2 Open *International Customers-1* from your sample files folder.

This file contains the beginning of a document:

> **Information for International Customers**
>
> We are happy to supply our products to any world location and to bill you in your own currency.
>
> We convert our prices using the following exchange rates:

3 Insert the *International Customer Rates-1* Excel Workbook at the end of the document as a linked object.

1. Click just to the right of the sentence: *We convert our prices using the following exchange rates:*

2. Press the **<Enter>** key to move down to the next line.

3. Click: Insert→Text→Object→Object.

    The *Object* dialog is displayed.

4. Click the *Create from File* tab.

5. Click the *Link to file* check box.

    ☑ Link to file

6. Notice the help text that has appeared:

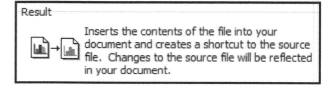

    Result

    Inserts the contents of the file into your document and creates a shortcut to the source file. Changes to the source file will be reflected in your document.

    This means that any changes to the Excel worksheet will immediately appear in the linked Excel object.

7. Click the *Browse...* button.

8. Navigate to the *International Customer Rates-1* workbook.

9. Click the *Insert* button.

10. Click OK

    The exchange rates are now displayed inside the Word document.

International Customers-1

note

Link and embed objects using Drag and Drop

You can simply drag and drop a range of cells from Excel to Word. Make sure that you <Ctrl>-click-drag if you want to copy the range. If you simply click and drag, you'll remove the range from the workbook!

To drag and drop, you'll need to arrange your screen so that you can see both the Excel and Word document windows at the same time.

When you drag and drop, Word has to guess whether you want to link or embed.

If you drag and drop a chart, Word will link. If you drag and drop a range of cells, Word will embed.

Because of this limitation, the other methods are preferable when you need to control linking and embedding.

We convert our prices using the following exchange rates:

Exchange Rates

Country	Multiply GBP Price by:	To get price in:
USA	1.59077	US Dollar
Australia	1.78756	Australian Dollar
Canada	1.68582	Canadian Dollar
Euro	1.08224	Euro
Hong Kong	12.32888	Hong Kong Dollar
Indonesia	15,164.60	Indonesian Rupiah
Japan	141.128	Japanese Yen
Singapore	2.22958	Singapore Dollar
Sweden	11.13615	Swedish Krona
Switzerland	1.63895	Swiss Franc
Thailand	53.18778	Thai Baht

4 **Test the link by changing values in the Excel workbook.**

Linked objects work in a different way to embedded objects.

When you double-click an embedded object you are able to edit it inside the Word document.

When you double-click a linked object Excel will open with the linked file open inside Excel.

1. Double-click the Excel object.

   Excel opens with the *International Customer Rates-1* workbook open.

2. Re-size the Excel and Word windows so that you can see both documents.

3. Change one of the exchange rates in the *International Customer Rates-1* workbook.

4. Click once in the Word document window to make it the active window.

5. Right-click the Excel linked object in the *International Customers-1* Word document.

6. Click *Update Link* on the shortcut menu.

   Values are normally only updated when you open the Word document. The *Update Link* command tells Word to refresh the data it is displaying.

   Notice that the values update to match those in the workbook.

5 **Close the Excel window.**

6 **Save the Word document as *International Customers-2*.**

Lesson 7-10: Understand the three different ways to share a document

> When an undertaking hath been committed to many, it caused but confusion, and therefore it is a saying... too many cooks spoils the broth.
>
> *B Gerbier , Principles of Building 24 (1662)*

Document sharing is one of the most confusing and complex Excel features.

To use document sharing properly, you need to understand the real-world problems that document sharing must overcome.

In order to understand the three different sharing methods Excel provides, we'll step outside the world of Excel and consider how we might have shared paper documents in the pre-computer age.

The lock method

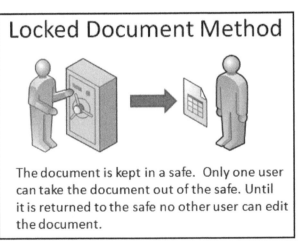

Locked Document Method

The document is kept in a safe. Only one user can take the document out of the safe. Until it is returned to the safe no other user can edit the document.

This is the simplest (and easiest) method to use. The feature is covered in: *Lesson 7-11: Share a workbook using the lock method.*

The merge method

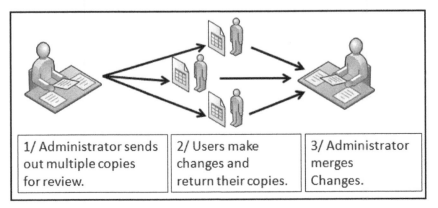

1/ Administrator sends out multiple copies for review.	2/ Users make changes and return their copies.	3/ Administrator merges Changes.

Excel allows you to send out multiple copies of a workbook by e-mail, and then merge all of the documents back into a master document when they are sent back with revisions. This feature is covered in: *Lesson 7-12: Share a workbook using the merge* method.

Sharing workbooks on a network

Sending e-mail documents for revision isn't the most efficient way to work. If you have a network, it is better to save the workbook onto a shared drive, and then to have many different people work on it *at the same time.*

This method is explained in: *Lesson 7-13: Share a workbook on a network.*

Using a network makes the process far easier as you don't need to manually merge the changes.

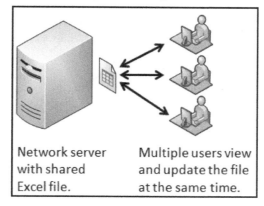

Network server with shared Excel file.

Multiple users view and update the file at the same time.

This method presents Excel with several challenges:

- If two users change the same cell at the same time – which change should succeed? In Excel terminology, we'd say: "which change should *win*"?

- How can we implement an audit trail so that we know which user changed which piece of data? In Excel terminology, we'd like to be able to *track changes.*

- How can a manager approve changes that users have made?

Excel rises to the challenge and provides comprehensive tools to cater for each of these requirements.

By the end of this session you'll completely understand how to use all of Excel's shared workbook features.

Lesson 7-11: Share a workbook using the lock method

This is the easiest method because it is outrageously simple to implement. You don't have to do anything at all other than to place your workbook on a shared drive.

Sometimes you will have a single workbook that must be viewed and updated by many different people. To do this, the workbook is placed on a shared network drive so that many different people can view and update it.

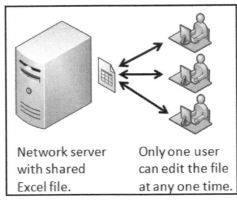

Network server with shared Excel file.

Only one user can edit the file at any one time.

Here's how things could go wrong if more than one user was allowed to edit the file at the same time:

1. Mike opens a workbook and makes some changes.

2. Before Mike has saved and closed the workbook, Mary opens the same workbook, makes some changes, saves, and closes the workbook.

3. Mike now saves his workbook, over-writing Mary's changes.

Excel prevents this from happening by preventing two users from opening the same book, in read/write mode, at the same time. Here's how it works:

1. Mike opens a workbook and makes some changes.

2. Mary tries to open the same workbook. The Excel policeman says:

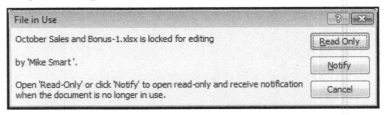

3. Mary really wants to change the workbook so she clicks *Notify*.

The workbook still opens but in *Read-Only* mode. She is able to read it but cannot save any changes (unless she saves a copy by changing the name of the workbook).

4. Mike saves and closes his workbook.

October Sales and Bonus-1

5. A little message pops up on Mary's desktop (it's the Excel policeman again):

6. Mary clicks the *Read-Write* button to open the workbook, makes her changes, saves, and closes the workbook.

In this lesson, you'll see Excel manage document locking to make sure that only one user is able to edit a workbook at any one time.

1 Open *October Sales and Bonus-1* from your sample files folder.

2 Open another instance of Excel.

While Excel is open, open Excel again. You will then have two instances of Excel open at the same time. This is to enable you to simulate another user attempting to open the workbook.

3 Arrange the screen so that you can see both Excel windows.

4 Attempt to open *October Sales and Bonus-1* in the second instance of Excel.

A warning dialog is displayed:

> **File in Use**
>
> October Sales and Bonus-1.xlsx is locked for editing by 'Mike Smart'.
>
> Open 'Read-Only' or click 'Notify' to open read-only and receive notification when the document is no longer in use.
>
> [Read Only] [Notify] [Cancel]

5 Click the *Notify* button.

The file opens in *Read Only* mode. In this mode you are unable to save any changes to the workbook. The title bar at the top of the window changes to inform you that you are in *Read-Only* mode.

> October Sales and Bonus-1.xlsx [Read-Only] - Microsoft Excel

6 Close the file in the first instance of Excel.

Eventually a dialog will appear. Be patient! It took six seconds to appear on my computer but may take a lot longer on yours.

> **File Now Available**
>
> 'October Sales and Bonus-1.xlsx' is now available for editing. Choose Read-Write to open it for editing.
>
> [Read-Write] [Cancel]

7 Click *Read-Write* to open the file for editing.

8 Close the second instance of Excel.

You don't have to save the file as you haven't changed it in any way.

Lesson 7-12: Share a workbook using the merge method

In *Lesson 7-11: Share a workbook using the lock* method, you explored Excel's default way of handing workbook sharing.

This method works but is very primitive. There are four problems:

1. There's no history to let you know which user made each change.

2. There's no review process to allow you to approve changes before they are applied.

3. Only one user can edit the document at the same time.

4. Every user must be connected to the network.

If all of the reviewers are connected to a network, you wouldn't want to use the merge method described in this lesson. It is more efficient to share the workbook on a network, (you'll learn about this in: *Lesson 7-13: Share a workbook on a network*).

In this lesson, we'll assume that all of the reviewers are not connected to a network. In this case, you would need to send review copies by e-mail and then merge any changes made when they were returned.

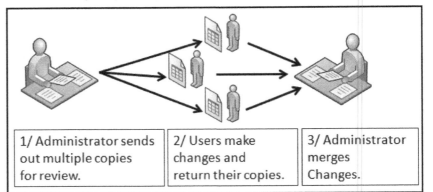

1/ Administrator sends out multiple copies for review.	2/ Users make changes and return their copies.	3/ Administrator merges Changes.

1 Open *October Sales and Bonus-1* from your sample files folder (if it isn't already open).

2 Save the file as *October Sales and Bonus-2*.

In a moment, this workbook will be converted to a shared workbook. When you do this it will demand to be saved.

By saving it with a new name you will avoid over-writing the original file, enabling you to repeat the following three lessons at a later date if required.

3 Enable workbook merging by converting the workbook to a shared workbook.

1. Click: Review→Changes→Share Workbook.

The *Share Workbook* dialog appears.

2. Check the *Allow changes by more than one user at the same time. This also allows workbook merging* check box.

October Sales and Bonus-1

☑ Allow changes by more than one user at the same time. This also allows workbook merging.

3. Click the OK button.

You are now prompted to save the workbook.

4. Click OK.

Notice that the title bar at the top of the Excel window now advises that this is a shared file.

October Sales and Bonus-2.xlsx [Shared] - Microsoft Excel

4 Make a copy of the workbook to send to your reviewer.

Save the workbook as: *Harry – October Sales and Bonus-2.*

This is the file that you would e-mail to Harry for review. You could also make more copies to send to other employees.

5 In Harry's review copy of the workbook change *Lucille Ashe's* sales to **23,200** and *John Bradshaw's* Sales to **27,500**.

1. Change *Lucille Ashe's* sales (cell C8) to **23,200**.

2. Change *John Bradshaw's* sales (Cell C10) to **27,500**.

6 Save the *Harry-October Sales and Bonus-2* workbook.

7 Add the *Compare and Merge Workbooks* command to the Quick Access Toolbar (see sidebar).

8 Merge the changes from the *Harry-October Sales and Bonus-2* workbook into the *October Sales and Bonus-2* workbook.

1. Close the *Harry-October Sales and Bonus-2* workbook.

A workbook cannot be merged from unless it is closed.

2. Open the *October Sales and Bonus-2 Workbook.*

3. Click the new *Compare and Merge Workbooks* button ⬤ on the *Quick Access Toolbar.*

4. Select the *Harry-October Sales and Bonus-2* workbook and click the *OK* button. (If you had multiple workbooks to merge you could hold the **<Ctrl>** button down and then select several files and merge them all at the same time).

Notice that cells C8 and C10 are highlighted to show that they have been changed.

5. Hover the mouse over cell C8 and notice that you are able to view the change history.

	C	D	E	F	G
7	26,900				
8	2⊕200	Mike Smart , 12/10/2009 12:04: Changed cell C8 from ' £17,400.00 ' to ' £23,200.00 '.			
9	16,800				

9 Save the workbook but keep it open for the next lesson.

note

How to add the *Compare and Merge Workbooks* command to the *Quick Access Toolbar*

The *Compare and Merge Workbooks* feature is yet another of those fantastically useful tools that most Excel users will never discover, because you won't find it anywhere on the Ribbon or dialogs.

In order to use it, you have to add a button to the *Quick Access Toolbar* or customize the Ribbon. (You'll learn how to create a custom Ribbon tab later in: *Lesson 8 19: Create a custom Ribbon tab*).

1. Click the drop-down arrow on the right of the *Quick Access Toolbar.*

2. Click *More Commands...* from the drop-down menu list.

3. Select *Commands Not in the Ribbon* from the *Choose commands from* drop-down list.

4. Select *Compare and Merge Workbooks...* from the command list.

5. Click the *Add>>* button.

6. Click the OK button.

You now have a new command button on the *Quick Access Toolbar* that will *Compare and Merge Workbooks.*

Lesson 7-13: Share a workbook on a network

In *Lesson 7-12: Share a workbook using the merge method*, you explored a way of distributing multiple copies of a workbook via e-mail for review.

If reviewers are connected to a network, there is a much better way of sharing a workbook that will avoid the need to manually merge workbooks.

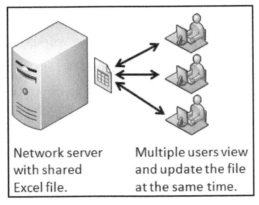

Network server with shared Excel file.

Multiple users view and update the file at the same time.

Because several users may edit the same workbook, there is a possibility that two users will change the same cell at the same time. This is called a *conflict*. When this happens, Excel must decide which user will "win" (their change is accepted) and which will "lose" (their change is rejected).

Excel also provides reviewing tools to allow you to change Excel's decision later. (Reviewing is covered in: *Lesson 7-14: Accept and reject changes to shared workbooks*).

note

How to find out who else has the workbook open

You can view a list of the other users who are currently working with a shared workbook.

1. Click:

Review→Changes→Share Workbook.

The *Share Workbook* dialog is displayed.

2. Click the *Editing* tab.

A list of all users who currently have the workbook open is displayed.

1   You should still have *October Sales and Bonus-2* open from the last lesson.

The three lessons beginning with: *Lesson 7-12: Share a workbook using the merge method* must be completed sequentially.

2   Open *October Sales and Bonus-2* again in another instance of Excel.

1.   While Excel is open, open Excel again.

2.   Open *October Sales and Bonus-2* in the new instance.

You now have two instances of Excel open at the same time, each viewing the same workbook.

This is to enable you to simulate two users opening the same workbook at the same time. For the rest of this lesson, I will call the first instance *User 1* and the second instance *User 2*.

3   Arrange the screen so that you can see both Excel windows.

4   Change Jane Anderson's sales (cell C6) to 22,000 in the *User 1* window.

You must begin this sequence of three lessons at: Lesson 7-12

	B	C			B	C
6	Anderson	22,000		6	Anderson	20,000
7	Armstrong	26,900		7	Armstrong	26,900

Notice that you cannot yet see the change in the *User 2* window.

5   Change Jane Anderson's sales (cell C6) to 24,000 in the *User 2* window.

	B	C			B	C
6	Anderson	22,000		6	Anderson	24,000
7	Armstrong	26,900		7	Armstrong	26,900

We now have a classic conflict. Both users have changed cell C6 but, until they save their changes, Excel doesn't have to resolve the conflict.

6   Save the *User 1* window.

Excel still cannot see a conflict because it doesn't yet know whether *User-2* will ever save changes.

You still cannot see *User-1's* change in the *User 2* window.

7   Save the *User 2* window.

Excel now detects the conflict and asks how it should be resolved.

Resolve Conflicts

Your changes on sheet 'Sales_Bonus':

Changed cell C6 from ' £20,000.00 ' to ' £24,000.00 '.   [Accept Mine]

Conflicting changes by Mike Smart - 11/10/2009 18:58:

Changed cell C6 from ' £20,000.00 ' to ' £22,000.00 '.   [Accept Other]

[Accept All Mine]   [Accept All Others]   [Cancel]

8   Click *Accept Mine* to accept *24,000* as the correct value.

9   Close the *User-1* window.

10   Change the conflict option so that the most recent save always wins.

A moment ago Excel asked you which change should win. This is the default way of handling conflicts. It is possible to change this behavior so that Excel simply saves the most recent change without bothering you.

1.   Click: Review→Changes→Share Workbook.

2.   Click the *Advanced* Tab.

3.   Click the *The changes being saved win* option button.

Conflicting changes between users
- ○ Ask me which changes win
- ● The changes being saved win

4.   Click the OK button.

11   Save the workbook but keep it open for the next lesson.

---

note

Automatically update changes made to a shared workbook

In an ideal world, all users of a shared workbook would see changes as soon as any user typed a value into a cell.

Unfortunately, Excel can't yet quite do that, but it can show you all changes made in the last five minutes.

Perhaps Excel will reduce this refresh rate in a later version. I know many users that would like to automatically refresh values every few seconds.

Here's how to switch auto-refresh on:

1. Click: Review→Changes→ Share Workbook.

2. Click the *Advanced* tab.

3. In the *Update Changes* section click the *Automatically every...* option.

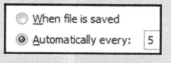

- ○ When file is saved
- ● Automatically every: [5]

Note that the minimum automatic refresh is 5 minutes but you can change it to a higher number if you wish.

Note also that you will only see other user's changes *when they save their workbook.*

Because you (and other users) may forget to save your changes, there's also an option to automatically save.

- ● Save my changes and see others' changes
- ○ Just see other users' changes

Lesson 7-14: Accept and reject changes to shared workbooks

Excel maintains an audit trail of every change made to a shared workbook. This is called the *change history*. Change history is useful for two reasons:

1. It allows you to review changes made by other users and reverse them if needed.

2. It provides an audit trail that can be automatically added to a *History* tab in the shared workbook (see sidebar on facing page).

1 **You should still have *October Sales and Bonus-2* open from the last lesson.**

The three lessons beginning with: *Lesson 7-12: Share a workbook using the merge method* must be completed sequentially.

2 **Review and accept all changes made to the workbook to date.**

1. Click: Review→Changes→Track Changes→Accept/Reject Changes.

2. The *Select Changes to Accept or Reject* dialog is displayed.

3. Click OK.

You are presented with details of the single edit made to cell C8.

4. Click *Accept* to accept the edit.

5. Click *Accept* to accept the next change (to cell C10).

You now see a different dialog showing details of all edits to cell C6. This is a different dialog because cell C6 has been changed three times.

note

Change history options

Because the history saves every single change to the workbook, a shared Excel file can get very large.

If file size is an issue, and if you can do without the history features, you may wish to switch it off.

History is maintained for 30 days by default, but you are able to increase or decrease this period.

To edit the *change history* options:

1. Click: Review→Changes→ Share Workbook.

2. Click the *Advanced* tab.

The *Track Changes* section allows you to edit the change history options.

You must begin this sequence of three lessons at: Lesson 7-12

The change history is displayed in a dialog so that you can decide which of the three edits to accept:

6.   Select the second item in the list (when the value in cell C6 was changed to 22,000).

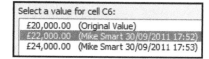

7.   Click the *Accept* button to accept the previous value of 22,000.

Notice that the value in cell C6 reverts to 22,000.

3   Understand *Track Changes* options.

Click: Review→Changes→Track Changes→Highlight Changes…

The *Highlight Changes* dialog is displayed showing several options that may be set when reviewing changes.

As is so often the case, the default options are nearly always what you need, but here's how you can use the other options.

> | ☑ Whe_n: | Not yet reviewed | ▼ |
> |---|---|---|
> | ☐ Wh_o: | Since I last saved | |
> | | All | |
> | ☐ Whe_re: | Not yet reviewed | |
> | | Since date... | |

The *When* options allow you to filter the change history based upon time. *Not yet reviewed* is the one you'll use most as you probably won't want to review the same changes twice.

> | ☑ Wh_o: | Everyone | ▲ |
> |---|---|---|
> | ☐ Whe_re: | Everyone | |
> | | Everyone but Me | |
> | | Mike Smart | |

The *Who* options allow you to focus upon a particular user, or to filter out your own changes as you do not normally need to review your own edits.

> | ☑ Whe_re: | $C$19:$C$29 | 🔲 |
> |---|---|---|

The *Where* option allows you to view changes on a selected range of cells. This could be useful if you wanted to know which users have edited a specific cell or cells.

> ☑ Highlight changes on _screen
> ☐ _List changes on a new sheet

Highlight changes on screen will surround each changed cell with a box and place a triangle in the top left corner. This allows you to view all changes by hovering the mouse cursor over the cell.

See sidebar for more information about the last option: *List changes on a new sheet.*

4   Save your work as *October Sales and Bonus-3.*

---

note

How to list all changes on a separate history worksheet

1. Click :Review→Changes→ Track Changes→ Highlight Changes...

2. Make sure that the *When, Who* and *Where* check boxes are not checked (to list all changes).

3. Check the *List changes on a new sheet* check box.

> ☑ _List changes on a new sheet

4. Click the OK button.

A history worksheet is created listing a full history of all changes made to the shared workbook.

▲	A	B	C
1	Action Number ▾	Date ▾	Time ▾
2	1	30/09/2011	17:38
3	2	30/09/2011	17:38
4	3	30/09/2011	17:52
5	4	30/09/2011	17:53

Session 7: Exercise

1 Open the *Spectrum Car Sales-1* Excel workbook from your sample files folder.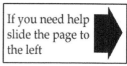

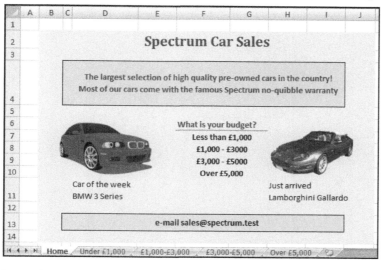

2 Hyperlink the *What is your budget?* cells (F7, F8, F9 and F10) to the relevant worksheets.

3 Hyperlink the *Car of the week BMW 3 Series* text (cell D11) to the *Under £1,000* worksheet.

4 Hyperlink the *Just arrived Lamborghini Gallardo* text (cell H11) to the *Over £5,000* worksheet.

5 Make the *e-mail sales@spectrum.test* text in cell D13 into an e-mail hyperlink that will send an e-mail to the e-mail address: *sales@spectrum.test* with the subject: *Car sales enquiry*.

6 Publish the entire workbook as a single file web page and view it in your browser.

7 Close your browser, save the workbook as *Spectrum Car Sales-2* and close Excel.

8 Open the *Stock List-1* sample file in Microsoft Word.

9 Place a linked object after the text in the *Stock List-1* word document that will show the contents of the *Over £5,000* worksheet in the *Spectrum Car Sales-2* workbook.

Here is our current stock list of cars in the over £5,000 category:

Cars over £5,000

All of these cars have a six month warranty

Make	Model	Year	Miles	Price
Ferrari	Testarossa 4.9 2 door	1990	26,500	£29,950
Rolls Royce	Silver Spirit II 6.8	1986	59,000	£8,000
Aston Martin	DB7 Volante 2 door convertible	1999	51,000	£24,750
Lamborghini	Gallardo 2 door Convertible	2004	36,000	£59,989

10 Save the Word document as *Stock List-2*.

Spectrum Car Sales-1   Stock List-1

If you need help slide the page to the left

Session 7: Exercise Answers

These are the four questions that students find the most difficult to answer:

Q 9	Q 6	Q 5
1. Open the *Spectrum Car Sales-2 workbook* in Excel.	1. Click: File→Save As	1. Select cell D13 on the *Home* worksheet.
2. Select the *Over £5,000* worksheet.	2. Select *Single File Web Page* as the *Save as type*.	2. Click: Insert→Links→Hyperlink.
3. Save and close the *Spectrum Car Sales-2* workbook.	3. Make sure that the *Entire Workbook* option button is selected.	3. Click *E-mail Address* on the left-hand selection bar.
4. Open the *Stock List-1* document in Microsoft Word.	Save: ⦿ Entire Workbook / ○ Selection: Sheet	4. Complete the dialog as follows:
5. Click just to the right of the *... £5,000 category:* text.	4. Click *Publish...*	E-mail address: / mailto:sales@spectrum.test / Subject: / Car sales enquiry
6. Press the **<Enter>** key to move to the next line.	5. Select *Entire Workbook* in the *Choose* drop-down list.	5. Click OK.
7. Click: Insert→Object→Object.	Choose: Entire workbook	This was covered in: *Lesson 7-5: Hyperlink to an e-mail address and enhance the browsing experience.*
8. Select the *Create from File* tab.	6. Make sure that the *Open published web page in browser* check box is checked.	
9. Click the *Browse* button and select the *Spectrum Car Sales-2* workbook.	7. Click the *Publish* button.	
10. Click the *Insert* button.	The entire workbook appears in your web browser as a tabbed web page.	
11. Check the *Link to File* check box.	This was covered in: *Lesson 7-2: Publish multiple worksheets as a web site.*	
12. Click the OK button.		
This was covered in: *Lesson 7-9: Link an Excel worksheet to a Word document*		

If you have difficulty with the other questions, here are the lessons that cover the relevant skills:

2,3,4 Refer to: *Lesson 7-3: Hyperlink to worksheets and ranges.*

Session Eight: Forms and Macros

> Any sufficiently advanced technology is indistinguishable from magic.
>
> *Sir Arthur C. Clarke (1917-2008)*
> *British science fiction author, inventor and futurist*

You can design Excel applications for users who have no Excel skills. When you create this type of application, you need to provide a simple and intuitive form-based user interface. The user interface should be so simple that the application can be used without any training.

In this session you'll create a powerful, form-based, Excel application with a simple and intuitive user interface.

You'll also learn how to record and run macros. Macros allow you to provide users with simple form controls that execute a complex sequence of Excel actions.

Session Objectives

By the end of this session you will be able to:

- Add group box and option button controls to a worksheet form
- Add a combo box control to a worksheet form
- Set form control cell links
- Connect result cells to a form
- Add a check box control to a worksheet form
- Use check box data in result cells
- Add a temperature gauge chart to a form
- Add a single input data table to a form
- Improve form appearance and usability
- Understand macros and VBA
- Record a macro with absolute references
- Understand macro security
- Implement macro security
- Understand trusted documents
- Record a macro with relative references
- Use shapes to run macros
- Run a macro from a button control
- Show and hide Ribbon tabs
- Add custom groups to standard Ribbon tabs
- Create a custom Ribbon tab

Lesson 8-1: Add group box and option button controls to a worksheet form

1   Open *Mortgage Calculator-1* from your sample files folder.

2   Add the *Developer* tab to the ribbon.

Because form controls are an advanced feature of Excel, Microsoft hides them from normal users. You must add the *Developer* tab to the Ribbon in order to reveal them.

1. Click: File→Options→Customize Ribbon.

2. Check the *Developer* check box in the right-hand pane.

3. Click OK.

The *Developer* tab is now visible on the Ribbon.

3   Delete row 5 and then insert two new blank rows so that there are four blank rows between *Property Price* and *Arrangement Fee*.

4   Add a *Group Box* control so that it completely fills cells B5:D6.

1. Click: Developer→Controls→Insert→Form Controls→ Group Box (Form Control).

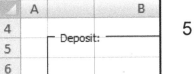

2. Hold down the **<Alt>** key. This will make the group box snap to the corners of the cells selected.

3. Carefully position the black cross cursor on the top left corner of cell B5.

4. Click and drag to the bottom right corner of cell D6 and release the mouse button.

A group box appears.

5   Change the caption of the group box to: **Deposit:**

1. Double click the *Group Box 1* caption on the border of the group box.

2. Delete the existing *Group Box 1* text and then type **Deposit:**

6   Add six option button controls to the group box.

1. Click: Developer→Controls→Insert→Form Controls→ Option Button (Form Control).

2. Click and drag inside the group box to add an option button. Keep the button small as you need space for six buttons and it is useful if they do not overlap. Be careful to keep the border of each option button inside the group box.

Mortgage Calculator-1

3. Repeat for the other five buttons. It is important that you add them in sequence from left to right. Your option group should now look like this:

7 **Change the option button captions to 5% to 30% (reading left to right).**

You need to use a special technique to rename an option button.

1. Right-click on the option button to select it.

    A box appears around the option button along with a shortcut menu.

2. Press the <Esc> key or click once again inside the control to close the shortcut menu (an even faster way to do steps one and two in a single operation is to double right-click the control).

3. Double-click the text next to the option button.

4. Delete the existing text and type **5%.**

5. Do the same for the **10%** to **30%** option buttons.

8 **Move and re-size the option buttons so that they are evenly spaced inside the group box.**

1. Select an option button and close the shortcut menu.

2. Use the arrow keys on the keyboard to move the option button to its new position.

3. Click and drag one of the white circles (sizing handles) on the border of the option button to re-size if necessary.

4. Your option group should now look like this:

9 **Add another set of option buttons to show terms from 5 to 30 years.**

1. Delete row 12 and then insert three new rows.

2. Add a group box control so that it completely fills cells B12:D14.

3. Add the option buttons. It is important that you add them in sequence (in ascending order).

10 Save your work as *Mortgage Calculator-2.*

Lesson 8-2: Add a combo box control to a worksheet form

1   Open *Mortgage Calculator-2* from your sample files folder (if it isn't already open).

2   Delete the contents of cell D16.

3   Remove the black border from cell D16.

    1.   Select cell D16.

    2.   Click: Home→Font→Borders→No Border.

4   Place a combo box control in cell D16.

    1.   Select cell D16.

    2.   Click: Developer→Controls→Insert→Form Controls→ Combo Box (Form Control).

    3.   Hold down the **<Alt>** Key. This will make the control fit perfectly in the cell.

    4.   Click just inside the top left border of cell D16 and drag to just inside the bottom right border.

    5.   The control is inserted into the cell (and fits perfectly).

	A	B	C	D
15				
16		Interest:		▼
17				

5   Create a new worksheet called *Data* to provide interest rate data from 2% to 15% in increments of 0.5%.

    1.   Create a new worksheet called *Data*.

| |◄ ◄ ► ►| | **Mortgage Calculator** / Data / |

    2.   Select the Data worksheet.

    3.   Type: **Interest Rates** into cell A1.

    4.   Type: **2.0**% into cell A2.

    5.   Type the formula: **=A2+0.005** into cell A3.

    6.   AutoFill cell A3 into cells A4:A28.

6   Format cells A2:A28 so that only one decimal place is shown.

    1.   Select cells A2:A28.

    2.   Click: Home→Number→Decrease Decimal.

	A	B
1	Interest Rates	
2	2.0%	
3	2.5%	
4	3.0%	
5	3.5%	

Mortgage Calculator-2

7   Create a range name for the interest rate values in cells A2:A28.

Range names were extensively covered in: *Session Four: Using Names and the Formula Auditing Tools*.

1. Select cells A1:A28.

2. Click: Formulas→Defined Names→Create from Selection.

3. Click OK.

8   Set the combo box's *Input Range* to reference the interest rate data.

1. Select the *Mortgage Calculator* worksheet.

2. Right-click the border of the combo box control.

3. Click *Format Control...* on the shortcut menu.

4. Select the *Control* tab.

5. Click in the *Input Range* box.

6. Type **Interest_Rates** into the *Input Range* box.

Input range:	Interest_Rates	

7. Click the OK button.

9   Test the combo box control.

1. Click away from the control to de-select it.

2. Click the drop-down arrow on the combo box.

3. Notice that the combo box displays all of the interest rates defined by the *Interest_Rates* range name.

10   Save your work as *Mortgage Calculator-3*.

Lesson 8-3: Set form control cell links

When working with forms, it is useful to separate the user interface from the input and result cells. The user interface is the part of the worksheet where the user enters values and views results. In this worksheet the user interface comprises of cells B3:D20.

Calculations are done in a different section of the worksheet where you will define *Input Cells* and *Result Cells*. You'll recognise this method of working from the lessons in: *Session Six: What If Analysis and Security.*

In this worksheet the *Input Cells* and *Result Cells* are shown in cells B23:D36. Later we will hide these rows from the user.

In this lesson we'll connect the *User Interface* with the *Input Cells.*

1   Open *Mortgage Calculator-3* from your sample files folder (if it isn't already open).

2   Link the user interface's *Property Price, Arrangement Fee,* and *Annual Income (after tax)* cells to the relevant *Input Cells.*

This is extremely easy as it can be done using simple cell references:

	B	C	D
23	**Input Cells**	**Value**	**Actual**
24	Property Price		=D3
25	Deposit		
26	Arrangement Fee		=D8
27	Term		
28	Interest		
29	Annual Income (after tax)		=D18

3   Connect the data from the *Deposit* group box to cell C25.

1.   Right-click the *5% Deposit* option button.

2.   Select *Format Control...* from the shortcut menu.

3.   Click the *Control* tab.

4.   Click in the *Cell link* box.

5.   Click in cell C25.

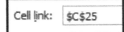

6.   Click the OK button.

4   Test the cell link.

1.   Click away from the option buttons to de-select.

2.   Left-click each option button in turn.

3.   Notice that numbers from 1 to 6 appear in cell C25 as each option button is clicked. Option 5% results in 1, option 10% results in 2… and so on.

Mortgage Calculator-3

If you find that the wrong numbers are appearing, it is because you added the option buttons in the wrong order. In this case you'll have to move the buttons around and change their captions, until you have the correct number associated with each button.

5   **Add a formula to cell D25 so that it displays the correct percentage for each option.**

1.   Type **=C25*.05** into cell D25.

2.   Test again. This time the actual percentage of the selected option button should display in cell D25.

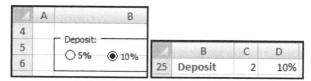

6   **Connect the data from the *Term* group box to cell C27.**

Do this in exactly the same way that you connected the *Deposit* group box to cell C25.

7   **Add a formula to cell D27 to show the actual term.**

1.   Type = **C27*5** into cell D27.

2.   Test the *Term* option buttons.

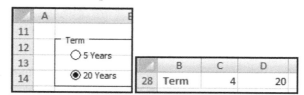

8   **Connect the data from the *Interest* combo box to cell C28.**

1.   Right-click the combo box control.

2.   Click *Format Control...* from the shortcut menu.

3.   Click the *Control* Tab.

4.   Click in the *Cell link* box.

5.   Click in cell C28.

Cell link:	$C$28

6.   Click OK.

9   **Test the *Interest* combo box cell link.**

Just like the option button controls, the value returned from the combo box is a number representing which option was selected. 2% returns the number 1, 2.5% returns the number 2... and so on.

10   **Add a formula to cell D28 so that it displays the correct interest rate.**

Type the formula **=(C28*0.5+1.5)/100** into cell D28.

11   **Test the combo box.**

12   **Save your work as *Mortgage Calculator-4*.**

Lesson 8-4: Connect result cells to a form

In the previous lessons we created a user interface using Excel's form controls.

The form now collects data from the user, and uses this data to update the input cells.

In this lesson we'll use the input cells to calculate the result cells, and then use the result cells to update the form.

1 Open *Mortgage Calculator-4 from* your sample files folder (if it isn't already open).

2 Add a formula to cell D32 that will calculate the *Amount Financed.*

   Amount Financed = Property Price – Deposit + Arrangement Fee

   To perform this calculation you need to type the formula:

   =D24-D24*D25+D26

   ...into cell D32.

3 Add a formula to cell D33 to calculate the *Monthly Repayment.*

   For this calculation we will use the PMT function that was covered in: *Lesson 3-3: Use the formula palette and the PMT function.*

   The function arguments will be:

Rate	D28/12
Nper	D27*12
Pv	D32
Fv	
Type	

4 Convert the negative *Monthly Repayment* to a positive value.

   The easiest way to do this is to place a minus operator in front of the function:

   f_x =-PMT(D28/12,D27*12,D32)

5 Add a formula to cell D34 to calculate the *Total Repaid.*

   Total Repaid = Monthly Repayment * 12 * Term

   To perform this calculation you need to type the formula:

   =D33*12*D27

   … into cell D34.

6 Add a formula to cell D35 to calculate the *Total Interest.*

   Total Interest = Total Repaid – Amount Financed

Mortgage Calculator-4

To perform this calculation you need to type the formula:

=D34-D32

... into cell D35.

7   Add a formula to cell D36 to calculate the *Repayment as % of Income*.

Repayment as % of Income =
Monthly Repayment * 12/Annual Income (after tax)

To perform this calculation you need to type the formula:

=D33*12/D29

... into cell D36.

8   Connect the *Amount Financed* result cell (D32) to the *Amount Financed* form cell (D10).

Type the following formula into cell D10:

=D32

9   Connect the *Monthly Repayment* result cell (D33) to the *Monthly Repayment* form cell (D20).

Type the following formula into cell D20:

= D33

10 Test the form.

Enter the values shown below into the form. The result cells should match those shown:

	A	B	C	D
3		**Property Price:**		350,000
4				
5		Deposit:		
6		○ 5% ○ 10% ○ 15% ◉ 20% ○ 25% ○ 30%		
7				
8		**Arrangement Fee:**		5,000
9				
10		**Amount Financed:**		285,000
11				
12		Term:		
13		○ 5 Years ○ 10 Years	○ 15 Years	
14		○ 20 Years ◉ 25 Years	○ 30 Years	
15				
16		**Interest:**	5.0%	▼
17				
18		**Annual Income (after tax):**		38,000

	B	C	D
31	**Result Cells**		
32	Amount Financed		285,000
33	Monthly Repayment		1,666.08
34	Total Repaid		499,824
35	Total Interest		214,824
36	Repayment as % of Income		53%

11 Save your work as *Mortgage Calculator-5*.

Lesson 8-5: Add a check box control to a worksheet form

In this lesson we will improve the form to model interest-only mortgages.

1   Open *Mortgage Calculator-5* from your sample files folder (if it isn't already open).

2   Left-align the text in cell B16.

     1.   Select cell B16.

     2.   Click: Home→Alignment→Align Text Left.

3   Move the combo box so that it appears directly after the *Interest:* text.

     1.   Right-click the combo box.

     2.   If a shortcut menu appears either press the **<Esc>** key or click once again inside the control to close it.

     3.   Use the arrow keys on the keyboard to move the combo box to its new position.

     4.   Your combo box should now look like this:

	A	B	C
15			
16		Interest: 5.0% ▼	

4   Add a check box control so that it completely fills cells C16:D16.

     1.   Click: Developer→Controls→Insert→ Check Box (Form Control).

     2.   Hold down the **<Alt>** Key. This will make the control fit perfectly in the cells.

     3.   Click just inside the top left border of cell C16 and drag to just inside the bottom right border of cell D16.

     4.   The control is inserted into the cells (and fits perfectly).

	B	C	D
15			
16	Interest: 5.0% ▼	☐ Check Box 20	

Your check box may have a caption such as *Check Box 19* as the control number is not consistently applied.

5   Change the check box caption to *Interest Only Loan*.

Change this in the same way you changed the option button captions in: *Lesson 8-1: Add group box and option button controls to a worksheet form*.

	B	C	D
15			
16	Interest: 5.0% ▼	☐ Interest Only Loan	

Mortgage Calculator-5

6   Add an input cell to link to the new check box.

    1.   Insert a row above row 29.

    2.   Type the text **Interest Only?** Into cell B29.

	B	C	D
28	Interest	7	5.0%
29	Interest Only?		
30	Annual Income (after tax)		38,000

7   Connect the data from the *Interest Only Loan* check box to cell D29.

    1.   Right-click the *Interest Only Loan* check box.

    2.   Select *Format Control...* from the shortcut menu.

    3.   Click the *Control* tab.

    4.   Click in the *Cell link* box.

    5.   Click in cell D29.

> Cell link: $D$29

    6.   Click the OK button.

8   Test the cell link.

    1.   Click away from the check box to de-select.

    2.   Click the *Interest Only Loan* check box a few times.

    When the box is checked, TRUE appears in cell D29. When the box is unchecked, FALSE appears in cell D29.

	C	D
16	☑ Interest Only Loan	

	B	C	D
29	Interest Only?		TRUE

	C	D
16	☐ Interest Only Loan	

	B	C	D
29	Interest Only?		FALSE

9   Save your work as *Mortgage Calculator-6*.

Lesson 8-6: Use check box data in result cells

1   Open *Mortgage Calculator-6* from your sample files folder (if it isn't already open).

2   Correct the *Monthly Repayment* result cell (D34) to allow for interest only loans.

1.   Click in cell D34.

2.   Click the *Insert Function* button to the left of the formula bar.

D34	▼	f_x	=-PMT(D28/12,D27*12,D33)

3.   The *Function Arguments* dialog appears.

The capital owed at the end of an interest only loan (Excel's terminology for this is: *Future Value*) will be the same as the *Amount Financed*. The *Future Value* will thus be:

Amount Financed * -1

A normal capital and repayment loan will have been repaid by the end of the term, so there will be no future value.

In order to make the PMT function return the correct value for both types of loan, we will have to use the IF logic function to set the future value. The IF function was covered in: *Lesson 3-5: Use the IF logic function.*

4.   Type the following formula into the *Fv* argument box:

Fv	IF(D29=TRUE, D33*-1,0)	

5.   This will set the *Future Value* to be the same as the **Amount Financed *-1** for an interest only loan, and to **zero** for a capital and repayment loan.

3   Correct the *Total Interest* result cell (D36) to allow for interest only loans.

A capital and repayment loan will incur interest of:

Total Repaid – Amount Financed.

Every payment in an *interest only* loan consists only of interest. This means that the *Total Interest* will be the same as the *Total Repaid.*

In order to correct the *Total Interest* result cell we will, once again, have to use an IF logic function.

1.   Click in cell D36.

2.   Delete the previous formula.

3.   Add an IF function. The function arguments are:

Mortgage Calculator-6

IF	
Logical_test	D29
Value_if_true	D35
Value_if_false	D35-D33

4   Test the check box.

I tested with the following form values:

	A	B	C	D
1		**Mortgage Calculator**		
2				
3		**Property Price:**		350,000
4		Deposit:		
5		○ 5% ○ 10% ○ 15% ● 20% ○ 25% ○ 30%		
6				
7				
8		**Arrangement Fee:**		5,000
9				
10		**Amount Financed:**		285,000
11		Term		
12		○ 5 Years ○ 10 Years ○ 15 Years		
13				
14		● 20 Years ○ 25 Years ○ 30 Years		
15				
16		**Interest:** 5.0% ▼ ☐ Interest Only Loan		
17				
18		**Annual Income (after tax):**		38,000
19				
20		**Monthly Repayment:**		1,880.87

When the *Interest Only Loan* box was unchecked the *Result Cells* were:

	B	C	D
32	**Result Cells**		
33	Amount Financed		285,000
34	Monthly Repayment		1,880.87
35	Total Repaid		451,410
36	Total Interest		166,410
37	Repayment as % of Income		59%

When the *Interest Only Loan* box was checked the *Result Cells* were:

	B	C	D
32	**Result Cells**		
33	Amount Financed		285,000
34	Monthly Repayment		1,187.50
35	Total Repaid		285,000
36	Total Interest		285,000
37	Repayment as % of Income		38%

5   Save your work as *Mortgage Calculator-7*.

Lesson 8-7: Add a temperature gauge chart to a form

Charting is covered in depth in the *Essential Skills* book in this series. Excel doesn't have a temperature gauge chart in its pre-defined range of charts. It is possible to create this type of chart by formatting a regular bar chart in a special way.

1   Open *Mortgage Calculator-7* from your sample files folder.

2   Add a bar chart to the worksheet with the single data value of *Repayment as % of Income.*

   1.   Select cell D37.

   2.   Click: Insert→Charts→Column→2D Column→ Clustered Column.

   3.   Right-click the center of the chart and then click *Select Data…* on the shortcut menu.

   4.   Click the *Edit* button above the *Legend Entries (Series)* list box.

   5.   Remove all of the text in the *Series values* box.

   6.   Click in the *Series values* box and then click cell D37.

   7.   Click OK and then OK again.

      You now have a chart with a single bar showing the loan affordability as a percentage of income.

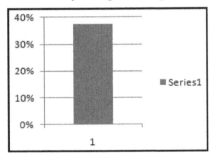

3   Change the vertical axis so that it begins at 0% and ends at 100%.

   1.   Click the chart to activate it.

   2.   Right click on the *Vertical (Value Axis).*

   3.   Click *Format Axis:* on the shortcut menu.

   4.   Set the *Minimum* and *Maximum* values to 0 and 1.

Minimum:	○ A<u>u</u>to	◉ F<u>i</u>xed	0.0
Maximum:	○ A<u>u</u>to	◉ Fi<u>x</u>ed	1

   5.   Click the *Close* button.

4   Remove the gap from the left hand side of the bar.

   1.   Right-click on the column and then click *Format Data Series…* from the shortcut menu.

   2.   Click *Series Options* on the left hand selection bar.

Mortgage Calculator-7

3. Change the *Gap Width* to *0%, No Gap* and then click *Close.*

5 Remove the *Legend* and *Horizontal Axis Labels* from the chart.

1. Click on the chart to activate it.

2. Click: Chart Tools→Layout→Labels→Legend→None.

3. Click: Chart Tools→Layout→Axis→Axes→ Primary Horizontal Axis→None.

6 Put a thin black line around the Plot Area.

1. Right-click in the center of the chart (but not on the bar or a gridline).

2. Click *Format Plot Area…* from the short cut menu.

3. Click *Border Color* on the left-hand selector bar.

4. Click the *Solid Line* option button.

5. Click the *Color* button and select *Black,* then click *Close.*

7 Re-size the chart so that it resembles a temperature gauge that is the same height as the form.

1. Click on the chart to select it.

2. Click and drag the bottom right-hand corner sizing handle to size as required.

3. Click and drag anywhere on the border of the chart that is not a sizing handle to move it to the required position.

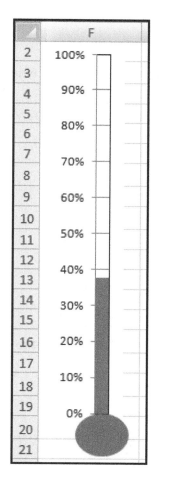

8 Remove the border around the chart.

1. Click on the chart to select it.

2. Right-click on the border of the chart.

3. Click *Format Chart Area…* on the shortcut menu.

4. Click *Border Color* on the left-hand selection bar.

5. Click the *No line* option button, and then click *Close.*

9 Add an oval shape to mimic the bulb at the bottom of a thermometer.

1. Click away from the chart to de-select it.

2. Click: Insert→Illustrations→Shapes→Basic Shapes→Oval.

3. Click and drag to draw an oval at the bottom of the chart.

4. Right-click the shape.

5. Click *Format Shape…* on the shortcut menu.

6. Click *Fill* on the left-hand bar and set a fill color that matches the color of the bar.

7. Click *Line Color* on the left-hand bar and then click *No line.*

8. Click the *Close* button.

Your chart should now look similar to the sidebar.

10 Save your work as *Mortgage Calculator-8.*

Lesson 8-8: Add a single input data table to a form

We covered single-input data tables in: *Lesson 6-1: Create a single-input data table*. In this lesson we'll recap this skill by adding a single-input data table to the form to show how repayments could increase if interest rates were to rise by up to 4% more than the current rate.

Mortgage Calculator-8

1   Open *Mortgage Calculator-8* from your sample files folder (if it isn't already open).

2   Add titles for each of the data table's columns.

Type labels into cells H2:L2 so that they are the same as the following:

	H	I	J	K	L
2	Interest	Monthly Repayment	Repayment as % of Income	Total Repaid	Total Interest

3   Merge cells H1:H2, I1:I2, J1:J2, K1:K2 and L1:L2.

1.   Select cells H1:H2.

2.   Click: Home→Alignment→Merge and Center→Merge Cells.

3.   Repeat for the other cell pairs.

4   Switch text wrapping on for cells H1:L1.

1.   Select cells H1:L1.

2.   Click: Home→Alignment→Wrap Text.

5   Arrange the labels so that they appear on two lines where necessary.

1.   Double-click just before the word *Repayment* in cell I1 (*Monthly Repayment*).

2.   Hold down the **<Alt>** key.

3.   Press the **<Enter>** key.

4.   Repeat for the other column labels.

5.   Re-size each column.

6.   Your column headers should now look like this:

	H	I	J	K	L
1		Monthly	Repayment	Total	Total
2	Interest	Repayment	as % of Income	Repaid	Interest

6   Add a formula to cell H3 that will show the interest rate selected on the form.

1.   Click in Cell H3.

2.   Add the formula: **=(C28*0.5+1.5)/100**

You need to refer to cell C28 rather than D28 to work-around an odd quirk in Excel data tables (see sidebar).

7   Add a formula to cell H4 that will show an interest rate 1% higher than the rate in cell H3.

1. Click in cell H4.

2. Add the formula: **=H3+0.01**

8   AutoFill the formula in cell H4 to cells H5:H7.

9   Format the formulas in cells H3:H7 so that they only display one decimal place.

1. Select cells H3:H7 and format the cells to show percentages.

2. Click: Home→Number→Decrease Decimal.

3. Click: Home→Number→Increase Decimal.

10   Add formulas to cells I3:L3 that will reference the relative result cells.

The correct formulas are:

	I	J	K	L
1	Monthly	Repayment	Total	Total
2	Repayment	as % of Income	Repaid	Interest
3	=D34	=D37	=D35	=D36

11   Add a single input data table to cells H3:L7.

1. Select cells H3:L7.

2. Click: Data→Data Tools→What-If Analysis→Data Table…

The *Data Table* dialog appears.

3. Click in the *Column input cell* box.

4. Click in cell D28.

5. Click OK.

Data Table

Row input cell:	
Column input cell:	$D$28

OK   Cancel

12   Copy the format in cells I3:L3 to cells I4:L7.

1. Select cells I3:L3.

2. Click: Home→Clipboard→Copy.

3. Select cells I4:L7.

4. Click: Home→Clipboard→Paste→Paste Special…

5. Click the *Formats* option button.

6. Click OK.

13   Resize the columns if necessary.

Your data table now looks similar to this:

	H	I	J	K	L
1		Monthly	Repayment	Total	Total
2	Interest	Repayment	as % of Income	Repaid	Interest
3	5.0%	1,529.94	48%	550,779	265,779
4	6.0%	1,708.72	54%	615,139	330,139
5	7.0%	2,091.23	66%	752,842	467,842
6	8.0%	2,714.12	86%	977,084	692,084
7	9.0%	3,603.67	114%	1,297,320	1,012,320

The actual values shown on your worksheet may differ depending upon the values selected.

14   Save your work as *Mortgage Calculator-9*.

Lesson 8-9: Improve form appearance and usability

An elegant form-based user interface enables you to create utilities for users with no Excel skills. The form should be so intuitive that staff training is not needed. In its present form the Mortgage Calculator might intimidate non-technical users. We need to do a few more things to make this into a really professional form. They are:

- Improve the appearance of the form.

- Hide irrelevant worksheets and cells. In this case we need to hide the *Input Cells, Result Cells* and the *Data worksheet*.

- Protect the form so that users cannot alter the functionality or layout.

1   Open *Mortgage Calculator-9* from your sample files folder.

2   Add a pie chart to show the *Amount Financed* and *Total Interest.*

   1. Click cell D33, hold down the **<Ctrl>** key and click cell D36.

   2. Click: Insert→Charts→Pie→3-D Pie→Pie in 3D.

   3. Move and re-size the chart so that it fills cells H9:L20.

   4. Right-click on the center of the Pie Chart.

   5. Click *Select Data...* from the shortcut menu.

   6. Click the *Edit* button at the top of the *Horizontal (Category) Axis Labels* list box.

   7. Click on cell B33, hold down the **<Ctrl>** key and click cell B37.

   8. Click OK, and then click OK again.

3   Surround the form area with two narrow padding columns.

   It is useful for a form to be clearly delineated from the worksheet. This is best achieved by adding two narrow padding columns to each border of the form (see the screen grab on the front cover of this book).

   The borders can then be shaded to clearly mark the form edges.

   1. Add two very narrow columns to the left of column A.

   2. Add two very narrow rows above row 1.

   3. Add two very narrow rows above row 24.

   4. Make columns P and Q very narrow.

4   Shade the form area (excluding controls and cells that the user will enter data into) light yellow.

   1. Click in cell D22.

   2. Set the background color to very light yellow.

   3. Double-click: Home→Paste→Clipboard→Format Painter.

   4. Click once in each cell that should be yellow (see cover of this book for guidance).

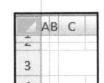

Mortgage Calculator-9

You may have to move the checkbox control in order to shade the cells behind it, and then move it back again.

5. Click: Home→Paste→Clipboard→Format Painter to switch the format painter off.

5 **Use a similar technique to format the worksheet to match the design shown (in color) on the cover of this book.**

You will have to add padding columns around the temperature gauge chart.

Sample file *Mortgage Calculator-10* has the end result as shown on the book cover. You can use different formatting and colors if you think that they look better.

6 **Switch off the gridlines.**

The gridlines are spoiling the appearance of the group boxes.

Click: View→Show→Gridlines.

7 **Unlock cells F5, F10, F20, E29, E31, E32 and F33.**

In a moment we will protect the workbook. At this point it will only be possible to change unlocked cells.

Notice that you have to unlock cells E29, E31 and E32 because a control cannot change a value in a locked cell.

1. Select all of the cells to be unlocked.

2. Right-click one of the selected cells.

3. Click *Format Cells…* from the shortcut menu.

4. Click the *Protection* tab and clear the *Locked* check box.

Cell locking and protection were covered in: *Lesson 6-11: Restrict the cells users are allowed to change.*

8 **Configure the charts to use data in hidden rows and columns.**

See sidebar if you are unsure how to do this.

9 **Hide the *Data worksheet*, *Input Cells* and *Result Cells* (rows 27:41).**

1. Right-click the Data tab and click *Hide* on the shortcut menu.

2. Select rows 27:41.

3. Right-click in the selected area and click *Hide* on the shortcut menu.

10 **Protect the worksheet.**

1. Click: Review→Changes→Protect Sheet.

2. Add a password if you want greater security.

3. Check the *Select Unlocked cells* check box.

4. Uncheck the *Select Locked cells* check box.

5. Click OK.

11 **Save your work as *Mortgage Calculator-10*.**

---

note

Charting data in hidden rows and columns

By default a chart cannot use source data that is in a hidden row or column.

To chart data in hidden rows and columns:

1. Right-click in the centre of the chart.

2. Click *Select Data...* on the shortcut menu.

3. Click the *Hidden and Empty Cells* button.

4. Check the *Show data in hidden rows and columns check box.*

☑ Show data in hidden rows and columns

5. Click OK and OK again.

Charting was covered in depth in the *Essential Skills* book in this series.

Allow all users of this worksheet to:
☐ Select locked cells
☑ Select unlocked cells

---

note

VBA is a programming language that can be used to write custom extensions to Excel

Microsoft Office is written in a very special way. It consists of several hundred objects all "glued" together with programming code. In: *Lesson 7 8: Embed an Excel chart object into a Word document*, you saw how easy it was to place one object inside another object.

Microsoft has documented all of the objects that make up Office, so that programmers can use Office objects in their own applications.

I regularly use Excel chart objects when I write accounting applications and need to display data as a graph. The users don't even know that I "borrowed" the functionality from Excel, and Microsoft don't mind a bit (as long as each computer has an Office licence).

Because all of the objects that make up Excel can be used in other computer programs, it is possible to add new features to Excel that Microsoft didn't anticipate you would want.

Here's an example:

Commodity and Foreign Exchange traders often want a live data feed connected to an Excel worksheet so that they can see up-to-the-second, constantly updating, stock market, commodity and foreign exchange prices in their worksheets. Excel can't do that "out of the box" but a competent VBA programmer can connect the feed into the worksheet in a matter of minutes.

VBA isn't an Excel-specific skill. The Visual Basic language can be used to add functionality to Excel, Word, PowerPoint, Visio, Project... and many other Microsoft and third party applications.

Lesson 8-10: Understand macros and VBA

Macros are a very misunderstood concept. Most books cause terrible confusion by mixing up the twin subjects of macros and the VBA (Visual Basic for Applications) programming language. You don't need to know how an engine and gearbox work to drive a car. VBA is a little like the engine and gearbox, you don't need to know anything about the VBA programming language to use macros.

Macros record keystrokes and mouse-clicks

The macro recorder is able to record (and playback) every mouse click or key stroke that you make. Here's how I would record a simple macro:

1. Start the recorder to record a macro called *Mike*.

2. Type my name into cell A5.

3. Press the **<Enter>** key.

4. Stop the recorder.

I've now recorded a macro that I can play back in future. The macro recorded the following key presses:

Press the **<M>** key, press the **<i>** key, press the **<k>** key, press the **<e>** key, press the **<Enter>** key.

Perhaps I'd like to play back the *Mike* macro in the future. This is what I might do:

- Click in cell B10.

- Run the *Mike* macro.

The word *Mike* then magically appears in cell B10 and the cursor moves down to cell B11. The macro player has pressed all of the keys for me!

The actual method that Excel uses, to save and play back your key presses and mouse clicks, is to automatically write VBA code. But you don't need to know anything at all about those technicalities in order to record and play macros.

1 Open a new blank workbook.

2 Begin recording a macro called *MyName* with a shortcut key of **<Ctrl>+<m>**.

    1. Click: View→Macros→Macros→Record Macro.

    2. Type **MyName** into the *Macro name* box.

        Note that macro names cannot have a space.

    3. Type a lower case **m** into the *Ctrl+* box.

    4. Select *This Workbook* in the *Store macro in* drop-down list.

note

A little knowledge is a dangerous thing

Alexander Pope, poet (1688-1744)

While I can teach you all you need to know about macros in less than an hour, I'd need several days to teach you to be a competent and professional Visual Basic programmer.

I run my Excel VBA programming courses across two to five days and still don't have enough time to cover really advanced topics (such as user defined classes). VBA is one of those subjects that it isn't useful to know a tiny bit about, so I am not going to attempt to teach you even a tiny bit in this book.

Of the hundreds of people I've taught in my Excel VBA programming courses, a large number found that the skills were not useful. Many of them would have benefited far more from my *Expert Skills* course.

Most of the problems that they had imagined needed custom VBA coding could be better (and more easily) solved by the correct use of the Excel features you've learned in this book.

The other options for this setting will be explained later.

5. Describe your macro in the *Description* box.

> Description:
> Puts my name into the active cell

6. Click the OK button – but do nothing else!

You are now recording your macro. There's no time element to a macro recording so you can be relaxed. The macro will record every key press and every mouse click, so it is important that you do not press any keys or click anywhere with the mouse.

3   Record a macro that will put your name into the active cell.

1. Type your name into the currently active cell.

Remember that every click and keystroke are recorded, so be careful not to move to any other cell. If you did, your name would always appear in the cell you had moved to when the macro was played.

> Mike

2. Press **<Ctrl>+<Enter>**.

3. When you press **<Ctrl>+<Enter>** you save the value into the cell without moving to the next line. This keystroke combination is very useful when recording macros.

4   Stop the macro recording.

You can do this in two ways:

Click: View→Macros→Macros→Stop Recording.

OR

Click the Stop button on the bottom left of the status bar.

> |◄ ◄ ► ►| Sheet1
> Ready ▣

It is a common error to forget to stop a macro recording. I've had Excel crash in my classes when a student had forgotten and then accidentally continued to record for a long period.

note

Learning more about VBA

In the near future, I plan to publish my Excel VBA course as a book and video.

By the time you read this book it may be available.

Search Amazon for:

Learn Excel 2010 VBA with The Smart Method.

5   Test the macro.

1. Click in any blank cell.

2. Click: View→Macros→Macros→View Macros.

The macro dialog appears listing only the *MyName* macro (as you have only recorded one macro so far).

3. Click the *Run* button.

Your name appears in the currently active cell.

4. Click in another blank cell and press **<Ctrl>+<m>**.

Once again your name appears in the currently active cell.

6   Close the workbook without saving.

note

Choosing where to store your macros

There are three possible places to store a macro:

Store macro in:

This Workbook

Personal Macro Workbook
New Workbook
This Workbook

Macros stored in *This Workbook* are also available to other workbooks – but only if the workbook containing the macro is open!

The *Personal Macro Workbook* is a special workbook called *Personal.xlsb*. This is stored in a folder called XLSTART buried deep in the file system where nobody is likely to find and change it.

Whenever you open Excel, the Personal Macro Workbook opens in the background (but it is hidden so you never see it). Because it is always open, every workbook has access to its macros at all times.

The only purpose of the Personal Macro Workbook is to act as a container to store macros that you want to be available to every workbook.

Remember that if you store macros in the Personal Macro Workbook, they will only work on your machine. If you e-mail a workbook that depends upon one of these macros, it will not work on the recipient's machine. In this type of scenario you'd want to store the macro in *This Workbook*.

You'll rarely want to use the *New Workbook* option. If you record a macro in a new workbook you would have to always make sure that it was open before you could access its macros.

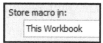

Expenses Claim-1

Lesson 8-11: Record a macro with absolute references

1   Open *Expenses Claim-1* from your sample files folder.

Imagine that this is a form you need to fill in every week. Every time you make an expenses claim, you have to add your *Employee Number* and other details. This isn't very efficient so you decide to record a macro that will automatically complete part of the form.

2   Begin recording a macro.

Click: View→Macros→Macros→Record Macro.

The *Record Macro* dialog appears.

3   Name the macro *FillInExpenseForm*.

Type **FillInExpenseForm** into the *Macro name* box.

Note that macro names cannot have a space. Always use mixed case for macro names and do not abbreviate. (For example, don't use names such as **FillExpFrm** – they will only confuse).

4   Assign a shortcut key of **<Ctrl>+<e>** to the macro.

Type a lower case **e** into the *Ctrl+* box.

See the sidebar on facing page for more about choosing macro shortcut keys.

5   Store the macro in *This Workbook*.

Note that there are three possible places to store a macro

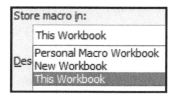

Normally you'll simply want to choose between *This Workbook* (when the macro is only useful in one workbook) and the *Personal Macro Workbook* (when the macro may be used by all workbooks). See the sidebar for more details.

This macro will only ever be used in the *Expenses Claim-1* workbook, so the most appropriate location is in *This Workbook*.

If there were many expense claim forms that all had the same data in cells B3, B5, B7, B9 and B11 you'd want to store the macro in the *Personal Macro Workbook* to make it available to all workbooks on your computer.

Store macro in:

This Workbook

6   Add a *Description* to the macro.

It is good practice to describe your macros so that other users will understand what they are used for. The description is displayed in the *Macro* dialog when the user runs the macro.

important

Choosing macro shortcut keys

Excel provides many shortcut keys (such as **<Ctrl<+<c>** to copy).

If you were to define **<Ctrl>+<c>** as your macro shortcut key you would override Excel's shortcut key and you'd no longer be able to use **<Ctrl>+<c>** to copy (as it would run the macro instead).

There are several strategies to avoid causing clashes with the built-in shortcut keys:

1. Use capital letters for shortcut keys. This will result in a shortcut key of:

<Ctrl>+<Shift>+<c>

You will then still be able to copy using the normal **<Ctrl>+<c>**.

2. Only run macros from the Ribbon.

Click:

View→Macros→Macros→ View Macros

You can also use the shortcut key **<Alt>+<F8>).**

This is quite an awkward way to access your macros.

3. Provide the user with buttons to run macros. You'll learn how to do this in: *Lesson 8-17: Run a macro from a button control.*

4. Add a button to the *Quick Access Toolbar* or *Ribbon* to run each macro. You'll learn how to do this in *Lesson 8-17: Run a macro from a button control (sidebar).*

Describe your macro in the *Description* box.

Description:
Fill in the Name, Department, Employee Number, Bank Account No and Sort Code in the Expenses Claim form

7 Record the macro.

1. Click the OK button.

2. Make cell B3 the active cell.

    This is a potential pitfall. If B3 is already the active cell (when you begin recording the macro) and you simply type your name, the recorder will place your name into whatever cell is the active cell when the macro is run. This may not be B3.

    For this reason you should click into a different cell, and then back again into cell B3 to explicitly record your intention to move the cursor to cell B3.

3. Fill in each box (with fictitious details). Here's the ones I used:

	A	B
3	Name:	Elvis Preseley
5	Department:	Rock and Roll
7	Employee Number:	EP999
9	Bank Account No:	398724789A
11	Sort Code:	32-77-63

    Make sure that you press the **<Enter>** (or **<Ctrl>+<Enter>**) key after entering the last cell or you'll stay in edit mode and won't be able to stop the macro recorder.

4. Click: View→Macros→Macros→Stop Recording.

8 Test the macro.

1. Delete the contents of cells B3:B11.

2. Click: View→Macros→Macros→View Macros.

    The macro dialog appears listing only the *FillInExpenseForm* macro (as you have only recorded one macro so far).

3. Click the *Run* button.

    All of the details that you previously recorded appear in the relevant cells.

4. Delete the contents of cells B3:B11.

5. Press **<Ctrl>+<e>**

    Once again the form is completed with the recorded details.

9 Don't save your work yet but keep the workbook open.

You need to understand more about security and workbook formats before you can save. You'll save this workbook in the next lesson: *Lesson 8-12: Understand macro security*

You must begin this sequence of two lessons at: Lesson 8-11

Lesson 8-12: Understand macro security

Why is security needed?

Macros are a wonderful Excel feature but they can also be dangerous. It is possible to record a macro that will damage your computer in many ways.

Macro security provides several methods to identify which macros you can trust and which you can't.

You shouldn't trust any macro enabled workbook that is sent to you across the Internet (unless it is digitally signed, you learned about digital signatures in: *Lesson 6-14: Add an invisible digital signature to a workbook*). Without a digital signature it is impossible to be sure of an e-mail sender's identity. It is extremely easy to send an e-mail with a forged name and e-mail address.

The *Excel Workbook* and *Excel Macro Enabled Workbook* formats.

Excel 2007/2010 have taken a huge leap forward in the battle against macro viruses. There used to be only one Excel workbook format (the .xlsx file). Now there are two:

- Excel Workbook (.xlsx file extension).

  This type of workbook can always be trusted, because it is incapable of storing a macro.

- Excel Macro Enabled Workbook (.xlsm file extension).

  You must ensure that you can trust the origin of this type of workbook as it is capable of carrying destructive macro viruses.

Four ways to trust a macro enabled workbook.

Excel 2010 provides four mechanisms for recognizing a trusted workbook.

- Make the workbook a *trusted document*. This is a brand new feature for Excel 2010. When a workbook becomes a trusted document you will no longer receive a warning when opening it. *Lesson 8-14: Understand Trusted Documents* covers trusted documents in depth.

  This is probably the easiest and best way to manage macro security.

- Place the workbook in a trusted folder.

  Excel allows you to designate a folder as a trusted location. You are then able to open macro enabled workbooks that are saved to this location without warnings or restrictions.

  You'll learn about trusted folders in: *Lesson 8-13: Implement macro security.*

■ Digitally sign the macro.

You learned about digital signatures in: *Lesson 6-14: Add an invisible digital signature to a workbook.*

Excel can be configured to run digitally signed macros from trusted publishers without warnings or restrictions. You'll discover how to do this in: *Lesson 8-13: Implement macro security.*

■ Warn the user before enabling a macro.

Excel warns you that a workbook contains macros and asks whether you wish to enable them. You'll see this working in: *Lesson 8-13: Implement macro security.*

1   *Expenses Claim-1* should still be open from the previous lesson.

In the previous lesson you recorded a macro within this workbook.

The workbook is currently an anomaly – a regular Excel Workbook that contains a macro. Excel cannot allow such a workbook to be saved.

2   Attempt to save the workbook.

Excel warns you (in a rather cryptic way) that you cannot save this workbook as a regular (macro free) Workbook.

3   Click the *No* button to close the dialog.

The *Save As* dialog appears.

4   Save the workbook as an *Excel Macro Enabled* Workbook named *Expenses Claim-2*.

1. Change the *Save as type* to: *Excel Macro-Enabled Workbook.*

2. Change the file name to: *Expenses Claim-2.*

3. Click the *Save* button.

You have now saved your first macro enabled workbook.

5   Close *Expenses Claim-2.*

note

Controlling macro security using digital certificates

In: *Lesson 6-14: Add an invisible digital signature to a workbook,* you learned that it is possible to obtain a digital certificate by paying a third-party authority an annual subscription.

By signing a workbook with a digital signature, it is possible to confirm that you are the *publisher* of the workbook.

In order for Excel to suppress the normal security warning five conditions must be met:

1. The workbook must be signed with a digital signature.

2. The macro must not have been changed since the digital certificate was issued.

3. The digital certificate must not have expired.

4. The digital certificate must have been issued by a certificate authority recognized as reputable by Microsoft.

5. The publisher must appear in your trusted publisher list.

When you open a workbook with a valid digital certificate you are prompted with the name of the publisher and asked whether you want to add the publisher to your trusted publishers list.

To view publishers currently appearing on your trusted publisher list:

1. Click: File→ Options→Trust Center→ Trust Center Settings...

2. Click *Trusted Publishers* on the left-hand selection bar.

You will then see a list of all trusted publishers and are able to view details of their digital certificates or remove them from the list.

Lesson 8-13: Implement macro security

1 Open *Expenses Claim-2* from your sample files folder.

Remember that this is a macro-enabled workbook. When you open it one of three things will happen:

- The workbook opens without warnings and macros are enabled.

- Excel displays a security warning (this is the default setting).

> ! Security Warning   Macros have been disabled.   **Enable Content**

- The workbook opens without warning, but the macros are disabled.

It doesn't matter which is the case on your computer at the moment. This lesson will show you how to set up the macro security options to any one of the above.

2 Set the Trust Center's Macro Settings to: *Disable all macros with notification.*

1. Click: File→Options→Trust Center.

2. Click the *Trust Center Settings...* button.

3. Click *Macro Settings* in the left-hand selection bar.

Macro settings are displayed.

4. Click the option: *Disable all macros with notification.*

This is the default setting for Excel so will probably already be selected.

This option displays a warning when a workbook containing macros is opened (unless it is digitally signed by a trusted publisher – see sidebar). It is the best setting for an informed user.

> **Macro Settings**
>
> For macros in documents not in a trusted location:
> - ○ Disable all macros without notification
> - ◉ Disable all macros with notification
> - ○ Disable all macros except digitally signed macros
> - ○ Enable all macros (not recommended; potentially dangerous code can run)

5. Click OK and OK again.

3 Close and re-open the *Expenses Claim-2* workbook and notice the warning that is displayed.

1. Open the *Expenses Claim-2* workbook.

Notice the warning that is displayed:

> ! Security Warning   Macros have been disabled.   **Enable Content**

Expenses Claim-2

Do not click the *Enable Content...* button (if you did this you would create a trusted document). Trusted documents will be covered in: *Lesson 8-14: Understand Trusted Documents.*

Note that you are now unable to run the *FillInExpenseForm* macro.

4   Set a trusted folder for your macro-enabled workbooks.

If you designate a folder for your trusted macro-enabled workbooks, Excel will know that they are trusted and not bother you with any warnings in future.

For extra security, the trusted folder should always be a non-shared folder on your local hard drive (not a network drive).

1. Create a folder for your trusted macro-enabled workbooks.

   I created a folder called; **C:/Trusted Files** just to illustrate how this works.

2. Click: File→Options→Trust Center.

3. Click the *Trust Center Settings...* button.

4. Click *Trusted Locations* on the left-hand selection bar.

5. Click the *Add new location...* button.

6. Click the *Browse...* button.

7. Navigate to the folder that your trusted files will be placed in.

8. Click the OK button.

9. Click OK and OK again to close the dialogs.

5   Test the trusted folder.

1. Save the *Expenses Claim-2* workbook into the trusted folder.

2. Close the *Expenses Claim-2* workbook.

3. Open the *Expenses Claim-2* workbook from the trusted folder.

   This time the workbook opens without warnings.

4. Delete the contents of cells B3:B11.

5. Run the *FillInExpenseForm* macro.

   (You learned how to do this in: *Lesson 8-11: Record a macro with absolute references).*

   The macro runs proving that it is enabled.

6   Close the *Expenses Claim-2* workbook.

Lesson 8-14: Understand Trusted Documents

In previous versions of Excel it was only possible to open a macro-enabled workbook without a prompt if it was either placed in a trusted document folder or digitally signed.

Most users had to deal with this prompt every time they opened a macro-enabled workbook:

> ⚠ **Security Warning**   Macros have been disabled.   [Enable Content]

The Excel 2010 designers realized that showing the prompt every time didn't really add any security. If you had decided to trust the workbook the first time you opened it, you were hardly likely to change your mind the next time. For this reason it was decided that Excel 2010 would remember which documents you have already trusted and open them without prompts forever more.

Despite the name, Excel does not make the workbook itself "trusted". It is a lot cleverer than that. It stores the location (or path), file name and file creation time in a table that is linked to your user name. This means that the macro-enabled workbook will no longer be trusted in any of the following cases:

- A different user logs onto your machine and tries to open the workbook (in this case the user name will be different).

- You change the file name or move the file to a different directory.

- A malicious user deletes the old file and replaces it with another of the same name (in this case the file creation time will not be correct).

1   Open *Expenses Claim-2 from* your sample files folder.

   Note that this file should be opened from your sample files folder and not the trusted folder.

   Because you have never clicked the *Enable Content* button for this file, the security message bar appears:

   > ⚠ **Security Warning**   Macros have been disabled.   [Enable Content]

2   Click the *Enable Content* button to allow macros to run.

3   Run a macro to prove that macros are enabled.

   1. Delete the contents of cells B3:B11.

   2. Run the *FillInExpenseForm* macro.

      (You learned how to do this in: *Lesson 8-11: Record a macro with absolute references*).

      The macro runs as intended because you had previously clicked the *Enable Content* button.

4   Close the *Expenses Claim-2* file and re-open it.

   This time the file opens without showing the security message bar because Excel knows that you have previously approved the file.

Company List-1

In other words, *Expenses Claim-2* has become a *trusted document*.

5 **Run a macro to prove that they are enabled.**

1. Delete the contents of cells B3:B11.

2. Run the *FillInExpenseForm* macro.

   The macro runs as intended because this is now a trusted document.

6 **Close *Expenses Claim-2*.**

7 **Clear your trusted documents list.**

As mentioned in the introduction to this lesson, no information is saved in the workbook file when you approve it. Instead a trusted files list is maintained by Excel.

Sometimes you may want to clear the trusted files list. When you do this all macro-enabled files will once again display the security message bar the first time they are opened (unless, of course, they are in a trusted folder or have a digital certificate).

1. Click: File→Options→Trust Center→ Trust Center Settings...→Trusted Documents.

   The *Trusted Documents* dialog appears.

Trusted Documents

Warning: Trusted Documents open without any security prompts for macros, ActiveX controls and other types of active content in the document. For a Trusted Document, you will not be prompted the next time you open the document, even if new active content was added to the document or changes were made to existing active content. Therefore, you should only trust documents if you trust the source.

☑ Allow documents on a network to be trusted

☐ Disable Trusted Documents

Clear all Trusted Documents so that they are no longer trusted   [Clear]

You can see that this dialog can also be used to permanently disable the *Trusted Documents* feature for network drives only or for all file locations.

2. Click the *Clear* button.

3. Click *Yes, OK* and *OK* again to clear the dialogs.

   All trusted documents in the trusted documents list are now cleared. This means that every macro-enabled workbook will now display the security message bar the first time they are opened.

8 **Open *Expenses Claim-2* from your sample files folder.**

Notice that the security message bar is shown because *Expenses Claim-2* is no longer a trusted document.

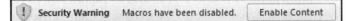

⚠ **Security Warning**   Macros have been disabled.   [Enable Content]

9 **Click the *Enable Content* button.**

Expenses Claim-2 has once again become a trusted document. This means that the security message bar will not display the next time you open it.

Lesson 8-15: Record a macro with relative references

1   Open *Company List-1* from your sample files folder.

This workbook contains a list of 88 companies. We want to use the company list for a mail merge.

We need the data in a form that Word can understand. Instead of:

	A
3	**Contact Name**
4	Alejandra Camino
5	Romero y tomillo
6	Gran Vía, 1
7	Madrid
8	28001
9	Spain
10	
11	
12	
13	Alexander Feuer
14	Morgenstern Gesundkost
15	Heerstr. 22
16	Leipzig
17	4179
18	Germany
19	

We need the format to be:

	A	B	C	D	E	F
3	**Contact Name**	**Company Name**	**Address**	**City**	**Post Code**	**Country**
4	Alejandra Camino	Romero y tomillo	Gran Vía, 1	Madrid	28001	Spain
5	Alexander Feuer	Morgenstern Gesundkost	Heerstr. 22	Leipzig	4179	Germany

This would take a long time to do manually, but we can convert all 88 records in less than five seconds by creating a macro recorded with relative references.

Relative reference macros record an offset from the active cell. Imagine that the active cell is A4 (Alejandra Camino). The relative macro will record the actions:

- Move one cell down
- Copy
- Move one cell up and one cell to the right.
- Paste

... and so on until all of Alejanra's details are moved to row 4. The macro will then delete the blank rows and be ready to start again with Alexander Feuer.

2   Set up the macro recorder to use relative references.

Click: View→Macros→Macros→Use Relative References.

3   Make Cell A4 the active cell.

View Macros
Record Macro...
Use Relative References

Company List-1

When recording a relative reference macro, it is vital that you select the active cell <u>before</u> beginning the recording.

4 Record a macro with the name *MoveAddress* and save it in *This Workbook* with the shortcut key <Ctrl>+<m>.

1. Click: View→Macros→Macros→Record Macro.

2. Type **MoveAddress** into the *Macro name* box.

3. Type a lower case **m** into the *Shortcut key* box.

4. Select *This Workbook* from the *Store macro in* drop-down list.

5. Click OK to begin recording the macro.

6. Click in cell A5 and cut.

7. Click in cell B4 and paste.

8. Continue until the complete address is pasted into row 4.

	A	B	C	D	E	F
3	Contact Name	Company Name	Address	City	Post Code	Country
4	Alejandra Camino	Romero y tomillo	Gran Vía, 1	Madrid	28001	Spain
5						

9. Select rows 5:12.

10. Right-click inside the selected cells.

11. Click *Delete* on the shortcut menu.

12. Click in cell A5 to make it the active cell.

	A	B	C	D	E	F
3	Contact Name	Company Name	Address	City	Post Code	Country
4	Alejandra Camino	Romero y tomillo	Gran Vía, 1	Madrid	28001	Spain
5	Alexander Feuer					
6	Morgenstern Gesundkost					

The macro will be run multiple times to convert all of the addresses. By placing the cursor in cell A5 before you stop recording, it will be in the right position to convert the next address.

13. Click: View→Macros→Macros→Stop Recording.

5 Convert the other 87 addresses by running the macro multiple times.

1. Make sure that A5 is the active cell.

2. Press **<Ctrl>+<m>**.

3. The next address is converted.

4. Hold down the **<Ctrl>+<m>** keys and let the keyboard automatically repeat.

5. The next 87 addresses are converted very quickly. On my computer it took less than five seconds!

	A	B	C	D	E	F
3	Contact Name	Company Name	Address	City	Post Code	Country
4	Alejandra Camino	Romero y tomillo	Gran Vía, 1	Madrid	28001	Spain
5	Alexander Feuer	Morgenstern Gesundkost	Heerstr. 22	Leipzig	4179	Germany

6 Save your work as a macro enabled workbook called: *Company List-2*.

Lesson 8-16: Use shapes to run macros

1   Open *Mortgage Calculator-10 from* your sample files folder.

2   Record a macro in *This Workbook* called *PrintWorkbook*.

1.   Click: View→Macros→Macros→Record Macro.

2.   Type **PrintWorkbook** in the *Macro name* box.

Macro name:

PrintWorkbook

3.   Describe what the macro does in the *Description* box.

Description:

Print the workbook

4.   Click the OK button.

5.   Click: File→Print→Print.

The worksheet will print out on your default printer.

Print

6.   Click: View→Macros→Macros→Stop Recording.

3   Save the workbook as a macro enabled workbook called *Mortgage Calculator-11*.

1.   Click: File→Save As→Excel Macro Enabled Workbook.

2.   Type: **Mortgage Calculator-11** in the *File Name* box.

3.   Click the *Save* button.

4   Record a macro in *This Workbook* called *SaveWorkbook* .

1.   Click: View→Macros→Macros→Record Macro.

2.   Type **SaveWorkbook** in the *Macro name* box.

Macro name:

SaveWorkbook

3.   Describe what the macro does in the *Description* box.

Description:

Save the workbook

4.   Click the OK button.

5.   Click: File→Save.

6.   Click: View→Macros→Macros→Stop Recording.

5   Add three shape controls to the worksheet.

1.   Click: Review→Changes→Unprotect Sheet (if the worksheet is protected).

2.   Re-size the chart to make space for a row of buttons underneath.

Mortgage Calculator-10

3. Click: Insert→Illustrations→Shapes→Rectangles→ Rounded Rectangle.

4. Click and drag on the worksheet to draw the button.

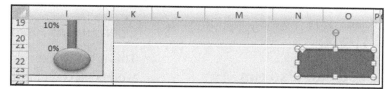

5. Click: Drawing Tools→Format→Shape Styles→ Shape Style Gallery→Intense Effect – Blue, Accent 1.

6. Copy and paste the shape twice.

7. Right-click on the right-most button.

8. Click *Edit Text* on the shortcut menu.

9. Type: **Save Quote** to add a caption to the shape.

10. Add **Print Quote** and **Go To Website** captions to the other two shapes.

6 Connect the *Save Quote* and *Print Quote* shapes to the *SaveWorkbook* and *PrintWorkbook* macros.

1. Right-click the *Save Quote* shape.

2. Click *Assign Macro…* on the shortcut menu.

3. Select the *SaveWorkbook* macro.

4. Click OK.

5. Follow the same procedure to assign the *PrintWorkbook* macro to the *Print Quote* shape.

7 Connect the Go To Website shape to the LearnMicrosoftExcel.com website.

1. Right-click the *Go To Website* shape.

2. Click *Hyperlink…* on the shortcut menu.

3. Click *Existing File or Web Page* on the left hand selection bar.

4. Type **www.LearnMicrosoftExcel.com** into the *Address* box.

5. Click OK.

8 Protect the worksheet.

9 Test the shapes.

1. Save, close and re-open the workbook.

2. Click the *Enable Content* button at the top of the screen to enable the macros. When you click upon each shape the relevant macro or hyperlink executes.

10 Save your work as *Mortgage Calculator-11.*

Lesson 8-17: Run a macro from a button control

note

You can also run macros from the Quick Access Toolbar

If you have general-purpose macros (saved in the Personal Macro Workbook) that you would like to run with a single click you can add them to the Quick Access Toolbar.

1. Click:File→Options→ Quick Access Toolbar.

2. Select *Macros* in the *Choose commands from* drop-down list.

3. Select the macro that you want to add to the Quick Access toolbar.

4. Click the *Add>>* button.

5. Select the macro in the right-hand pane.

6. Click the *Modify...* button to change the icon and tip text for the macro.

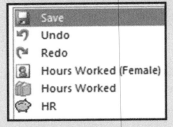

7. Click OK.

The macros can then be run from the *Quick Access Toolbar* with a single click.

You can also add macro buttons to the Ribbon in a similar way. You'll learn how to do this in: *Lesson 8-20: Create a custom Ribbon tab.*

1 Open *Human Resources-2 from* your sample files folder.

This is the workbook created in: *Lesson 6-8: Create custom views.* The workbook contains three custom views:

- Hours Worked

- Hours Worked (Female)

- HR

It is not obvious that the workbook contains custom views. You want users to be more aware of the feature, and to make the feature easier to use, by adding button controls to move between the custom views.

2 Record macros in *This Workbook* that will show each custom view.

1. Click: View→Macros→Macros→Record Macro.

2. Type **ShowHoursWorkedView** in the *Macro name* box.

3. Describe what the macro does in the *Description* box.

> Description:
> Display the hours worked custom view.

4. Click OK to begin recording the macro.

5. Click: View→Workbook Views→Custom Views.

6. Select the *Hours Worked* view.

7. Click the *Show* button.

8. Click: View→Macros→Macros→Stop Recording.

9. Create a *ShowHoursWorkedFemaleView* macro that will display the *Hours Worked (Female)* custom view.

10. Create a *ShowHRView* macro that will display the *HR* custom view.

3 Add a button control to cell A8 with the caption *Hours Worked* that will run the *ShowHoursWorkedView* macro.

1. If the *Developer* tab is not shown in the Ribbon click: File→Options→Customize Ribbon and check the *Developer* check box in the right-hand pane.

2. Click: Developer→Controls→ Insert→ Form Controls→Button (Form Control).

3. Click and drag in the top of cell A8 to add a button.

Human Resources-2

note

Create a macro that runs automatically when a workbook is opened

In this lesson's workbook you might want the opening view to always be the HR view, no matter which view was selected when the workbook was last saved.

You are able to do this by creating a macro that automatically runs when the workbook is opened.

To do this simply record a macro named *Auto_open* that selects the HR view.

The name of the macro tells Excel to run it automatically when the workbook is opened.

	A	B	C	D
7	Button 1			
8		Johnny Caine	George Marley	Betty Anan
9	Hourly Rate	18.20	12.57	12.67

4. The *Assign Macro* dialog appears.

5. Select the *ShowHoursWorkedView* macro.

6. Click OK.

7. Click on the face of the button, delete the existing text and type: **Hours Worked**.

	A
7	Hours Worked

4 Add another button control to cell A8 with the caption *Hours Worked (Female)* that will run the *ShowHoursWorkedFemaleView* macro.

5 Add another button control to cell A8 with the caption *HR* that will run the *ShowHRView* macro.

	A	B	C	D	E	F	G
1	**Payroll**						
2							
3	**Payroll Rules**						
4	Tax	32%					
5	Social Security	8%					
6	Pension	5%					
7							
8	Hours Worked / Hours Worked (Female) / HR	Johnny Caine	George Marley	Betty Anan	Paris Winfrey	Ozzy Dickens	Johnny Roberts
9	Hourly Rate	18.20	12.57	12.67	11.33	9.56	15.83
10							
11	Hours Worked						
12	Monday	9	10	10	10	7	7

6 Test the workbook.

Click on each of the command buttons. The workbook should display each custom view as the command buttons are clicked.

7 Save your work as a macro-enabled workbook with the name *Human Resources-3*.

Lesson 8-18: Show and hide Ribbon tabs

When Excel 2007 introduced the Ribbon, many users missed the ability to customize Excel's user interface.

Excel 2003 and earlier used a menu/toolbar interface and it was possible to create any number of custom toolbars. Users of older versions felt a little short-changed when they discovered that Excel 2007 only allowed them to customize one toolbar (the Quick Access toolbar).

This has all changed in Excel 2010 as you now have the ability to customize both the Quick Access Toolbar and Ribbon.

You can:

- Show and hide Ribbon tabs.

- Add your own custom command groups to standard Ribbon tabs. Microsoft has (fortunately) prevented users from adding or removing items from the standard Ribbon command groups.

- Add your own custom tab(s) to the ribbon and add custom command groups to them.

1   Open *Mortgage Calculator-11* from your sample files folder.

   The Mortgage Calculator has a very simple user interface that non-Excel users will find easy and intuitive to use.

   The screen still looks intimidating to a non-Excel user (even though most of the Ribbon buttons are grayed out).

   If we hide all of the standard Ribbon tabs the screen will seem a lot simpler.

2   Hide all of the standard Ribbon tabs.

   1. Right-click anywhere on the Ribbon and *select Customize the Ribbon…* from the shortcut menu.

      The *Excel Options* dialog appears with the *Customize Ribbon* pane selected.

   2. Select *Main Tabs* in the *Customize the Ribbon* drop-down list on the right-hand pane of the dialog:

      Customize the Ri**b**bon: ⓘ

      | Main Tabs | ▼ |

   3. Clear the check boxes next to each of the main tabs:

note

Other ways to open the *Customize Ribbon* dialog

The easiest way to open the Customize Ribbon dialog is to right-click anywhere on the Ribbon and then select *Customize the Ribbon…* from the shortcut menu as described in the lesson text.

It is also possible to do the same thing by clicking:

File→Options→ Customize Ribbon

Mortgage Calculator-11

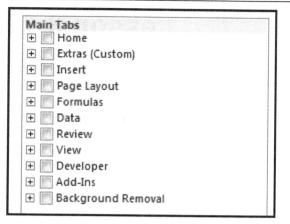

4. Click the OK button.

The User Interface is now a lot cleaner with only the *File* tab displayed:

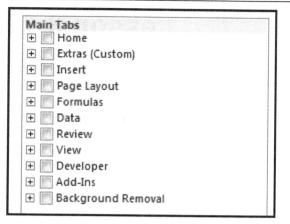

note

Ribbon customizations are set at application level

When you customize the Ribbon you are customizing Excel itself and not the current workbook.

For applications such as the Mortgage Calculator it would be great if you could save customizations that only applied to the current workbook.

Unfortunately you cannot easily do this in Excel 2010 but perhaps we'll see this feature in a future Excel release.

3   **Bring the tabs back again.**

1. Right-click on the *File* tab and select *Customize the Ribbon...* from the shortcut menu.

2. The *Excel Options* dialog appears with the *Customize Ribbon* pane selected.

3. Check each of the check boxes that you unchecked earlier.

4. Click the OK button.

5. The standard Ribbon tabs are restored.

note

Why it is a bad idea to customize standard Ribbon tabs.

A common attraction at fairgrounds is the "reverse steering bicycle". The showman has a bicycle that has special steering. When the handlebars are steered left the bicycle turns right, and when steered right the bicycle turns left.

The showman competently rides the bicycle, demonstrating how easy it is, and challenges the public to ride just five meters to win a prize. Of course, nobody that takes the challenge is able to ride the bicycle.

This works because the showman has learned to ride the bicycle with reverse steering. Because riding a bicycle is a subconscious process, nobody that has learned to ride a regular bicycle can ride a reverse steering bicycle. In computer-speak the bicycle has a non-standard user interface. As a side-effect the showman will also be unable to ride a normal bicycle!

Excel 2003 used fully customizable toolbars (the predecessor of Ribbon tabs). It was possible to freely add and remove toolbar buttons.

A common problem in my Excel 2003 classes was caused by users that had extensively customized the standard toolbars. They were then unable to work with the unfamiliar standard Excel 2003 user-interface on the classroom computers. They had effectively turned themselves into reverse cyclists!

For this reason I have always taught my Excel 2003 students to refrain from customizing the standard toolbars, but to feel free to create their own custom toolbars.

Passwords-1

Lesson 8-19: Add custom groups to standard Ribbon tabs

While I was very pleased that Excel 2010 introduced the ability to add new custom tabs to the Ribbon, I was less pleased to find that users can also add and remove command groups on the standard Ribbon tabs.

In my opinion it would be a great idea to refrain from doing this (see sidebar). Despite my opinion this lesson demonstrates the new feature.

1   Open *Passwords-1* from your sample files folder.

This workbook has been created so that the user does not forget passwords. Unfortunately the passwords used are very insecure; in fact they are among the world's top 20 commonly used passwords. It would be very easy to hack into this user's sites!

	A	B
3	Web Site	Password
4	YouTube.com	qwerty
5	Facebook.com	123456
6	PayPal.com	letmein

The user has wisely decided to change the passwords to secure ones (secure passwords were discussed in: *Lesson 6-9: Prevent unauthorized users from opening or modifying workbooks*). In order to do this the user has created a secure password generator (see facing page sidebar if you are interested in how this works).

2   Generate a new password and copy it to cell C4.

1.   Press the <F9> key to generate a new password.

2.   Copy the password in cell C21.

3.   Right-click in cell C4.

4.   Click: Paste Options→Values from the shortcut menu.

Paste Options:

3   Apply the strikethrough style to the old password.

1.   Click in cell B4.

The strikethrough style is very useful when you have replaced text but still wish to retain it. Unfortunately this style is not included on the Ribbon and it is necessary to use the dialog launcher to access it.

2.   Click: Home→Font→Dialog Launcher→Strikethrough.

	A	B	C
3	Web Site	Password	
4	YouTube.com	~~qwerty~~	2UE5vl@y77e7

3.   Click OK.

note

How the secure password generator works.

The secure password generator is constructed using skills covered in earlier lessons in this book.

Look at the *Password Characters* worksheet. This contains a table named *Password*. The first column contains sequential numbers and the second contains all of the letters, numbers and special symbols that may be used in the generated password. You learned about tables in: *Session One: Tables, Ranges and Databases*.

Return to the *Passwords* worksheet and unhide rows 23 to 34. You learned how to do this in: *Lesson 6-7: Hide and unhide worksheets, columns and rows*.

Look at the formula in cell A23. This uses the RANDBETWEEN() function in conjunction with a VLOOKUP() function to return a random letter from the *Passwords* table. You learned about VLOOKUP() in: *Lesson 3-22: Use a VLOOKUP function for an exact lookup*.

Look at the formula in cell C21. This uses the CONCATENATE() function to construct the password from the random characters in cells A23:A34. You learned about the CONCATENATE() function in: *Lesson 3-19: Use the TEXT function to format numerical values as strings*.

It is standard behaviour for a worksheet to recalculate when the <F9> key is pressed. Each time this is done the RANDBETWEEN() function generates new random numbers which, in turn, lookup new random letters. This is discussed in depth in: *Lesson 3-17: Understand calculation options (manual and automatic)*.

4   Add a custom group called *Special Formatting* to the right of the *Font* command group in the *Home* Ribbon.

   1.   Right-click the Ribbon and select *Customize the Ribbon...* from the shortcut menu.

   The *Customize the Ribbon* dialog appears.

   2.   Select the *Home* tab in the right-hand pane of the dialog.

   3.   Click the *New Group* button.

   A new group appears within the *Home* tab.

   4.   Click the *Rename...* button and type **Special Formatting** into the *Display Name* text box.

   5.   Click OK.

   6.   Use the up and down arrow buttons to move the group so that it appears after the *Alignment* group.

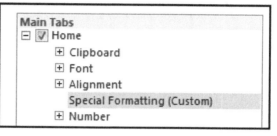

5   Add a *Strikethrough* command to the *Special Formatting* custom group.

   1.   Select *Commands Not in the Ribbon* at the top of the left pane of the dialog.

   2.   Select the *Strikethrough* command from the left-hand list.

   3.   Click the *Add>>* button.

   The *Strikethrough* command now appears within the *Special Formatting* custom group.

   4.   Click OK.

   The *Home* Ribbon now contains a *Special Formatting* custom group with a single *Strikethrough* command.

6   Add a new secure password for *Facebook.com* and strikethrough the old password using the new Ribbon command.

	A	B	C
3	Web Site	Password	
4	YouTube.com	~~qwerty~~	2UE5vl@y77e7
5	Facebook.com	~~123456~~	S#yQk1rH#!pS

7   Save your work as *Passwords-2*.

Lesson 8-20: Create a custom Ribbon tab

Excel has many really useful features that hardly any user will ever discover. A good example is the Speak Cells feature covered in: *Lesson 4-16: Use Speak Cells to eliminate data entry errors.* The only way to access these features is by adding commands to either the Quick Access Toolbar or Ribbon.

In this lesson we'll create a special Ribbon tab containing my own favorite selection of hidden Excel features. You may find that you want to keep this Ribbon permanently.

The Ribbon we will create is shown in the sidebar.

1   Open a new blank workbook.

2   Create a custom Ribbon tab called *Extras.*

   1.   Right-click the Ribbon and select *Customize the Ribbon…* from the shortcut menu.

      The *Customize the Ribbon* dialog appears.

   2.   Click the *New Tab* button at the bottom of the right-hand pane.

      A new custom tab and single new custom group appear in the *Main Tabs* window.

> ⊟ ☑ New Tab (Custom)
>   New Group (Custom)

   3.   Select the new tab and click the *Rename…* button.

      Be careful to click the *New Tab* and not the *New Group* item.

      The *Rename* dialog appears.

   4.   Type **Extras** into the *Display Name* text box.

> Rename   ？ ✕
>
> Display name: Extras
>   OK   Cancel

   5.   Click OK.

> **Main Tabs**
> ⊞ ☑ Home
> ⊞ ☑ Insert
> ⊟ ☑ Extras (Custom)
>   New Group (Custom)
> ⊞ ☑ Page Layout

3   Add six more custom groups to the *Extras* tab.

   Click the *New Group* button six more times.

4   Name the new custom groups: *Hyperlinks, Speak, Collaboration, Format, Widgets, Quick Paste* and *File/Print.*

   1.   Select the first *New Group.*

   2.   Click the *Rename…* button.

The *Rename* dialog appears.

Notice that you are able to select a symbol as well as define a name. The symbols will display when the application window is made so narrow that the commands have no room to display... like this:

Note that the new *Format* command group has only one command meaning that no symbol is ever shown.

3. Select the cloud symbol and type **Hyperlinks** into the *Display Name* text box.

4. Click OK

5. Repeat for the other command groups.

5   Add *Forward* and *Back* commands to the *Hyperlinks* command group.

In: *Lesson 7-5: Hyperlink to an e-mail address and enhance the browsing experience,* you discovered how useful a forward and backward button were when constructing workbooks that had hyperlink-based navigation systems.

1. Select the *Hyperlinks* custom group in the right-hand pane of the *Customize the Ribbon* dialog.

2. Select *Commands Not In the Ribbon* in the drop-down list above the left-hand pane.

3. Click the *Forward* command in the left-hand pane.

4. Click the *Add>>* button.

5. Repeat for the *Back* command.

6   Add all of the other commands to the relevant Ribbon groups.

If you don't find a command in the *Commands Not in the Ribbon* group look in the *All Commands* group.

7   Save your Ribbon Customizations to a file.

You may wish to share your custom ribbon with other users or to load it onto a different computer.

1. Right-click the Ribbon and select *Customize the Ribbon...* from the shortcut menu.

    The *Customize the Ribbon* dialog appears.

2. Click the *Import/Export* button at the bottom of the right-hand pane.

3. Click *Export all Customizations* in the drop down list.

4. Name the customizations *Extras Bar* and click *Save.*

Choose commands from: ⓘ

Commands Not in the Ribbon ▾

Session 8: Exercise

1   Open *Gala Dinner-1* from your sample files folder.

2   Add combo box, group box, option button and check box form controls, so that the user interface looks like this:

	A	B
1	**Gala Dinner Ticket Order**	
2		
3	**No Of Tickets:**	▼ (22.50 each)
4		
5		┌ Dietary Preference ──────
6		◉ All types of food
7		○ Vegetarian
8		○ Vegan
9		
10	Drinks:	☐ Water (2.50 per person)
11		☐ Wine (5.50 per person)
12		
13	Total Cost:	

3   Add a new worksheet called *Data*.

4   Add a named range to the *Data* worksheet called *Tickets* containing the numbers 1-10.

5   Set the *Input range* of the combo box control to the *Tickets* range name.

6   Link the combo box and check box controls to the input cells (B19, B20 and B21).

7   Add formulas to the result cells (B24, B25, B26 and B27) to calculate the total cost of the order.

8   Add a formula to cell B13 so that it displays the same value as cell B27 and hide rows 18 to 27.

9   Record a macro named *PrintOrder* in *This Worksheet* that will print the worksheet.

10   Add a button control to the form that will run the *PrintOrder* macro.

	A	B
1	**Gala Dinner Ticket Order**	
2		
3	**No Of Tickets:**	2 ▼ (22.50 each)
4		
5		┌ Dietary Preference ──────
6		○ All types of food
7		◉ Vegetarian
8		○ Vegan
9		
10	Drinks:	☐ Water (2.50 per person)
11		☑ Wine (5.50 per person)
12		
13	Total Cost:	56.00
14		
15		Print Order

11   Save your work as a *Macro-Enabled Workbook* named *Gala Dinner-2.*

Gala Dinner-1

If you need help slide the page to the left

Session 8: Exercise Answers

These are the four questions that students find the most difficult to answer:

Q 9	Q 7	Q 6	Q 3 & 4
1. Click: View→Macros→ Macros→Record Macro…	The correct formulas are:	1. Right-click the combo box.	1. Click the *Insert Worksheet* tab at the bottom left of the screen to insert a new worksheet.
2. Type **PrintOrder** into the *Macro name* box.	*Ticket Cost* (B24): **=B19*22.5**	2. Click *Format Control…* on the shortcut menu.	2. Double-click on the tab and change the worksheet name to *Data*.
3. Select *This Workbook* from the *Store macro in* drop-down list.	*Water Cost* (B25): **=IF(B20=TRUE, B19*2.5,0)**	3. Click the *Control* tab.	
4. Click the OK button.	*Wine Cost* (B26): **=IF(B21=TRUE, B19*5.5,0)**	4. Click in the *Cell Link* box.	3. Select the *Data* worksheet and type **Tickets** into cell A1.
5. Click: File→Print.	*Total Cost* (B27): **=SUM(B24:B26)**	5. Click in cell B19.	3. Type the numbers 1 to 10 in cells A2:A11.
8. Click the *Print* button.	This was covered in: *Lesson 8-6: Use check box data in result cells.*	6. Click the OK button.	4. Select cells A1:A11.
11. Click: View→Macros→ Macros→Stop Recording.		7. Follow the same steps for the check boxes, linking the *Water* check box to cell B20 and the *Wine* check box to cell B21.	5. Click: Formula→ Defined Names→ Create from Selection.
This was covered in: *Lesson 8-17: Run a macro from a button control.*		This was covered in: *Lesson 8-3: Set form control cell links.*	6. Click OK.
			You have now created a named range called *Tickets* that references cells A2:A11.
			This was covered in: *Lesson 4-4: Automatically create range names in two dimensions.*

If you have difficulty with the other questions, here are the lessons that cover the relevant skills:

2   Refer to: *Lesson 8-1: Add group box and option button controls to a worksheet form* and *Lesson 8-2: Add a combo box control to a worksheet form.*

5   Refer to: *Lesson 8-2: Add a combo box control to a worksheet form.*

8   The correct formula is: **=B27.** To hide the rows select them, right-click and select *Hide* from the shortcut menu.

10   Refer to: *Lesson 8-17: Run a macro from a button control.*

Appendix A: Skills Covered in the Essential Skills Course

> You have to learn to crawl before you can walk.
> You have to learn to walk before you can run.
>
> *Proverbs, unknown authors*

In order to get the most out of this book you should already be very comfortable with Excel's main features. We also have an *Essential Skills* course for absolute beginners.

ISBN: 978-0-9554599-7-9
310 pages.

ISBN: 978-0-9554599-8-6
370 pages. (This book).

This (Expert Skills) book assumes that you have already mastered the skills taught in the *Essential Skills* book.

So how do you know if your skills are already advanced enough to tackle this book?

This appendix lists the objectives for each of the seven sessions in the *Essential Skills* course.

If you already have all (or at least most) of the skills taught in the *Essential Skills* course you are ready to upgrade your skills to Expert level with this course.

Essential skills course outline

Session 1

- Start Excel and check your program version
- Maximize, minimize, re-size, move and close the Excel window
- Understand the Application and Workbook windows
- Download the sample files and open/navigate a workbook
- Save a workbook
- Understand common file formats
- Pin a workbook and understand file organization
- View, move, add, rename, delete and navigate worksheet tabs
- Use the Versions feature to recover an unsaved Draft file
- Use the Versions feature to recover an earlier version of a workbook
- Use the Ribbon
- Understand Ribbon components
- Customize the Quick Access Toolbar and preview the printout
- Use the Mini Toolbar, Key Tips and keyboard shortcuts
- Understand views
- Use full screen view
- Use the help system

Session 2

- Enter text and numbers into a worksheet
- Create a new workbook and view two workbooks at the same time
- Use AutoSum to quickly calculate totals
- Select a range of cells and understand Smart Tags
- Enter data into a range and copy data across a range
- Select adjacent and non-adjacent rows and columns
- Select non-contiguous cell ranges and view summary information
- Re-size rows and columns
- AutoSelect a range of cells
- Use AutoSum to sum a non-contiguous range
- Use AutoSum to quickly calculate averages
- Create your own formulas
- Create functions using Formula AutoComplete
- Use AutoFill for text and numeric series

- Use AutoFill to adjust formulas
- Use AutoFill Options
- Speed up your AutoFills and create a custom fill series
- Use the zoom control
- Print out a worksheet

Session 3

- Insert and delete rows and columns
- Use AutoComplete and fill data from adjacent cells
- Cut, copy and paste
- Cut, copy and paste using drag and drop
- Use Paste Values
- Increase/decrease decimal places displayed
- Transpose a range
- Use the multiple item clipboard
- Use Undo and Redo
- Insert, View and Print cell comments
- Understand absolute, relative and mixed cell references
- Create a template
- Use a template
- Freeze columns and rows
- Split the window into multiple panes
- Check spelling

Session 4

- Format dates
- Understand date serial numbers
- Format numbers using built-in number formats
- Create custom number formats
- Horizontally and Vertically align the contents of cells
- Merge cells, wrap text and expand/collapse the formula bar
- Understand themes
- Use cell styles and change themes
- Add color and gradient effects to cells
- Add borders and lines
- Create your own custom theme
- Create your own custom cell styles

- Use a master style book and merge styles
- Use simple conditional formatting
- Manage multiple conditional formats using the Rules Manager
- Bring data alive with visualizations
- Create a formula driven conditional format
- Insert a Sparkline into a range of cells
- Apply a common vertical axis and formatting to a Sparkline group
- Apply a date axis to a Sparkline group and format a single Sparkline
- Use the format painter
- Rotate text

Session 5

- Create a simple chart with two clicks
- Move, re-size, copy and delete a chart
- Change the chart layout and add a data table
- Format chart element fills and borders
- Format 3-D elements and align text
- Move, re-size, add and delete chart elements
- Change a chart's source data
- Create a chart with numerical axis
- Deal with empty data points
- Add data labels to a chart
- Highlight specific data points with color and annotations
- Add gridlines and scale axis
- Emphasize data by manipulating pie charts
- Create a chart with two vertical axis
- Create a combination chart containing different chart types
- Add a trend line
- Switch chart rows/columns
- Add a gradient fill
- Create your own chart templates

Session 6

- View the same workbook in different windows
- View two windows side by side and perform synchronous scrolling
- Duplicate worksheets within a workbook
- Move and copy worksheets from one workbook to another

- Hide and unhide a worksheet
- Create cross-worksheet formulas
- Understand worksheet groups
- Use find and replace

Session 7

- Print Preview and change paper orientation
- Use Page Layout view to adjust margins
- Use Page Setup to set margins more precisely and center the worksheet
- Set paper size and scale
- Insert, delete and preview page breaks
- Adjust page breaks using Page Break Preview
- Add auto-headers and auto-footers and set starting page number
- Add custom headers and footers
- Specify different headers and footers for the first, odd and even pages
- Print only part of a worksheet
- Add row and column data labels and grid lines to printed output
- Print several selected worksheets and change the page order
- Suppress error messages in printouts

Index

G

T

X

Y